A New Gospel for Women

Katharine C. Bushnell (1855–1946)

Source: Clara C. Chapin, ed., *Thumb Nail Sketches of White Ribbon Women* (Chicago: Woman's Temperance Publishing Association, 1895).

A New Gospel for Women

Katharine Bushnell and the Challenge of Christian Feminism

KRISTIN KOBES Du MEZ

OXFORD
UNIVERSITY PRESS

OXFORD
UNIVERSITY PRESS

Oxford University Press is a department of the University of
Oxford. It furthers the University's objective of excellence in research,
scholarship, and education by publishing worldwide.

Oxford   New York
Auckland   Cape Town   Dar es Salaam   Hong Kong   Karachi
Kuala Lumpur   Madrid   Melbourne   Mexico City   Nairobi
New Delhi   Shanghai   Taipei   Toronto

With offices in
Argentina   Austria   Brazil   Chile   Czech Republic   France   Greece
Guatemala   Hungary   Italy   Japan   Poland   Portugal   Singapore
South Korea   Switzerland   Thailand   Turkey   Ukraine   Vietnam

Published in the United States of America by
Oxford University Press
198 Madison Avenue, New York, NY 10016

© Oxford University Press 2015

Library of Congress Cataloging-in-Publication Data
Du Mez, Kristin Kobes.
A new gospel for women : Katharine Bushnell and the challenge of Christian
feminism / Kristin Kobes Du Mez.
pages cm
ISBN 978-0-19-020564-5 (hardback : alk. paper)   1. Bible and feminism.   2. Bible–
Criticism, interpretation, etc.   3. Women in the Bible.   4. Women–Religious aspects–
Christianity.   5. Feminism–Religious aspects–Christianity.   6. Bushnell, Katharine C.
(Katharine Caroline), 1855–1946.   I. Title.
BS680.W7D86 2015
230.082—dc23
2014035461

1 3 5 7 9 8 6 4 2
Printed in the United States of America
on acid-free paper

For Zachary Izaac, Eva Lucia, and Louisa Isadora
"Where the Spirit of the Lord is, there is liberty."

Contents

Preface

The Book of Genesis, According to Katharine Bushnell

In the beginning . . . God created Adam, a male-female being, and it was very good. God charged Adam to watch and protect the Garden of Eden, but in time Adam began to lose perfection, and God decided that it was not good that Adam should be alone. To prevent further falling into imperfection and to restore Adam to original goodness, God took from Adam's side and separated out the woman.

Before the woman had been formed, God had commanded Adam not to eat of the tree of knowledge of good and evil. But a Serpent came to the woman and tempted her. Though she had heard from Adam not to eat of the tree, she succumbed to the Serpent's tempting, and ate. The man, too, ate of the tree, not through the Serpent's tempting, but at the woman's invitation.

After they had eaten they became aware of their nakedness and were ashamed, and when they heard God approaching, they hid. God knew of their sinfulness, and questioned them. Adam and the woman both confessed: "I did eat," and both told of the immediate influence that led to the eating. The woman spoke of the Serpent, and Adam, (whose job it had been to protect the garden, presumably from serpents and other sources of harm), spoke not of the Serpent, but of his companion. But Adam did not stop there: "The woman," he said to God, "whom *you* put here with me, caused me to sin." Unlike the woman, who rightly blamed Satan, Adam blamed God—a betrayal that initiated humanity's Fall into sin. Lurking nearby, Satan rejoiced that Adam had shielded him from blame.

Thus the man advanced to the side of the Serpent, becoming a false accuser of God. But the woman, by exposing the character of Satan before his very face, created an enmity between herself and Satan. God proposed to widen the breach she had made, saying to Satan: "I will put enmity between thee and the woman, and between thy seed and hers. It will bruise thy head, and thou will bruise his heel." The Word of God called the woman Eve, "the mother of all living"—of all who were spiritually living.

As Satan's declared enemy and as the progenitor of the coming destroyer of Satan, Eve became the target of Satan's wrath. Satan set out to cripple her, inciting her husband against her and inflicting pain upon her childbearing.

For man's disobedience and rebellion, God exiled him from the garden. But Eve, too, chose to turn away from her God and follow Adam out of Eden. And so Eve became the first woman of many to turn from her Creator to her husband, and to forsake her heavenly calling for the sinful submission to man.

Paraphrased from Katharine C. Bushnell, *God's Word to Women: One Hundred Bible Studies on Woman's Place in the Divine Economy* (Oakland, CA: Katharine C. Bushnell, 1923; repr. Peoria, IL: Cosette McCleave Jolliff and Bernice Martin Menold, n.d.).

Acknowledgments

IT WAS A winding footnote trail that first led me to Katharine Bushnell's *God's Word to Women*, and after reading only a few pages it became clear to me that Bushnell's book was unlike any other I had encountered in the history of feminist theology. So began the journey to uncover the story behind this fascinating book, to bring to light the history of its remarkable author, and to determine how both the book and the author could have faded so quickly from historical memory.

Along the way my research has been nurtured and supported by a number of different institutions and individuals. The project initially took shape under the guidance of two superb graduate mentors, George Marsden and Gail Bederman. George's wisdom, generosity, and sense of humor sustained me throughout my graduate education and beyond, and he continues to serve as a model scholar and friend. Gail Bederman first introduced me to the field of women's history, and her enthusiasm was contagious. She has continued to provide unsparing support and encouragement at crucial junctures throughout my academic career. For both of these relationships, and for the congenial environment of the University of Notre Dame's History Department, I am immensely grateful. During the initial stages of this project I was also privileged to benefit from the mentorship of Regina Kunzel and the hospitality of Williams College, and from the intellectually engaging setting of the Five College Women's Studies Research Center, where I first began to situate my research in the context of global feminism.

Throughout my academic journey I have been fortunate to have found myself in exceptionally supportive intellectual communities, and none more so than my current academic home, Calvin College, where I have been blessed with witty, generous, and compassionate colleagues. My colleagues in the History Department deserve special mention, and I have benefited as well from conversations with passionate and insightful

Gender Studies faculty. I am also grateful for the institutional support Calvin College has provided me over the course of this project—for essential funding provided by the Calvin College Alumni Travel Grant, for the support of the Calvin Institute for Christian Worship, for release time provided by a Calvin Research Fellowship and a sabbatical leave, and finally for assistance in bringing the book to completion from the Calvin Center for Christian Scholarship. I am thankful as well to the Calvin College McGregor Scholars Program for funding my student research assistant, Jared Warren, and to Jared for the exemplary dedication and skill with which he pursued this project.

At earlier stages of the project I received essential support from the University of Notre Dame's Zahm Travel Grant and the Schlesinger Library Research Support Grant. And at a critical later stage I benefited from the generous support provided by the Louisville Sabbatical Research Grant. This grant enabled me to return to the archives, expand the scope of the book, and craft the book into its present form. It is my hope that this work will indeed play a small part in strengthening the Christian church in North America, and beyond.

Over the years I have also been fortunate to receive friendly, prompt, and expert assistance from numerous librarians and archivists. I am particularly grateful to the staff at the Radcliffe Institute's Schlesinger Library (Harvard University); the Women's Library (London); the British Library; the Frances Willard Memorial Library & Archives; the Northwestern University Library; the University of Wisconsin, Oshkosh, Archives & Area Research Center; the Denver Public Library; the Yale Divinity School Library; Yale University's Sterling Memorial Library; the University of California, Berkeley's Bancroft Library; the Drew University Library, and the University of Liverpool's Sydney Jones Library. And I am thankful to Kathleen Struck of Calvin College's Hekman Library for the extensive interlibrary loan assistance she has provided.

At later stages of the project I benefited from the insights of members of the Society of Biblical Literature's Working Group on Female Biblical Interpreters, as well as from my participation in the international symposium on Women's Movements and the Bible in the Nineteenth Century (Bern, Switzerland). I am also grateful to Timothy Gloege, Christiana de Groot, Lavonne Schaafsma Zwart, Joel Carpenter, and Nevada DeLapp for their instructive comments on individual chapters, and to Alicia Smit and Jenna Hunt for assistance in the final stages of editing. I am particularly indebted to James Bratt, George Marsden, Marion Taylor, and Margaret

Bendroth, for their careful and insightful reading of the entire manuscript, and to my anonymous readers who offered thoughtful and perceptive comments.

I am thankful as well to Philip Law for his early interest in this undertaking, and to many others who provided assistance at various points along the way—to Jonathan Britton, Andrea Hensen, Greg Veltman, and Larry Herzberg, for their assistance in my research queries, and to Gay Anderson, Barbara Collins, Mimi Haddad, Ruth Hoppin, Gladys Masore, Zaphania Masore, Carrie Miles, and Lisa Thompson, for sharing with me their knowledge of Bushnell and of her continuing relevance today. Over the years my interactions with individuals near and far who have been influenced or inspired by Katharine Bushnell's work have supplied me with a steady source of encouragement.

I would also like to offer special thanks to my parents, Helen and Wayne Kobes, who have always supported me in my academic endeavors, and who provided timely babysitting assistance for my final research trip to London.

And I would be remiss not to thank Zachary, Eva, and Louisa for their graciousness and understanding throughout this lengthy process. All three came to be over the course of this project, and since two of the three have "published" their own research projects during this time, they couldn't help but wonder why mine was taking so long. In all honesty, they did have a bit to do with extending the project's timeline, but the delightful distractions they provide on a daily basis have been a source of endless entertainment and immeasurable joy. It is to these three that I dedicate this book. If nothing else, I hope it may someday inspire them to turn to the pages of their own Bibles with greater curiosity about God's word to women, and men.

Finally, my deepest thanks belong to Jack—for his enthusiastic support for this project from its earliest stages, for his unflagging encouragement over the long haul, for timely research and technical support, and for never wavering in his conviction that Katharine Bushnell's was a story that needed to be told. He has lived with this book as long as I have, and has been a true partner in this endeavor.

Note on Sources

In citing Katharine Bushnell's *God's Word to Women*, I have followed the author's practice in referring to paragraph numbers rather than pages. Unless otherwise noted, I have cited a reprint of her 1923 edition (Katharine C. Bushnell, *God's Word to Women: One Hundred Bible Studies on Woman's Place in the Divine Economy* [Oakland, CA: Katharine C. Bushnell, 1923; repr. Peoria, IL: Cosette McCleave Jolliff and Bernice Martin Menold, n.d.]), since this is one of the editions most widely available today.

A New Gospel for Women

Introduction

THIS BOOK TELLS the story of Katharine Bushnell (1855–1946), a remarkable figure in the history of American social reform, women's rights, and feminist theology. Inspired by her Methodist faith, Bushnell was at the forefront of late nineteenth-century social reform, first as a medical missionary, then as a temperance worker, and finally as an international social purity activist. At the height of her career, the name of Kate Bushnell was a "household word" within the world of Anglo-American reform, but by the early decades of the twentieth century, she had largely faded from prominence. In most circles today she has been all but forgotten. Her story, however, illuminates a pivotal period in the history of Christianity and feminism in America.

Bushnell formulated her ideas and rose to prominence at a time when Christianity and feminism were more closely aligned than at any other time in American history. In believing that Christianity was essential to the advancement of women, Bushnell was not alone; particularly in the context of Western expansionism, the apparent superiority that Anglo-American women enjoyed over their "degraded heathen sisters" seemed to provide compelling evidence of Christianity's role in elevating the status of women. But what set Bushnell apart from the vast majority of her contemporaries was her conviction that Christianity itself required reform—that a feminist corrective was urgently needed in order to re-establish an authentic Christian faith. For Bushnell, Christianity and feminism were not only compatible, but each was essential to the other.[1]

In her efforts to reform Christianity, Bushnell set out to undo centuries of male bias in order to reveal the emancipatory message at the heart of the Christian gospel. Drawing on her knowledge of biblical languages and her extensive research into the history of biblical interpretation, Bushnell sought to provide a new theology for women and men. In 1916, after dedicating more than a decade to the task, she published the first edition of *God's Word to Women*, a collection of startling reinterpretations of the Christian Scriptures.[2] Even today, *God's Word to Women* stands as one of the most innovative and comprehensive feminist theologies ever published.

In one hundred meticulously researched and tightly argued lessons, Bushnell recast the message of the Bible as one of liberation for women. God had created women to be strong, courageous, and independent, she insisted. But men, in rebellion against God, had subordinated women to themselves, and Bushnell accused biblical translators and interpreters of collaborating in man's rebellion by portraying women's subordination as the will of God. In her own hands, the Bible told a very different story. From the first chapters of Genesis through the book of Revelation, Bushnell demonstrated how the Scriptures revealed God's love for women, how they established women's God-given authority, and how, in light of the disastrous effects of women's tragic subordination to men, they foretold of women's ultimate spiritual and social redemption in Christ.

What is perhaps most remarkable about *God's Word to Women* is that Bushnell pressed her revolutionary claims while upholding the authoritative truth of the Scriptures. She considered every word of the biblical text "inspired, infallible and inviolable."[3] However, she rejected modern translations as patriarchal corruptions of the true word of God, and turned instead to Hebrew and Greek texts as the basis of her theological revisions. Bushnell was thus able to craft a radical feminist theology without abandoning her staunch commitment to the authority of the Scriptures. For this reason, *God's Word to Women* has enduring appeal among Christians seeking a biblical theology of liberation for women that is compatible with a conservative hermeneutic.

By reconstructing the story of Bushnell's *God's Word to Women*, this book contributes to ongoing efforts to recover the history of female biblical interpretation. Those familiar with this history know that it is often one of erasure and neglect; time and again, women have wrestled with the Christian Scriptures and have penned intriguing and insightful commentaries, only to have their work quickly forgotten, leaving each generation to begin the task anew. The resurgence of modern feminism in the 1960s and 1970s spawned efforts to uncover this lost history of feminist biblical interpretation, and of feminism more generally.[4] In subsequent years, evangelical or "biblical" feminists joined in this recovery effort, in some cases motivated by a desire to locate their own work within a longer historical tradition in order to distance it from the taint of "secular feminism" that, in the eyes of many conservatives, clung to the project of contemporary feminist theology.[5] More recently, the burgeoning field of reception history has helped spur further research into how women have read the Bible in different times and places.[6] Together, these developments have provoked a lively present-day interest in the ways in which women have interpreted the Bible, past and present.[7]

A New Gospel for Women contributes a fascinating and critical chapter to the history of feminist biblical interpretation, but this project is not merely an exercise in recovery. In many ways, it is about forgetting as much as remembering. The story of Bushnell's life and work, and her subsequent disappearance from the historical record, together illuminate the dynamic and often thorny relationship between faith and feminism in modern America. While one purpose of this book is to provide an accessible introduction to Bushnell's theology, then, that introduction comes with a caveat. Occasionally those interested in the history of Christian feminism, particularly those identifying as Christian feminists, have exhibited a willingness to pluck examples of biblical feminism from the past in order to apply those teachings to contemporary situations. On the one hand, this practice is perfectly understandable. For faith communities who believe the Bible to be the inspired word of God, biblical interpretation, and not just the Bible itself, can take on an air of timelessness; if the Holy Spirit is not bound by time, neither is the insight wrought by the Spirit.

The Christian faith, however, is a deeply historical faith. Rooted in the incarnation, the interjection of a timeless God in human history, the faith is always enculturated, received in a specific time and place, and "addressed to the setting in which it is produced."[8] By locating Bushnell and her theology in a specific time and place, this book seeks not only to recover Bushnell's contributions to the history of theology, but also to articulate the ways in which her particular location both shaped and constrained her theology, and to uncover how a shifting historical context affected the memory of her life and the legacy of her work. Bushnell may well prove inspirational to Christians today, particularly to those committed to a biblical faith oriented toward social justice activism and gender equality. Yet at the same time, her story illuminates the difficulties confronting those who seek to apply historical theologies to contemporary contexts vastly different from the settings in which they were produced.

As Bushnell's story makes abundantly clear, her theology was deeply rooted in the context in which she lived, the world of late-Victorian evangelical reform. It was Bushnell's work on behalf of women the world over that compelled her to study the Scriptures and to develop her gendered critique of traditional Christian theology. Her reform work introduced her to women in tawdry houses of prostitution in Wisconsin lumber camps, in British army brothels in colonial India, and in the "vice dens" that sprang up throughout East Asia wherever Western influence was present, and in each case she observed *Christian* men treating women with astonishing cruelty. Not only did Christian men commit despicable acts against women, Bushnell noted, but they often did so with impunity, continuing to be revered in their communities as respectable Christian gentlemen. It was in the face of such damning evidence that Bushnell came to conclude that Christianity itself must be to blame—or, more precisely, the Christianity handed down by generations of men.

In order to locate the theological roots of the abuse of women at the hands of seemingly upstanding Christian men, Bushnell turned to the Scriptures. Her initial reading of the account of the first woman, Eve, in the book of Genesis, together with the writings of the Apostles, convinced her that the Bible did indeed appear to endorse woman's subordination, and through her subordination her abuse, for Bushnell considered the two indistinguishable.[9] The more she searched the Scriptures, the more she came to believe that the abuse of women she had observed in her travels was in fact closely linked to that most sacred institution, Christian marriage. Men could not make women "obedient slaves" within the marriage relation, she surmised, without coming to see all women in that light.[10]

But it made no sense to Bushnell that Christians who claimed to confess Christ's atonement would nevertheless insist that women perpetually atone for the sins of Eve—that men who preached a gospel of humility and grace would nonetheless usurp power and authority over their fellow human beings. Bushnell was unable to accept that a God of justice and grace would condemn one-half of the human race to subordination and abuse, and the other half to domination and brutality. Yet she refused to abandon the Christian faith in its entirety. Rather, she rejected the "whole fossilized system of theology" that had been wrought by "masculine egotism" as a patriarchal perversion of the true faith.[11] She turned instead to Hebrew and Greek texts in order to uncover the unadulterated word of God, and after years of rigorous theological investigations, she published her findings in *God's Word to Women*.

A product of the late Victorian era, Bushnell remained confident that theology shaped society, and she was optimistic that her theological revisions would accomplish dramatic change within the Christian church, and within society at large. She sought, for example, to undermine powerful Victorian social conventions. Unlike the vast majority of her contemporaries, she considered patriarchal marriage, the celebration of female virtue and domesticity, and the very notion of a separate woman's sphere to be manifestations of man's rebellion against God. Convinced that the time had come for women to claim their redemption in Christ, Bushnell believed that by offering a theological foundation for a new vision of Christian womanhood, she could help usher in a new era for women.

Yet few readers today are familiar with Bushnell's path-breaking work. Despite garnering enthusiastic reviews from a number of biblical scholars, *God's Word to Women* failed to achieve the religious and social transformation that Bushnell had envisioned. As it turned out, the book appeared at a transitional moment in the history of Christianity and feminism in America. Bushnell began her career during the late Victorian era, a period that might well be considered the "golden age" of Christian feminism in America. Women of Bushnell's generation helped forge this alliance. By combining the egalitarian impulses of revivalist Protestantism with conventional notions of femininity, enterprising women carved out a space for themselves in the burgeoning world of evangelical reform; venturing far beyond the domestic sphere, many of these women came to embrace women's rights, particularly women's suffrage, as essential to their efforts to reform the world. In some cases these women then turned their feminist convictions back upon their religious inheritance and, like Bushnell, sought a theology of female empowerment suited to the spirit of the age.

By the turn of the twentieth century, however, the once-vibrant world of evangelical female reform had begun to wane, and with it the alliance between faith and feminism that Bushnell and women like her had helped achieve. The causes were various: economic and social change, the mounting authority of modern science, escalating divisions within American Protestantism, and the professionalization of reform all played a part, so that by the early twentieth century connections between Christianity and the women's rights movement had become increasingly strained. This rift revealed itself both in the growing secularization of the women's movement, and in the declining power that Protestant women wielded within their own churches.

Nowhere was this parting of ways between Christianity and feminism more evident than when it came to issues of sexuality. During the closing decades of the nineteenth century, many Protestant reformers and women's rights activists had united around the cause of social purity, a movement that for a time rivaled temperance in popularity in the world of female reform. Social purity reformers thought that by eliminating the sexual double standard—the Victorian ideal that upheld far loftier standards of purity for women than for men—they could significantly improve the condition of women. Rather than advocating greater sexual license for women, purity reformers insisted that men, as well as women, ought to exercise sexual restraint. This ideology not only accorded with traditional notions of Christian morality, but in a world in which sex often placed women in peril (exposing them to unwanted pregnancies and disease, and entrapping them in potentially abusive relationships), many reformers and women's rights activists alike believed that an egalitarian ideal of purity would best protect and empower women.

But as the Victorian order gave way to the modern era, purity came to seem increasingly outmoded, and a new generation of feminists, bolstered by the authority of modern science, began to advocate a new sexual ethic, one based not on restraint, but rather on the liberation of female sexuality. The majority of evangelical reformers, however, continued to advocate purity and restraint. In this way, women who had once identified as progressive "New Women" found themselves maligned as conservative reactionaries, increasingly out of step with their former allies in the women's movement. By the time of her death in 1946, Bushnell had become one such obscure and marginalized figure. Her dream for religious and social revolution had gone unrealized, and the memory of her life's work quickly faded.

Given Bushnell's prominence in the world of nineteenth-century reform and her pioneering work in feminist theology, her virtual disappearance from the modern historical record is striking. Even as a new wave of feminist activism swept the nation in the 1960s and 1970s, prodding a generation of feminist historians to mine the past for inspirational forebears, Bushnell's life and legacy went largely unnoticed by scholars and activists alike. In light of her unrelenting resistance to a sexual ethic based on liberation rather than restraint, together with her zealous insistence on the authority of Scripture, the once-radical critic of Victorian society seemed more a relic of a time gone by than a compelling feminist foremother.

In this regard, Bushnell's legacy can be contrasted instructively with that of another once-forgotten figure of the same era, Elizabeth Cady Stanton. Like Bushnell, Stanton had penned a feminist critique of patriarchal Christianity, and she, too, had deemed theological change essential to the emancipation of women. But the two women parted ways when it came to their theological methods. Whereas Bushnell adhered to a conservative hermeneutic, Stanton and her *Woman's Bible* co-authors embraced the possibilities of higher criticism. Lacking expertise in the biblical languages, Stanton exhibited few qualms when it came to picking and choosing from among biblical texts, underscoring passages that seemed to empower women, reinterpreting those that constrained them, and in cases where the latter proved too difficult, handily dismissing entire portions of the Scriptures.[12] Her confused and piecemeal approach to the Scriptures, however, together with her rather misleading title—for *The Woman's Bible* was in fact a collection of commentaries rather than a new Bible—provoked such an uproar among Christians that its publication proved counterproductive to Stanton's radical aims. Confirming associations of women's rights with heresy, at least in the minds of conservatives, the book for a time turned out to be "the most devastating weapon in the antisuffrage arsenal."[13]

By convincing a generation of women's rights activists of the wisdom in avoiding entanglements with religion altogether, the storm of controversy surrounding Stanton's book contributed to the growing estrangement of Christianity and feminism in America, and it cast a chilling effect on feminist biblical interpretation within the larger women's movement for decades to come. Discussions of the Christian Scriptures did not disappear entirely from suffragist literature in the wake of Stanton's *Woman's Bible*, but they did appear less frequently and came to play a more marginal role in the movement, as both suffragists and antisuffragists alike came to prefer other battlegrounds.[14] Turning away from more expansive and potentially contentious reform efforts, women's rights leaders instead chose to focus more narrowly on suffrage—precisely the turn of events that Stanton had been trying to thwart. In the aftermath of the *Woman's Bible* controversy, then, the women's movement became both more secular, in the sense that the subject of religion receded into the background of public debates over women's rights, and more conservative, in that a more profound social critique was forfeited in favor of expediency.

Even as Stanton's book alienated many feminists of her own time, over half a century later her work would resonate with a new generation of feminist activists. Republished in 1972, *The Woman's Bible* served as a source of inspiration for modern feminists seeking comprehensive social revolution, many of whom were once again eager to throw off the constraints of traditional Christianity. Much as it had in the aftermath of its initial publication, the reappearance of Stanton's *Woman's Bible* again bolstered associations of feminist theology with unorthodoxy, and helped to perpetuate divisions, real and perceived, between Christianity and modern feminism. These divisions were heightened by the concurrent re-emergence of American evangelicalism, a movement that would come to define much of its political agenda in terms of a strident antifeminism. As feminists once more sought to liberate female sexuality in their pursuit of equality, conservative evangelicals decried feminists' permissive sexual ethic and instead championed "family values" harking back to an idealized Victorian era. Stanton's book, then, ended up reinforcing a narrative that pitted women's rights against Christianity—a narrative that continued to obscure the work of Christian feminists like Bushnell, who undoubt-edly seemed too Christian for many feminists, and too feminist for many Christians. As in the early decades of the twentieth century, it once again seemed difficult, if not impossible, to be both Christian and feminist.[15]

But Bushnell had not been entirely forgotten. In the decades after her death, a small number of evangelical and Pentecostal women and men had kept Bushnell's legacy alive. As the evangelical resurgence of the 1970s made unmistakably clear, the secularization of American society that had seemed all but inevitable in the 1920s had not in fact come to pass, and for those who continued to adhere to a conservative hermeneu-tic, *God's Word to Women* provided powerful biblical arguments support-ing women's right to preach and teach. By the 1970s and 1980s, a new generation of evangelical feminists had begun to find within Bushnell's biblically based critique of patriarchy not only a justification for women's ecclesiastical rights, but also a compelling foundation for a Christian man-date to combat the abuse of women.

In recent years, this renewed interest in Bushnell's work has begun to expand across the globe. Bushnell's own theology was deeply rooted in her global encounters. Her experiences both as a foreign missionary and as an international purity activist were integral to the development of her feminist critique of traditional Christianity. And so it is fitting that her work is finding a new audience today among the rapidly expanding com-munity of global Christians, many of whom share with her a conservative hermeneutic and yet are seeking alternatives to patriarchal familial and societal structures. Through the efforts of missionaries and the reach of the Internet, women and men in Africa, Asia, and the Americas are reading Bushnell's work with interest, finding within it a biblical critique of their own patriarchal traditions and a defense of women's religious authority. At the same time, religious organizations battling human trafficking are finding in Bushnell's writings a biblical call to address the abuse of women worldwide. As it did in her own day, Bushnell's work speaks powerfully to Christians who hold conservative theological commitments, but find within the Scriptures the good news of women's spiritual and social emancipation.

And yet, as much as Bushnell's theology demonstrates anew the promise of Christian feminism, her life and work also reveal the considerable challenges confronting Christian feminists today. Even at the time Bushnell first published *God's Word to Women*, the world in which she had formulated her ideas was rapidly falling away. Changes wrought by modern feminism had rendered all but obsolete the nineteenth-century women's movement in which Bushnell had played such a formative role. At the same time, escalating tensions between liberal and conservative Protestants were indelibly altering the American religious landscape. Given these social and religious transformations, it makes sense that Christian feminists today are often drawn to their nineteenth-century predecessors in their own search for inspirational forebears, to a time when Christianity and feminism were often closely aligned. In doing so, however, they risk depicting both Christianity and feminism as static constructs, and in this way they may ultimately fail to provide a solid historical foundation for those who wish to reconcile the two today.

Bushnell lived nearly ninety-one years; understanding how her ideas could be enthusiastically received by one generation and all but forgotten the next illustrates the dynamic history of both Christianity and feminism in America. By situating Bushnell's theology securely within its historical context, this study seeks both to illuminate the sources of her ideas and to examine the difficulties she faced as her late-Victorian world gave way to a distinctly modern one. Only when this tangled history is appreciated can one begin to grasp how Bushnell's ideas might speak to the present generation.

Part history, part biography, and part historical theology, this book is crafted to introduce Bushnell to multiple audiences—to theologians and historians of biblical interpretation, to historians of sexuality, feminism, and American religion, to interested Christians, and to the general reader. The first four chapters locate Bushnell historically and historiographically within the world of late-Victorian global evangelicalism. Chapter 1 tells of Bushnell's early years and positions her at the epicenter of an emerging Protestant women's culture, one that fostered the development of a distinctly Christian feminism. Chapters 2 and 3 examine Bushnell's involvement in the world of female reform, first as a missionary to China, and then as a temperance and social purity activist, in the United States and around the world. These chapters trace how Bushnell's growing feminist consciousness emerged as a result of her international reform work, and how her work on behalf of women the world over contributed to her growing suspicions of traditional Christianity. The two chapters also situate Bushnell in terms of the literature on gender, missions, and empire, in an effort to better articulate the ways in which she was both an agent and a critic of imperialism, a product of Victorian Christianity and a participant in the world of global evangelicalism. Chapter 4 then explores how Bushnell ultimately came to conclude that Christianity itself, or rather a pernicious distortion of Christianity, was to blame for the cruelty and misogyny exhibited by Western, Christian, "civilized" men, and it describes how Bushnell dedicated the remainder of her life to uncovering what she believed to be God's true word to women.

Chapters 5 and 6 depart from this historical narrative in order to offer a synopsis of Bushnell's extraordinary rereading of the Christian Scriptures. Bushnell's own writing, while meticulously researched and painstakingly written, is often repetitive, and at times convoluted. By offering a concise summary of her central arguments, these chapters assist both in the recovery of her work, and in clarifying precisely how her theology reflected the context in which it was produced. The final two chapters then consider the reception of Bushnell's work in light of the dramatic transformations taking place both within American Protestantism, and within the modern women's movement. Chapter 7 discusses the diminishing audience for *God's Word to Women* in the context of an increasingly polarized religious landscape. With the rift between fundamentalists and modernists widening, a theology that was both feminist and conservative would find few eager readers. At the same time, the estrangement of biblically oriented conservatives and socially oriented progressives eroded the dynamic Protestant women's culture of which Bushnell had long been a part. The final chapter outlines Bushnell's staunch opposition to contraception, and to Margaret Sanger, the "priestess of a new morality," and situates her mounting isolation in the context of shifting conceptions of religion, morality, and modern feminism in twentieth-century America.

The lessons Bushnell offers various audiences today are many, but each must be refracted through the particularities of time and place, with appreciation for the historical distance between Bushnell's time and our own. Even as *God's Word to Women* continues to find new readers nearly a century after its initial publication, Christian feminists today face an enduring challenge: the need to fashion a robustly Christian sexual ethic, one based not on a Victorian moral system, but rather one suited to the realities of the modern world. Ultimately, Bushnell's story can reveal both the promises and perils of Christian feminism today.

I

A *Paradise for Women*

THE SEVENTH OF nine children, Katharine Bushnell was born in 1855 to William Francis and Mary Fowler McKean Bushnell.[1] Like so many of their fellow Americans, the Bushnells had ventured to the American Midwest in order to make a life for themselves. They settled in Peru, Illinois, a small town at the junction of the Illinois River and the Illinois and Michigan Canal. Completed just a few years earlier, the canal had opened up vital shipping lines between the Great Lakes and the Gulf of Mexico, and William Bushnell, a carpenter and contractor, helped build the town that sprang up around the strategic port. Before long, however, Peru fell victim to the boom-and-bust cycles that plagued nineteenth-century America. Periodic floods, fires, and cholera outbreaks took their toll on the community, but more devastating still was the proliferation of railroads that dramatically diminished the canal's significance. By the 1870s, Peru had stagnated. Charred and abandoned buildings cluttered the landscape, and no one seemed to possess the means or the initiative to rebuild them.[2] In 1871, undoubtedly in search of a better location in which he could ply his trade, William Bushnell submitted what turned out to be the lowest bid for the construction of a lighthouse on Evanston's Grosse Pointe promontory, a particularly treacherous shoreline along Lake Michigan a few miles north of Chicago. With government contract in hand, he and his wife Mary left the struggling town and resettled their family over one hundred miles away, in Evanston, Illinois.[3]

It is hard to imagine a location that could have better prepared Katharine Bushnell for her future work, for in perhaps no community in America were the connections between Protestant Christianity and the women's movement more evident than in Evanston in the 1870s. Inspired by their Christian faith, Evanston's women pioneered efforts in education and voluntary work for women. They were enthusiastic supporters of the women's foreign missionary movement, and they would be instrumental in transforming temperance into the leading cause of nineteenth-century American women. In Evanston, Bushnell would be welcomed and nurtured by a vibrant community of women, and the formative years she would spend in Evanston would prepare and empower her to launch her own remarkable career.

A Methodist Mecca

With just over 3,000 inhabitants, Evanston was slightly smaller than Peru at the time, but with a population that had nearly quadrupled over the previous decade, it was an up-and-coming town. In Evanston, the Bushnell family not only found vastly improved economic conditions, but they encountered a more hospitable religious environment as well. Devout Methodists, the Bushnells proudly traced their ancestry back to John Rogers, a sixteenth-century Bible translator martyred for his opposition to the Church of Rome.[4] With regard to their Methodist faith, the Bushnells were not exceptional. At the time of the nation's founding Methodists had numbered fewer than a thousand members, but in ensuing decades the denomination experienced what seemed like miraculous growth, thanks in large part to intrepid circuit riders who fanned out across the Western backcountry. Preaching a gospel of simplicity, purity, and personal responsibility, the itinerant evangelists found a receptive audience among Americans struggling to piece together a hardscrabble existence, and by the middle of the nineteenth century over one-third of the nation's church members counted themselves as Methodists.[5]

Methodism had reached the frontier outpost of Peru in 1838, just five years after settlers had displaced the local Indians. Though Methodism would find a warm welcome in many Western communities around this time, such was not the case in Peru. As one delightful story recounts, early on "about a dozen young reprobates" interrupted in dramatic fashion the town's first religious meeting. Disgruntled with the newly arrived Methodist preacher's refusal to preach only "piety and righteousness in the abstract," the young men conspired to light up well-filled tobacco pipes the moment the preacher began to reprove the community for some of their more questionable practices. They then proceeded to smoke the preacher out of the log-shanty church—though not, apparently, before he managed, between spasms of coughing, to "[hurl] back some rather unchristian anathemas upon the graceless and sacrilegious scamps."[6] As it turned out, such inauspicious beginnings portended well the challenges that Methodism would face in the community. The year before Katharine Bushnell's birth, Methodists had managed to erect a large meetinghouse in Peru, but the cost of the new building proved too much for the congregation, and they ended up selling the building and disbanding for a time. Though the church formed again the year before the Bushnells departed, the congregation remained small, barely able to retain a pastor.[7] Not surprisingly, Methodism had little influence on the city's social mores; Peru was at that time home to three breweries, seven taverns, and forty "Lager Beer and Drinking Saloons."[8]

Evanston, on the other hand, was known as "the great Methodist Mecca of the Northwest."[9] Methodists all, its founders had initially set out in the early 1850s to establish a Methodist college in Chicago, but their concern over what they perceived to be the city's excessive poverty and moral corruption prompted them to resolve instead to build both town and school. Selecting a plot of land thirteen miles north of the city, they charted out a town with wide streets, expansive lots, and beautiful parks—one in which they hoped to fashion an environment more conducive to their idea of moral living. In doing so, Evanston's founders represented a new generation of American Methodists. Whereas earlier Methodists had eschewed material wealth and social status, this generation had seen their worldly ambitions prosper; demonstrating a new affinity for capitalism, they helped transform Methodism from a countercultural movement embraced by those on the margins of society, into the predominant religion of America's emerging middle class.[10]

Evanston's founders saw no conflict between prosperity and faithfulness, and they happily combined their faith in God with civic boosterism, their missionary zeal with a pragmatic interest in land speculation. Although a few dissenting voices sought to call the faithful back to an earlier, simpler Methodism, by mid-century growing numbers of Methodists had come to deem wealth and status entirely compatible with moral fervor; indeed, for many Methodists, middle-class values and religious virtue would become all but indistinguishable.

Even as they achieved worldly respectability and influence, this new generation did not abandon their reformist zeal. Rather than focusing on personal discipline and material simplicity, however, they instead directed their efforts at transforming the society in which they now held a significant stake. Through reform movements, voluntary agencies, and institution-building, middle-class Methodists set out to purify their society. Evanston's Methodist inhabitants certainly did not hesitate when it came to applying their faith to social behaviors, both within their own community and in the world beyond. Staunchly abolitionist in the 1850s, the town would also become a hub of national temperance reform and prohibition efforts. (From its earliest days, Evanston had been a "dry" town—both school charter and city ordinance prohibited the sale of alcohol within four miles of the college.) With its churches, schools, restrictive ordinances, and zealous inhabitants, Evanston stood apart from other Midwestern boom-time communities. In the words of one observer, arriving at Evanston was like "entering the holy precincts of a cloister."[11]

Enterprising Women

Moving from Peru to Evanston opened up new opportunities for the entire Bushnell family, but for young Kate (as Katharine was often called), who early on exhibited "a robust, religious character, and more than ordinary intellect,"[12] this move must have seemed nothing less than providential. Just as she was entering young adulthood, Bushnell found herself in a place that her new neighbor Frances Willard described as "a paradise for women."[13] As Willard explained, the town was "remarkable in nothing if not in the ability, individuality and enterprise of its women."[14] As future president of the Woman's Christian Temperance Union, Willard attributed the "mutual respect, generous admiration and helpful good will between the brothers and sisters of the human household" that prevailed in Evanston to the absence of saloons.[15] Because men were not holed up in saloons and bars, she reasoned, a social space existed for mixed intellectual pursuits that fostered a sense of mutuality and respect between women and men.[16] In fact, residents' temperance convictions and their progressive attitudes toward women could both be attributed to the community's Methodist heritage. Like other evangelical revivalist traditions, early Methodism's emphasis on the transformative power of the Holy Spirit, its tradition of a strong laity, and its repudiation of social hierarchies and conventional notions of propriety worked together to endow women with significant religious and social authority.[17]

Evanston's women, then, drew upon a rich tradition of spiritual egali-
tarianism and female empowerment. But they confronted a conflicting
set of expectations as well. As growing numbers of Methodists moved
away from their revivalist roots and instead came to court social respectability and worldly status, they began to abandon traditional sources
of women's spiritual authority in favor of the Victorian ideal of female
domesticity. Historians have long documented the nineteenth-century
"cult of domesticity" that elevated women's roles as especially pious and
self-sacrificing mothers and wives,[18] but few have appreciated the role that
Methodism played in helping to establish the dominance of the domestic
ideology for middle-class women. It was no coincidence that what became
known as the "Methodist Age" in American religious history was concurrent with the rise of American domesticity, for as growing numbers
of Methodists sought positions of worldly respectability, they tended to
define respectability for women primarily in terms of domesticity. Indeed,
many middle-class Methodists came to consider the family circle, with the
Christian wife and mother at its heart, to be divinely instituted, a model
for "all rule, authority, and power."[19] In this way the home came to rival the
church as the center of the Methodist faith, and for women, domesticity
became elevated to a spiritual calling.[20]

There remained within Methodism a countermovement, however. In
the 1830s, a New York City woman named Phoebe Palmer had begun to
reinvigorate old-school Methodism's revivalistic and egalitarian message
with her "holiness" teachings. Drawing on the traditional Methodist conception of sanctification, Palmer called upon Christians to be transformed
to a life of holiness through a "second blessing," a supernatural act of
the Holy Spirit that would bring about "entire sanctification," or "perfection," and Palmer required all those who experienced this "baptism of
the Holy Spirit" to testify to their experience—women as well as men.
She proclaimed her teachings through holiness meetings, speaking tours,
periodicals, and books, and before long the movement had spread to other
denominations and across the nation, taking hold particularly among
inhabitants of small Midwestern towns and in the rural South.[21]

Some holiness converts were able to incorporate holiness teachings
into their respectable, middle-class faith, but for many believers, holiness spirituality proved more disruptive. By calling Christians, regardless of gender, to a life of piety, and by requiring all to testify publicly to
the work of the Spirit, holiness teachings undercut the gender distinctions upon which the cult of domesticity depended, and helped propel

a new generation of Methodist women into leadership positions in their churches and communities. To Palmer these tensions were clear; she castigated those Protestants like Catharine Beecher and Henry Ward Beecher who preached a Victorian "gospel of gentility" in place of the pure gospel message, and her teachings proved instrumental in mobilizing half a century of female missionary and reform work.[22]

In Evanston these conflicting strands came together. On the one hand, Evanston was designed by and for members of the Methodist middle class as a place where domesticity could flourish. But its bourgeois inhabitants also had access to an egalitarian religious language that enabled some women to expand or transgress conventional boundaries of domesticity. In Evanston's homes, middle-class mothers, daughters, and grandmothers came together to explore their religious heritage and investigate the ways of holiness; as older women shared their wisdom with younger women, they equipped and empowered the rising generation to devote their lives to social sanctification, at home and abroad. In this way Evanston came to serve as a crucible for Protestant women's activism in nineteenth-century America, and around the globe.[23]

Tensions between the community's quest for respectability and its egalitarian impulses were evident at its very founding. Unlike earlier generations of Methodists who had shunned higher education, the religious entrepreneurs who founded Evanston saw higher education as a means to enhance their denomination's stature and extend its influence. Already in 1855 they completed the first building at Northwestern College and welcomed the school's first ten students, and they opened Garrett Biblical Institute to four young men training for the ministry. Most remarkably, that same year they also founded Northwestern Female College and preparatory school, which in its first year drew fifty-one women eager to extend their education.[24] At that time "a woman's college course equal to that arranged for young men was unheard-of, except at Oberlin and Antioch, Ohio,"[25] and the priority that Evanston's citizens assigned to women's higher education was not without controversy. A number of wealthy and influential men viewed the prospect of a female college with "disgust and scorn," fearing that a college associated with "the unscholarly name of woman" would detract from the community's respectability and "cheapen and degrade" all institutions of higher learning for men; besides, many doubted that girls had "the intellect to grasp live mathematics and dead languages."[26] It was only after several Methodist ministers lent their support to the project that it came to pass that Evanston's young women "began to study Homer and Horace while the Indian's trail was yet visible along the shore."[27]

As an early center for women's higher education, Evanston quickly became home to an array of vibrant women's organizations. The community's women first found common cause in a fundraising effort for Garrett Biblical Institute. Ten years after its founding, the school was still housed in a plain wooden structure along the lake, and when James Smart, the school's new financial agent, arrived in town, he turned to the community's women for help. Noting that 1866 marked the centenary of American Methodism, Smart resurrected the story of Barbara Heck, the "Foundress of American Methodism." Heck had earned this appellation one hundred years earlier after confronting Philip Embury, the first Methodist minister to arrive in America, while he was playing cards with a group of "reckless comrades." In no uncertain terms the Irish laywoman had chided the wayward minister to "preach to us or we all go to hell together." Suitably convicted, Embury complied, and Methodism quickly took root in American soil.[28] "A sensible man," Smart proposed that Evanston women coordinate a national effort to solicit funds for the construction of Heck Hall, an impressive new building to house the Institute, and Frances Willard, a 26-year-old schoolteacher, was selected as corresponding secretary of the newly formed Methodist Women's Centenary Association.[29]

Smart's good sense paid off, as the women succeeded in raising $25,000 for the construction of Heck Hall. The benefits were not merely financial; Willard later reflected on how Methodist women gained a new "sense of power" from their Centenary accomplishments.[30] Additionally, as corresponding secretary, Willard had effectively introduced herself to thousands of Methodist women across the nation, and had acquired important organizational skills that would prepare her to lead a national women's organization in the years ahead.

It was not long before Methodist women put their newfound power to use in a movement that would sweep the globe in the name of Christ: the women's foreign missionary movement. Although American Protestants had engaged in foreign missions for decades, it was only in the wake of the Civil War that the foreign missionary movement emerged as a powerful force in American Protestantism, and women's efforts were crucial to the movement's success.[31] In the past, women had supported missions through "female cent societies" and auxiliary mission societies, but the funds they raised had been channeled into male mission boards over which they had little influence. Women themselves generally only went abroad as missionary wives, not as missionaries in their own right.[32] But as Victorian Protestants began to elevate the religious and social significance of female domesticity, they came to see the conversion of "heathen mothers" as key to the Christianization of families and communities. As a writer in the inaugural issue of *The Heathen Woman's Friend* explained to her fellow Methodist women in 1869, "We know too how inestimable is the value, and how incalculable the influence of a pure Christian home, and if the influences of such homes are so indispensable in a Christian land, what must be their importance among a people, the depth of whose degradation is, as we are often assured, altogether beyond our realization?"[33]

Male missionaries, however, were making little headway in their efforts to evangelize the women of non-Christian cultures, particularly in the case of the sometimes secluded women of "the Orient," and so they urged mission boards to send female missionaries.[34] Many newly educated, single young women embraced this opportunity. Employing the rhetoric of maternal self-sacrifice, they found ample justification for the expansion of their own duties as a means by which to rescue and "uplift" their heathen sisters.[35] Claiming "the world their household," they set out to "admit the light of the Gospel" to heathen women's "benighted hearts and homes."[36]

The American Civil War served as a further catalyst for the expansion of middle-class women's roles beyond a narrowly defined domestic sphere.[37] As men went off to war, many women took over men's tasks on the home front and organized extensive wartime relief efforts. When the war ended, it not only left tens of thousands of women widowed, but also countless women eager to employ their newly acquired skills. At the same time, new household technologies like domestic plumbing, sewing machines, and improved stoves and furnaces, coupled with the availability of foreign-born domestic help and a declining birth rate, began to liberate middle-class women from the bondage of perpetual housework and child care.[38] As the writer in *The Heathen Woman's Friend* put it, Providence had now freed women, newly awakened to their latent power and responsibilities, to take up "new and yet grander undertakings" as missionaries themselves, or as members of supporting organizations back home.[39]

Propelled by the Wesleyan missionary impulse and accustomed to holding in tension domesticity and female empowerment, Methodist women quickly outpaced their counterparts in other denominations in the foreign missions enterprise. Just four years after the end of the Civil War, Methodist women in Boston came together to organize the Woman's Foreign Missionary Society (WFMS) of the Methodist Episcopal Church.[40]

Although the WFMS would eventually receive widespread denominational support, its pioneering members faced opposition and even ridicule: "bishops were disturbed, missionary secretaries perplexed, editors
confounded, and leading men, generally, failed to comprehend the situation." Despite the church's hesitancy "to obey God's marching orders and
take up a new enterprise," however, the women persisted, and the organization quickly expanded throughout the Northeast and the Midwest,
where the "untrammeled zeal of the west issued a hearty welcome to this
new enterprise of Methodist women."[41] Evanston's women organized a
WFMS in 1870, the year before the Bushnell family arrived, and by the
next year the North-Western Branch of the WFMS already boasted 66
auxiliaries and 3,750 members drawn from Illinois, Michigan, Indiana,
and Wisconsin. In light of the remarkable expansion of the WFMS, even
its staunchest critics would come to acknowledge that the women's work
must indeed be the work of the Lord.[42]

The WFMS, in turn, served as an important training ground for its
members. Through their involvement in the WFMS, women acquired new
administrative skills and a new confidence in their own abilities. Women
whose church involvement had been limited to "an occasional class and
prayer-meeting testimony . . . church suppers, festivals and social enter-
tainments," found themselves learning, and soon teaching, "the meaning
of Constitution and By-laws, how best to conduct monthly and quarterly
meetings, how to disseminate missionary intelligence, raise funds; how,
when, and to whom to make reports."[43] American women often spoke of a
debt they owed their "heathen sisters" in terms of their obligation to bring
the gospel to foreign lands, but they were also deeply indebted to those
women whose very existence opened up new avenues for their own initia-
tives. As a motto offered by one of the pioneering members of the WFMS
declared: " 'The Bible in every heathen home, and every woman in our
church helping to carry it there.' For Christ's sake, for the sake of heathen
women, for our own sake, we must push this work forward."[44]

Living upon Alpine Heights

And so it was that the seventeen-year-old Bushnell came to call home a
town bustling with religiously dedicated, newly empowered, and globally
oriented women. Although details surrounding her first year in Evanston
are scant, enough fragmentary evidence exists to begin to piece together
probable early influences. It was likely only shortly after Bushnell and

her family arrived in Evanston that the city hosted the itinerant holiness preacher, Maggie Van Cott.[45] Van Cott, who in 1869 had become the first woman licensed to preach in the Methodist Episcopal Church, had no qualms about the appropriateness of female preaching: "I believe my tongue is my own," she explained, "and I will use it when I please, where I please, and as I please."[46] In Evanston she led a revival described as "the most memorable ever known," and although it is unclear if Bushnell participated in this revival, she is unlikely to have remained unaware of the religious fervor that Van Cott's presence stirred in her hometown, especially among its women.[47] Likely not coincidentally, it was to this time that Bushnell dated her own conversion experience, marking her decision to formally commit her life to Christ.[48]

It was Bushnell's new neighbor, Frances Willard, who was to exert the greatest influence over Bushnell during her time in Evanston. Recently returned from extensive travels in Europe and the Middle East, Willard, already a leader among Evanston's women, had begun to reflect publicly on the condition of women in foreign lands, and also in her own country. Though by comparison she found the lot of American women preferable, Willard nevertheless argued on behalf of the advancement of women in the United States, as well as abroad. Calling for a "new chivalry of justice," she insisted that rather than requiring men's benevolent protection, women instead needed men to support their education and advancement.[49] During this period in which Willard was beginning to articulate her views on women, she and Bushnell enjoyed "many a delightful interview as teacher and pupil," and Willard later recalled that she had "no stronger or more chivalric ally than this gifted, individualized, forceful young nature."[50]

Bushnell had ample opportunity to demonstrate her fierce loyalty to her mentor once Willard took up the presidency of the newly established Evanston College for Ladies. It turns out that Evanston's first women's college had failed to live up to original hopes to provide an education equal to that available to male students, and so after coordinating the fundraising efforts for Heck Hall, Evanston's women determined that "the next work of this kind that we do will be for girls."[51] They selected Willard to lead the new college and assigned her the preliminary task of raising funds for the institution. Willard initially succeeded in securing contributions from a number of wealthy Chicago businessmen, but when the Great Fire swept through Chicago that year it forced the majority of her donors to renege on their promises. Willard had no choice but to allow the school to come under the authority of Northwestern University, and she was subsequently appointed dean of Northwestern's Woman's College (which was not in fact a college but rather a dormitory and seminary for female students), and professor of English and "art and aesthetics" at the university.[52]

This arrangement might have proved satisfactory, had Charles Fowler not been recently appointed president of Northwestern. As far as Willard was concerned, a less amenable candidate could hardly have been found. Not only did she consider Fowler ambivalent at best toward the advancement of women, but she also had personal reasons to regret his appointment; a decade earlier she had broken off her engagement to Fowler, and according to an early Willard biographer, he had never forgiven her the offense. Whatever his motivations, Fowler appeared to challenge Willard's leadership at every turn. Particularly contentious was a public dispute over Willard's ongoing efforts to monitor female students' behavior, a system of self-reporting that she had designed to protect her students against allegations of impropriety, and to convince wary parents of their daughters' safety and security. Only twelve years earlier, however, Willard herself had chafed under the stifling regulations and seemingly arbitrary rules she encountered at the Female College, and had in fact looked for opportunities to break those rules at every turn. Not wanting to provoke such rebellion, Willard instituted an experimental system of self-government based on a "Roll of Honor" meant to encourage proper conduct. In introducing the system to the students, she instilled in them a sense of their own significance: coeducation "was a new movement, a step forward in woman's advancement," she reminded them, and "greater interests than they had dreamed of depended upon their conduct."[53] Although a sympathetic biographer claims that Willard's female charges were committed to the project and devoted to her leadership, a number of male students treated the "Roll of Honor" with ridicule and contempt.[54]

To make matters worse, Elizabeth Cady Stanton happened to be visiting Chicago at the time, and upon hearing Northwestern students championing "equal rights" for their female classmates, and without full knowledge of the situation, the renowned women's rights activist publicly criticized Willard. Willard never forgot this slight. Taking advantage of the dispute, Fowler, together with a faction of the Board of Trustees that had never fully supported coeducation, used the circumstances to undermine Willard's authority, and a number of her male students proved more than happy to assist in this effort.[55] Unaccustomed to reciting their lessons to a woman, these "roistering youths" took pleasure in devising ingenious ways to "try her mettle," even once entrapping a howling cat in her desk drawer.[56] Though Willard bore her students' pranks with fortitude, her tensions with Fowler and the Board, coupled with the humiliation of being stripped of much of her authority, eventually became too much to bear. In 1874 she resigned from the institution she had worked so hard to build. At the time she was despondent and unsure of how to proceed, both personally and professionally. As it happened, however, her departure from women's higher education would free her to assume leadership of the next great movement for women that was beginning to take hold across the nation.

Even as Willard endured the antics of her rebellious male students, she continued to enjoy warm, nurturing relationships with the young women in her charge. One of Willard's students at the Evanston College for Ladies described well the adoration many of her students felt for her, and the impression she made on them in the formative period of their lives: "Such broad views of life and destiny as she opened to our sight; such high ideals of character as she set before us; such visions of the heights to which we might climb, of the noble deeds we might achieve, and, with it all, such a deep and weighty sense of responsibility for the use we made of life with its gifts and opportunities. . . . It was like living upon Alpine heights to be associated with her."[57] So intense was the affection and devotion Willard elicited from her students that some observers felt it "bordered on the uncanny"; a few critics even attributed to Willard "a kind of occult magnetism." But her close friend and biographer Anna Gordon accounted for her appeal otherwise, explaining that "her power was only that [of] a great soul, full of the spirit of Christ"—the same power that would make Willard "the organizer and leader of the womanhood of her time, and the commanding figure of this century."[58]

Bushnell was among Willard's most devoted disciples, and Willard's influence on her life and work would be pronounced. Although in all likelihood Bushnell lived at home while she attended classes at the preparatory school and college, and thus was not directly involved in the debates regarding rules for female students, she nonetheless observed the battles close at hand. Not only was her allegiance to Willard cemented during this time, but her sympathy for her embattled mentor may well have begun to foster in her a wariness of male power, a wariness that would only intensify in years to come. For her own part, Willard noted that from that time on, whenever she could, she worked to "help [Bushnell's] fortunes forward."[59]

Moral Medicine

Willard was not the only Evanston neighbor to have a formative influence on Bushnell during this period. Dr. James Stewart Jewell, a professor at the Chicago Medical College and a family friend of the Bushnells, also played an instrumental role in Bushnell's education. A noted specialist in nervous and mental diseases, Jewell also happened to take a keen interest in biblical studies, and Bushnell became a frequent and welcome guest in the Jewell home. Though Bushnell had initially begun a course of study in classical languages, under Jewell's direction she decided to switch to the study of medicine. Jewell tutored his eager pupil for two years and prepared her to enroll in the Chicago Woman's Medical College, which had opened its doors a few years earlier. There Bushnell studied under Dr. Sarah Hackett Stevenson, who in 1876—around the time Bushnell enrolled in medical school—had become the first woman admitted to the American Medical Association.[60] Bushnell's medical education was well-rounded. She served as a resident physician at the Chicago Hospital for Women and Children, a position that brought her into frequent contact with the city's destitute women, and was for a time in full charge of the hospital. She also spent three months in the Eye and Ear Infirmary, and graduated in February 1879, the youngest in her class by three years.[61]

As part of a pioneering generation of female physicians, Bushnell and many of her classmates were embarking on a career in medicine as an expression of Christian service. Practitioners of "moral medicine," they followed in the footsteps of Elizabeth Blackwell, who in 1849 had become the first woman to be licensed as a doctor in the United States, and who insisted that female physicians had a "glorious moral mission" to fulfill. Rather than imitate the methods and practices of male physicians, Blackwell believed that women could revitalize the profession "by recognizing the inseparable connection of the double elements of human nature . . . the soul and the body." By developing "the moral aspect of the physician's noble work," women could find their "especial *raison d-etre* and necessary place as co-workers in a progressive society." It was this moral medicine that drew Bushnell to the profession, and years later Blackwell herself would express admiration for Bushnell, her "brave medical sister," for carrying on this legacy.[62]

Bushnell trained for her career in moral medicine not only through her formal schooling, but also as an active member of Evanston's lively, intergenerational women's community. It was in this setting that she became thoroughly schooled in holiness Methodism. On Sunday and Thursday afternoons, for example, Bushnell could often be found at the home of Melinda Hamline, a holiness advocate, and good friend of Phoebe Palmer. The widow of Bishop Leonidas Lent Hamline, the first editor of *The Ladies Repository* and a "noted champion of women's rights,"[63] Melinda Hamline had moved to Evanston after her husband's death in 1865, where she was welcomed as a heroic woman of the faith in her own right. "Mrs. Bishop Hamline," as she was known at the time, quickly assumed a position of leadership among the community's women, and helped establish the holiness movement in Evanston.[64] In 1866 she brought Palmer to Evanston to lead a series of meetings,[65] and in the years that followed she continued to hold regular holiness meetings in her home. Through these meetings she offered her friends "strong words of helpfulness" that "were an inspiration and a benediction," and equipped "many a young soul . . . for its [spiritual] warfare."[66] Much admired by Evanston's women, Hamline nonetheless envied the new opportunities available to the young women of Bushnell's generation, and she rejoiced that she had lived long enough to glimpse a new day for women that promised possibilities unknown to her generation.[67]

Even as Bushnell sat at the feet of spiritual matriarchs like Hamline, she was already revealing herself to be "a missionary in spirit." She began organizing Sunday evening prayer meetings for college girls, "drawing them to a higher, purer life of real happiness and usefulness," and was "constantly seeking to uplift and help those whose acquaintance with Christ was more limited than hers."[68] Upon graduation, Bushnell initially intended to undertake further clinical work and postgraduate study. However, the community of women that had welcomed and nurtured her had other plans for this promising young woman. Desiring that she become a missionary not only in spirit but in fact, members of the Women's Mission Board at her church induced her to accept a position as a medical missionary to China.

Bushnell's years in Evanston had been formative ones, and had prepared her well to take up one of the most adventurous opportunities available to an educated young woman in her day. Trained in medicine and inspired by her religious formation, Bushnell could lay claim to the authority of modern science, to the moral authority of womanhood, and to the egalitarian power of the Spirit. And so it was that the well-educated but relatively inexperienced twenty-four-year-old would take her first steps on a global stage, leaving Evanston to embark on a journey halfway around the world. Her career in missions would not, however, last long, and over fifty years later she would reflect that, had she not believed that "all things work together for good to them that love God," she would consider this venture "the mistake of [her] life."[69]

2

Virtue, Vice, and Victorian Women

AS KATHARINE BUSHNELL set sail for China in the fall of 1879, she did so confident in her faith, and in her authority as a woman to advance the cause of Christ the world over. For Bushnell there was little conflict between Christianity and the advancement of women. She had pursued a career in medicine as an outgrowth of her Christian commitment, and she understood her missionary calling as a means by which to bring the advantages of Christianity to women in foreign lands. Bushnell had come of age and had formulated her ideas during a pivotal period in the history of Christianity and feminism; over the closing three decades of the nineteenth century, significant factions within Anglo-American Protestantism and the women's rights movement would help align Christianity and feminism more closely than at any time, before or since. For many feminists during this era, "a better feminist world meant a more spiritual, more Christian one."[1]

Three popular movements helped establish and promote the compatibility of faith and feminism at this juncture: the women's missionary movement, temperance reform, and the social purity crusade. Together, these three causes would extend the attention and efforts of countless Victorian women far beyond the domestic realm, introducing them to practical and moral necessities for the advancement of women, and in turn strengthening the religious identity of the American women's movement. Bushnell would participate in critical ways in each of these three endeavors. And although she never abandoned her belief in the compatibility of Christianity and feminism, her work in missions, temperance, and purity would reveal to her the complexities that characterized any alliance between the two.

The first of these three undertakings, the women's missionary movement, helped align Christianity and women's rights by expanding the opportunities available to enterprising women like Bushnell, and by empowering those who remained at home by assigning Western, Christian women unique roles in the evangelization of the world, and as emissaries of a higher civilization. Championing "Woman's Work for Woman," female missionaries helped forge a vision of global sisterhood that purported to unite women the world over, elevating gender over race and nation. In doing so, they helped lay the groundwork for a gender-based activism that would draw countless women into the realm of social reform in the late nineteenth and early twentieth centuries.

As the clearest example of such gender-based activism, temperance reform emerged as the second great movement bringing Christian women together to work on behalf of their sex. By presenting temperance work as a Christian duty, temperance leaders swelled their ranks with Christian wives and mothers, thereby introducing tens of thousands of American women to civic engagement more generally, and to the women's rights movement in particular. Though not all temperance crusaders supported all efforts for women's rights, a significant number of temperance women did come to embrace suffrage as a critical means by which they could reform society, effectively transforming suffrage from a radical cause to a respectable endeavor.

Finally, the social purity campaign represented the third key alliance between Christianity and feminism at the end of the nineteenth century. Closely linked to temperance reform, the social purity movement brought together a diverse group of women and men who sought to abolish prostitution and the sexual double standard. Working together with women's rights activists in their efforts to protect society's most vulnerable women and advocate for moral equality, Christian purity reformers not only became attuned to societal injustices that contributed to women's oppression, but they also helped transform sex from a taboo subject to one of respectable, even pious conversation.

Together, these three movements helped to unite Christianity and feminism in a mutually supportive relationship. To a degree this alliance strengthened the movement for women's rights, vastly expanding its ranks and fostering feminist critiques of traditional Christian doctrines concerning women's societal roles and religious authority. But the alliance could also work at counter purposes. For example, by reinforcing the notion that Western, Christian women enjoyed positions far superior to women across the globe, the missionary impulse could at times stifle efforts to reform Western social and religious traditions. And the influence of Christian women who had come to women's rights through temperance and purity reform could hinder more radical approaches to the emancipation of women from taking hold within the broader women's movement.

Missions, temperance, and social purity, then, had the potential to both confirm and disrupt traditional notions of Christianity, gender, sexuality, and morality.[2] For Bushnell, each of these movements would eventually end up illuminating the shortcomings of traditional Christianity—most particularly, the shortcomings and hypocrisies of Christian men. Though she would never waver in her belief that Christianity and feminism must go hand in hand, Bushnell's work in missions, temperance, and purity would lead her to radically alter her notion of what Christianity entailed.

Mission to China: 1879–1882

In November 1879, Bushnell arrived in the city of Kiukiang (Jiujiang),[3] a "treaty port" along the Yangtze River. In the wake of the Treaty of Tianjin, signed in the midst of the Second Opium War (1856–1860), Western powers had forcibly opened up Kiukiang to foreign trade, and to Christian missions. Quickly emerging as a center of trade in both rice and opium, the city also came to serve as headquarters for the Methodist Episcopal Church's Central China Mission. Several years before Bushnell's arrival, the Methodist Woman's Foreign Missionary Society (WFMS) had established a boarding school in Kiukiang. The local inhabitants, however, were suspicious of the missionaries' intentions. Initially refusing to entrust their daughters to the mission school, they later attacked and destroyed the fledgling institution.[4] Undeterred, members of the WFMS determined that "medical aid is the wedge which shall give entrance to many homes and hearts," and they sent instead for female medical missionaries.[5] These new arrivals wasted no time in setting up a dispensary in order to treat Chinese patients, but an excessive workload, together with an enervating climate and frequent exposure to illness, soon took a toll on the missionaries' health. Back home, the WFMS scrambled to send additional workers. Bushnell, "energetic and devoted," had been selected for this task.[6]

Gender, Missions, and Empire

Although medical missionaries were still somewhat rare in the 1870s (only around 3 percent of American women missionaries were trained as physicians),[7] they represented a new approach to missions. Over much of the century, the "anti-civilizing" theories of Rufus Anderson, secretary of the American Board of Commissioners for Foreign Missions, had shaped the foreign mission venture. Insisting that missionaries preach "nothing but Christ," Anderson had discouraged missionaries from "Westernizing" indigenous Christians in any way. The growing emphasis on the Christian home, however, and the ensuing recruitment of female missionaries, helped to replace this "anti-civilizing" framework with a more holistic approach.[8] Barred from preaching, women missionaries instead focused their efforts in the areas of education and medicine, and, particularly in the case of missionary wives, in modeling the virtues of Victorian domesticity.[9] Advancing a "Woman's Work for Woman" theory of mission, female missionaries offered medical care and training, English language lessons, and access to Western education more broadly to indigenous women and children. Rather than aspiring to accommodate the gospel to local cultural settings, missionary women embraced a transformative gospel, one that promised to bring the blessings of Western civilization to heathen societies.[10] In some cases, by bringing practical skills and cultural knowledge along with gospel teaching, women helped open up once hostile settings to the gospel message.[11]

Within this framework, evangelization necessarily entailed cultural conversion, the adoption of Western social values and practices. In this regard, the foreign missionary movement can rightly be seen as a powerful expression of cultural imperialism.[12] Indeed, from the 1960s to the 1990s, there emerged a scholarly consensus castigating foreign missionaries as agents of cultural imperialism.[13] Along with their male colleagues, missionary women were understood to be implicated in the imperial project. As "purifiers of empire," missionary women played a critical role in legitimating Western expansion as a benevolent enterprise.[14] And women's domestic identities were central to this justification for empire. As Amy Kaplan explains, somewhat paradoxically it was through their exclusion from the public realm of commerce and politics that women participated most actively in American expansionism. Catherine Beecher made this point explicitly in A Treatise on Domestic Economy, arguing as early as the 1840s that it was by "exhibiting to the world the beneficent influences of Christianity" through the graces of female domesticity that women could advance America's global mission.[15] As domesticity became inextricably linked to Anglo-Saxon racial identity, and to the blessings of Christianity and Western civilization, American expansionism could be justified in terms of bringing the unmitigated blessings of "true woman-hood" to women the world over.[16] "Imperial domesticity" thus provided a powerful justification for Christian missions and Western expansionism, and the two were closely linked.

Essential to this justification, and indeed at the very heart of "Woman's Work for Woman," was the depiction of foreign women as victims in need of redemption. In critical ways, missionary women's justification for the expansion of their own duties thus "actively depended on the subordination of their heathen sisters," on perpetuating a view of the "degraded female Other."[17] Perhaps nowhere is this attitude better illustrated than in Western responses to the Chinese custom of foot-binding. Evocatively symbolizing the oppression that women suffered in "heathen" cultures, foot-binding powerfully reinforced Westerners' conviction that Christianity had eman-cipated Western women from such cruel and oppressive practices. This emancipatory narrative was central to the missionary impulse, and to the women's missionary movement. In this regard, initial global encounters only served to bolster Anglo-American Protestants' sense of cultural supe-riority, and of the redemptive effects of Christianity on Western culture.

It was through a "missionary-imperial feminism," then, that Western women carved out new opportunities for themselves, sometimes at the expense of their "heathen sisters."[18] Premising their work on an imag-ined global "sisterhood," Western women situated themselves as sav-iors to non-Western or "heathen" women, and in this way justified their own advancement in education, and their expanding public roles.[19] In Bushnell's case, not only was the perceived oppression of Chinese women essential to raising support for her mission to China, but the need for female doctors to treat Chinese women was pivotal in opening up medical training for American women, at a time when the profession was largely deemed a masculine endeavor.[20] In many ways, then, the advancement of Western women became deeply implicated in imperial conquest, a legacy that Western feminists continue to confront today.[21]

Western women's engagement with their "heathen sisters" was not, however, an unequivocal source of empowerment. For even as they advanced their own cause by exercising power over women less power-ful than themselves, Western women frequently ended up ignoring the deeply engrained patriarchy within their own society.[22] By indicting "heathen" patriarchy, missionary women both implicitly and explicitly ended up affirming gender relations at home; as one British missionary woman exclaimed, "to think of the difference" between themselves and their heathen counterparts "was to excite feelings of grateful wonder."[23] Quick to decry the failings of "heathen" societies, many missionary women remained blind to the shortcomings of their own. Within the framework of "missionary-imperial feminism," for example, domesticity came to be seen not as a set of restrictions placed on women's activities, but rather as a key marker of "civilization."[24] By turning the attention of Western women outward to the comparatively greater oppression of "heathen" women, missionary discourse frequently cloaked the limitations that Victorian ideology imposed upon Western women.[25]

The influence of this domestic-imperial ideology stretched far beyond the mission field, as a generation of Protestant women came to understand their faith—and their world—in terms of the female missionary experience. By the early twentieth century, over three million women were dues-paying members of a women's missionary society, making the woman's missionary movement "the largest grassroots movement of women in the United States."[26] Consuming vast quantities of an expansive missionary literature, a significant portion of American women became conversant in a "missionary ethnology" that drew clear distinctions between Western and non-Western women, and that emphasized the emancipatory nature of Christianity.[27] Missionary letters and journals introduced women to "an entire vocabulary that implied the degradation of women: zenanas and harems, the seraglio and the bagnio; female infanticide and suttee; concubinage and polygamy; bride sale; foot-binding and ear and nose boring; consecrated prostitution and sacrifice . . . child marriage and slavery."[28] This literature attributed the wrongs suffered by women globally to faulty religion, but placed the wrongs suffered by American women "in contradistinction to Protestant Christianity." According to historian Joan Jacobs Brumberg, then, "the mass of American women came to use cross-cultural information to support rather than challenge gender and family arrangements in their own country." After all, compared to their oppressed sisters around the globe, Western women seemed to have little reason to complain. As a result, Brumberg asserts, "churchgoing American women, largely preoccupied with ameliorating what they considered to be the degraded condition of their non-Christian sisters, were generally skeptical, if not downright hostile, to the emergence of an indigenous feminist political movement and its critique of sexual subordination at home."[29]

The influence of missionary encounters on sending cultures, however, points to the complex nature of cultural interactions that a simplistic framework of cultural imperialism obscures, which in turn allows for a more nuanced understanding of the connections between gender, power, and imperial conquest. In recent years, scholars of American foreign relations, and of Christian missions, have contested any presumed unidirectionality in the case of Western imperial encounters, rejecting frameworks that imply "a one-way imposition of power from sending to receiving cultures, ignoring the ability of people in the receiving cultures to interpret and adapt the transmitted messages."[30]

To begin with, attention to the agency of non-Western peoples to receive, resist, and adapt what Westerners sought to impose upon them allows for a more complex understanding of the process of cultural exchange, even in an imperial context, and contributes to a more nuanced understanding of the missionary enterprise. A multidirectional model of cultural exchange, for example, better allows for the agency of indigenous converts, and of non-Western women who worked with Western missionaries and reformers, without dismissing them merely as "dupes of cultural imperialism."[31] But a multidirectional framework also allows for a more dynamic understanding of the sending culture, and of the influences of global encounters on the missionaries themselves. As Jane Hunter notes, even as "imperialism was dependent on domesticity as a way of inspiring, legitimating, and redeeming its projects," women's missionary experience also "fed back into American culture and ideology" and "ultimately represented a source of *challenge* to the dominant nationalist culture."[32]

Work within the field of missiology, too, offers useful correctives to a simplistic characterization of Christian missions as an uncomplicated imperial project. Drawing on Christian history and theology, for example, Andrew Walls explains that within the Christian gospel itself reside opposing tendencies: an "indigenizing principle," and a "pilgrim principle." The gospel is always incarnated, Walls argues, received in a particular time and place, and "indigenized" in particular cultural settings.[33] Yet at the same time, the gospel has a transformative element; followers of Christ are meant to be transformed, set apart from the culture in which they live. "Along with the indigenizing principle which makes his faith a place to feel at home," Walls explains, "the Christian inherits the pilgrim principle, which whispers to him that he has no abiding city and warns him that to be faithful to Christ will put him out of step with his society; for that society never existed, in East or West, ancient time or modern, which could absorb the word of Christ painlessly into its system."[34] In this way, the gospel can be seen both "as prisoner and liberator of culture," and both tendencies remain equally rooted in the gospel itself.[35]

Nineteenth-century Protestantism reflected well these conflicting tendencies. At the beginning of the century, the Christian gospel had seemed inextricably linked to Western culture. Over the previous three centuries, from the time the long-isolated West had begun in earnest to encounter non-Western peoples, "circumstances dictated that Christianity became more European than it had ever been before, and did so just at the point when Europe became more Christian than it had ever been before." As Walls explains, "Events so welded Christianity and the West together, and the domestication of Christianity in the West was so complete, the process of acculturation there so successful, that the faith seemed inseparable from the categories of European life and thought."[36] Then and now, this thorough enculturation of Christianity within Western culture during an age of global encounter has obscured the longer history of world Christianity, a history that unmistakably demonstrates that Christianity was not originally, nor has it ever been exclusively a Western faith. At the height of the Western missionary movement, however, "Western Christians had long grown used to the idea that they were guardians of a 'standard' Christianity."[37]

In critical ways, this idea of Christendom justified and propelled colonial conquest, sanctifying imperial expansion under the cloak of spreading the Christian gospel to "heathen lands." The missionary movement was indeed deeply implicated in imperial conquest. And yet at the same time, foreign missions, and colonialism itself, effectively contributed to the erosion of Christendom. As missionaries worked to express the gospel in other languages and to share a universalizing message of redemption in varying cultural settings, questions of faith and culture became manifest. Often finding themselves working at cross purposes with representatives of the "official" colonial presence, missionaries increasingly came to discern "a principle of separation between the religion of Christendom and its political, military, and economic power."[38] Western colonialism thus paradoxically helped to force "a distinction between Christianity and Christendom."[39] The missionary movement can thus be seen both as "the last flourish of Christendom," and as "a departure from Christendom or perhaps an Abrahamic journey out of it."[40]

Within the American missionary movement, both the indigenizing and the pilgrim principles were evident. On the one hand, evangelical Christianity's emphasis on sin and atonement dictated that all people were fallen and in need of redemption, regardless of race, class, or nation. Evangelicals had in fact frequently demonstrated a knack for critiquing the culture in which they found themselves.[41] But as the revivalist tradition moved from the margins to the mainstream, many evangelicals had abandoned this critical stance. Believing that the trappings of "civilization" represented the outgrowth of Christianity's long-standing influence in Western culture, they considered this cultural baggage essential to, and indeed inseparable from, the faith. On the mission field, many missionaries carried with them and maintained a supreme confidence in Western culture, and global encounters frequently ended up confirming and bolstering Westerners' sense of religious and cultural superiority.

At times, however, missionary encounters led to a more critical introspection that attuned missionaries to the enculturation of their own faith. This seemed particularly to be the case among those influenced by holiness teachings. Accustomed to positioning themselves as "outsiders" within their own culture, holiness Christians tended to divide the world not between the civilized and the savage, but rather between the saved and the unsaved—a traditional evangelical distinction that cut across culture, race, and nation. Aware that God's power often manifested itself through weakness, they were not surprised when indigenous Christians evidenced powerful workings of the Spirit, and they remained open to the possibility that God could use the faith of non-Westerners to bring spiritual revival to the West.[42] And many remained skeptical of the promises of civilization, knowing from experience that "civilization is a strange tree that brings forth good and evil fruit; it blows hot and cold; it helps save some and it damns many whom it touches."[43]

The influence of holiness Christianity ran deep within the Methodist WFMS. As Dana Robert notes, "a substantial percentage of female missionaries of the Methodist Episcopal Church were sanctified or had concrete experiences of a higher Christian life," and meetings of the WFMS were often infused with holiness teachings.[44] More closely attuned to the limits of "civilized society" than many of their contemporaries, Methodist holiness missionary women, and their supporters back home, were better positioned to critique the elevation of domesticity that other Protestants considered essential to the faith, and to the missionary enterprise. For holiness women, then, interactions with a global "sisterhood" of believers could at times advance, rather than stunt, a nascent feminist consciousness.[45]

Even so, holiness convictions and a belief in the superiority of Western civilization were not mutually exclusive, particularly among women who combined holiness theology with a mission to sanctify society, both at home and abroad. As a holiness Methodist woman, Bushnell was a product of these conflicting impulses. Without dismissing or downplaying the ways in which Bushnell was both agent and beneficiary of Western imperial hegemony, then, a more complex, multidirectional framework of cultural exchange better illuminates Bushnell's experience on the mission field, and the ways in which her global encounters would reveal to her the contours of Christianity and culture in the late Victorian era.

Days of Severe Trial

Arriving in Kiukiang in the fall of 1879, Bushnell was "happy in the prospect of [her] work," which would involve tending to the medical needs of Chinese women and children. Wishing to first learn the language and take time to put her medical supplies in order, Bushnell initially made every effort to avoid seeing patients. She soon found it impossible, however, to turn away the many patients who came to her door. By early spring she had treated 32 patients and written 249 prescriptions, and by that summer she was seeing over 100 patients and dispensing over 200 prescriptions in one month alone.[46] At first glance, the demand for Bushnell's services appears to reinforce missionary narratives that portrayed Chinese women as victims, suffering from a lack of access to medical care. Although consistent with images of a benevolent imperialism and effective in raising funds among sympathetic American churchgoers, this characterization was not entirely true. As Connie Shemo makes clear, "Scholars have demonstrated the existence of a sophisticated body of literature devoted to the health of women within traditions of Chinese medicine," and Chinese women had a variety of options available to them for medical care.[47] Bushnell's own reports reveal that her treatments were not always superior to those of Chinese practitioners. Indeed, Western medicine was ineffective in addressing a number of illnesses at that time, including tuberculosis. (Bushnell herself recounted that she was unable to cure a woman suffering from tuberculosis who had traveled "fifteen miles in a wheelbarrow" to see her.)[48] In a few areas, however—particularly in the case of surgeries, and in the treatment of eye diseases—Western medicine often produced superior results. It was, in fact, in treating the grandmother of the "second greatest official" in Kiukiang for an eye problem that Bushnell garnered some attention among the local population.[49]

It was a more unusual event, however, that established Bushnell's reputation far and wide, and dramatically increased the demand for her services. One hot summer night, thieves broke into her mission compound and gravely injured the gateman, leaving him for dead. Much to the amazement of a crowd of curious onlookers, Bushnell promptly attended to the gaping wound that extended from his forehead to his mouth, tying up the severed arteries and stitching his nose back together, as the man slipped in and out of consciousness.[50] In the end the gatekeeper recovered, but rumors quickly spread throughout the city and the surrounding country that he had actually died seven times that night, only to have been brought back to life each time by Bushnell's medicine.[51] Due to her sudden fame and increased patient load, Bushnell found it necessary to retreat for a time to a bungalow in the mountains until things quieted down. Although she enjoyed her brief respite, while there she sustained an injury to her spine that would ail her for years to come. Nevertheless, it was not long before she returned to Kiukiang and resumed her demanding duties.[52]

In the course of one year, Bushnell treated 70 respiratory diseases, 83 alimentary system diseases, 8 diseases of the nervous system, 122 febrile disorders, 7 urinary and renal disorders, 9 heart diseases, 42 gynecological and obstetrical conditions, 115 eye and ear conditions, 122 venereal conditions, and 62 "miscellaneous medical" conditions, in addition to performing 76 surgeries.[53] Her mission clinic, however, was chronically understaffed. She administered anesthesia herself and nursed inpatients in an empty apartment or on her veranda, all while running a dispensary out of her home.[54]

Before long, Bushnell began to suffer from "nervous prostration, caused by anxiety and overwork."[55] Making matters worse, Bushnell found the hot summers nearly unbearable. Over fifty years later, she would recall "with horror" the "intense, sickly heat" that would settle on the region each summer. "Every one," she remembered, "both missionaries and natives, suffered, and most of them were seriously, some dangerously, sick with remittent fever and other pests."[56] These were "days of severe trial" for Bushnell, according to a writer for the WFMS, during which she "learned new lessons of the wonderful love that never forsakes, which were of incomparable value."[57] Despite such opportunities for spiritual growth, Bushnell's colleagues pleaded with supporters back home to send assistance: "The medical work is winning its way to the hearts of this reserved people as nothing else could do," wrote one of her fellow missionaries, but "Dr. Bushnell is working much too hard. She sadly needs help. Pray for us, and pray for the medical workers most of all." The writer pleaded with her readers to "stir up some of our girls to this all-important work."[58] Bushnell herself, in a letter to *The Chicago Medical Journal and Examiner*, petitioned American medical professionals to encourage their "charitably disposed Christian medical students" to go to China, where they could both "heal the sick and preach the gospel to the poor."[59]

In 1881 the WFMS responded by sending Ella Gilchrest, a close friend and former classmate of Bushnell's, to the mission in Kiukiang. No stranger to hard work, Gilchrest had supported herself through high school, college, and throughout her time at the Chicago's Woman's Medical College. Two years Bushnell's junior in school, she and Bushnell had worked together at the Chicago Hospital for Women and Children, and it had been under Bushnell's guidance that Gilchrest had converted to Christianity; her "development in holy things were [sic] so rapid and clear that in a few short weeks she evinced the strength and beauty of full Christian womanhood." After graduating as valedictorian of her class in February 1881, Gilchrest responded to the Lord's call, and no doubt to her friend's urging, and set sail for China. Bushnell later recollected Gilchrest's arrival in Kiukiang: "the Chinese were sick and dying on every side; and, though we did not mean to overburden her, necessity threw every heavy burden on her willing shoulders." Gilchrest soon became ill with chronic bronchitis, but even then, "she treated from twenty to seventy dispensary patients a day, putting up all their prescriptions with her own hands, and besides looking up hospital cases and making out visits," all while spending several hours each day studying Chinese, her evenings reading medicine, and her Sundays teaching Sunday school and helping with the mission work.[60] Not surprisingly, both Gilchrest's and Bushnell's health deteriorated, and in the spring of 1882 the two friends found it necessary to return to America.

Defeated and dejected, Bushnell had much to ponder in the weeks she spent crossing the Pacific with her ailing friend. On the one hand, she had accomplished much. She had treated hundreds of patients and become conversant in the Chinese language, and while in Kiukiang she had mentored Shi Meiyu, a young Chinese girl who would go on to become a prominent Chinese medical missionary.[61] At the time, however, it seemed to Bushnell as though her missionary career had ended in failure.[62] Overwhelmed with exhaustion, she was at a loss as to what to do next. As it turned out, however, her years in China had planted the seeds for what would eventually become her life's work.

Sex-Biased Translation

Two-and-a-half years earlier, Bushnell had commenced her missionary career confident in the superiority of Western, Christian culture, eager to bring both the gospel and the advantages of modern medicine to the benighted Chinese. Her initial encounters with the Chinese had done little to disrupt this confidence. As a medical doctor, she was often dismissive of Chinese "superstitions," and she judged the Chinese utterly lacking in "real knowledge of the fundamental branches of medicine." (She found the use of bat or sparrow feces for ophthalmological purposes particularly revolting.)[63] She was also bewildered by her patients' unpredictable behavior, noting that "we receive indiscriminately from them glowing compliments, tearful gratitude, indifference, distrust, and even insult, and their conduct toward each other is as variable as towards the foreign physician." Her assessment of the Chinese was most favorable when their practices aligned most closely with Victorian values, particularly when she witnessed glimpses of what she deemed proper domestic affections. Reflecting on "the virtues and failings of the Chinese patient," she could only conclude that "Christianity would benefit any and all of them greatly."[64] Despite her background in holiness Methodism, then, Bushnell's attitudes toward Chinese women, and the confidence she placed in Christianity and Western civilization, initially seemed to conform to the contours of imperial domesticity.

Only a few weeks after arriving in China, however, Bushnell's faith in the emancipatory power of Western Christianity began to waver. The catalyst for this change was a Chinese translation of the Bible. Though still a novice in the language, Bushnell was working to decipher a text when she happened upon a seeming discrepancy between the Chinese translation of Philippians 4:2–3, and the King James Version, with which she was familiar. In that passage the Apostle Paul mentions two women, Euodia and Syntyche, with whom he "labored in the gospel." The Chinese translation, however, had switched the helpers from female to male. She checked several other Chinese translations and discovered that they, too, obscured the fact that Paul's fellow laborers were women.[65]

When Bushnell confronted a male missionary about this discrepancy, he explained that "undoubtedly it was so rendered because of pagan prejudice against the ministry of women." What seemed to him a logical and pragmatic decision was for Bushnell a shocking revelation. It "had never before entered [her] mind that such a thing could be," that the gospel of Christ could be blatantly distorted to align with cultural prejudices. It soon occurred to her that if devoted Christian missionaries could so easily justify a "sex-biased" Chinese translation, other translations of the Bible might also bear the mark of prejudice. She began to compare her Chinese and English Bibles to her Greek Testament, and soon discovered additional signs "that pointed in the same direction." She turned to the Old Testament Scriptures as well, first investigating a Greek translation, and then taking up a study of Hebrew. From that point on, Bushnell devoted her spare moments to a meticulous examination of the Greek and Hebrew Scriptures in search of further instances of male bias that had corrupted the English text.[66]

In spite of—or perhaps because of—the formative years she had spent as a part of Evanston's vibrant women's community, Bushnell had initially displayed little awareness of the limitations that Western, Christian tradition placed upon women. Despite her exposure to holiness teachings, for instance, she apparently held rather conventional views on women's roles in the church, considering it "neither desirable nor necessary for women to preach the Gospel; it was unbecoming." But her discovery of the distorted Chinese Bible would begin to change her opinions "as to woman's part in the Gospel."[67] Her growing skepticism toward traditional Christianity would then begin to embolden her to question Victorian conventions, and indeed the very foundations of Western culture. Though she did not immediately shed all cultural prejudice, she did begin to reassess many truths that Westerners held dear. From this point on, any confidence she expressed in the superiority of Christianity was profoundly muted by her conviction that the Christianity practiced and preached by the vast majority of Western Christians reflected a troubling distortion of the true faith. Rather than confirming her sense of Western superiority, then, Bushnell's cross-cultural experiences revealed to her the enculturation of the gospel in her own society, and ultimately enabled her to develop a prophetic critique of her inherited Christian tradition.

The Woman's Christian Temperance Union

Before Bushnell could begin to sort out the significance of these experiences, she needed to tend to more immediate concerns. After arriving in

San Francisco at the end of their sea voyage, she and Gilchrest traveled on to Denver, where Bushnell set up a medical practice and worked to regain her own health while caring for her sick friend. Bushnell, however, "had not studied medicine for its own sake, but as a help in Christian work,"[68] and soon became discontented with her practice, but she found an opportunity for more fulfilling work with the Colorado branch of the Woman's Christian Temperance Union (WCTU). Temperance had only recently emerged as the centerpiece of women's reform efforts, thanks in large part to the remarkable expansion of the WCTU under the leadership of Bushnell's friend and former teacher, Frances Willard.

The origins of the WCTU can be traced to the winter of 1873–1874, when women in cities and towns across the Midwest initiated a seemingly spontaneous "Woman's War" against alcohol.[69] Women and men had been active in temperance reform since the 1830s, but as the movement had come to emphasize the political process over moral suasion, women had become increasingly marginalized.[70] Women, however—lacking access to divorce or the means to support themselves—often bore the brunt of their husbands' drunkenness. The Civil War only exacerbated women's concerns, arousing fears that husbands and sons might return home with a taste for alcohol, and the years after the war seemed to bring additional threats in the form of hundreds of thousands of beer-drinking Southern and Eastern European immigrants arriving on American shores each year.[71]

In the face of these perceived perils, women took matters into their own hands that winter, dramatically descending upon local saloons to protest the consumption of alcohol. Evanston, a dry community, was not directly involved in this Woman's Crusade, and Willard was at the time embroiled in her battle over the direction of the Woman's College. But by the spring of 1874 she had resigned her position as dean, and while visiting friends in Pittsburg she decided to observe a group of crusaders who had been protesting local saloons for several months. Warmly welcomed at the crusade headquarters, Willard soon found herself accompanying the crusaders to a saloon, where, surrounded by barrels of alcohol, glittering decanters, sawdust floors, "abundant fumes," and "a crowd of unwashed, unkempt, hard-looking men," she experienced her "Crusade baptism."[72] The next day she left Pittsburgh, and within a week she had become president of the Chicago WCTU; five years later, in the fall of 1879 (right around the time Bushnell arrived in China), Willard was elected president of the national organization. By the end of the next decade, the WCTU had become the largest women's organization of its time.[73]

Despite her Methodist upbringing, Willard herself had never exhibited a zealous interest in temperance, but she understood that the Woman's Crusade had "transformed the temperance movement into the paramount women's issue of the day,"[74] and she glimpsed an unprecedented opportunity to mobilize women across the nation and around the world. Her years in Evanston had prepared her well for her new task. Highly educated and conversant in the mores of middle-class Methodism, she was also experienced in organizational tactics and institution-building; her close affiliation with members of the WFMS may well have provided her with an administrative model for expanding the WCTU across the nation, and her holiness background had introduced her to techniques such as camp meetings and drawing-room Scripture readings, which she then adapted to the temperance cause. More significant still, holiness teachings had instilled in her a sense of women's religious empowerment, helping her to craft the movement's emphasis on moral purity irrespective of gender, and providing her with the courage to transgress traditional notions of respectability when necessary.[75]

Purity and Power

In many ways, the doctrine of holiness helped Willard develop and promote a cohesive temperance worldview that resonated powerfully with Victorian Protestants. Historians have suggested that the holiness quest for spiritual perfection appealed to so many nineteenth-century Americans because it offered individuals a sense of control over the self; in a world that seemed increasingly disorderly, one in which the boom and bust cycles of industrial capitalism appeared to have severed the traditional relationship between virtue and reward, holiness Christianity provided believers with a sense of power over their spiritual lives, at the very least. Temperance might well be seen as a manifestation of this same impulse. By embracing a moral order that celebrated self-restraint, Victorians could reassert order and control in the midst of uncertainty. Alcohol, by signifying a lack of control, constituted a source of pollution, of social evil.[76] In more practical terms, it also threatened the economic basis of a new industrial economy, one that depended on the discipline and self-control of both managers and workers.[77]

Temperance reform swept the nation in such dramatic fashion, then, because it addressed an array of cultural needs. For Protestants, temperance signified the outward evidence of inner transformation, linking individual conversion to society at large; in essence, it gave social and political expression to evangelical belief.[78] More broadly, temperance reform offered Victorians a tangible way to reclaim a sense of orderliness in an increasingly disorderly world. But at its heart, temperance remained a women's movement—one rooted in evangelical and holiness Christianity and premised on a largely antagonistic view of women and men.[79] For middle-class Victorian women who had been relegated to the domestic realm, the movement enabled them to transform their own powerlessness into a powerful crusade to purify society. By advocating personal restraint, women could both secure their own freedom and assert a form of control over wayward husbands and sons. In this way, temperance drew together Christians and feminists in common cause in the late Victorian era, and for a time the movement would define the shape that both Christianity and feminism would take.

A deft and charismatic leader, Willard quickly garnered the support of thousands of eager and ambitious women, and it was not long before she expanded the purpose of the WCTU by introducing a "Do-everything policy"; under her leadership, the organization eventually boasted thirty-nine separate departments and advanced causes ranging from dress reform to world peace. Not long after taking charge of the organization, Willard began advocating women's suffrage as a crucial means to carry out the WCTU's ambitious agenda.[80] At that time, few respectable middle-class women supported suffrage, or women's rights more broadly, for to think in such terms seemed to violate the virtue of self-sacrifice at the very center of the Victorian ideal of Christian womanhood.[81] But Willard made a compelling case that wives and mothers needed the vote in order to protect their homes from the evils of alcohol. By framing suffrage in terms of "home protection," she helped transform women's suffrage from a disreputable cause to a religious duty, thereby bringing thousands of women into the suffrage fold.[82] Many women who joined her "White Ribbon Army" initially had little notion of Willard's expansive program, but she soon won them over. As one of her followers explained, "If Frances Willard should push a plank out into the ocean and should beckon the White Ribbon Army to follow her out to the end of it, they would all go without a question!"[83]

Willard promoted suffrage vigorously, but also strategically, leading her "army" by degrees. As an early biographer explains, "Had she announced in 1876 for full suffrage, the entire Union would have been alienated. Then she only asked for their support on the temperance ballot—a most reasonable suggestion! But once the Union declared for this, she advanced to equal rights, and by the time the Union again caught up with her, she was declaring for a woman president."[84] Willard herself credited the WCTU with "enlisting in the suffrage movement that important person, the average woman"—the woman who had never read John Stuart Mill or the *Woman's Journal*, who believed she had all the rights she needed and had no desire to vote. She succeeded in making the average woman think it her duty to want to vote, and as she put it, "When the average woman wants it, the broad shouldered, good-natured average man will give it."[85]

It is not clear if Bushnell was involved in the initial meetings of the Chicago branch of the WCTU, but several of her close friends were, and when she joined Denver's chapter it did not take her long to feel at home in the organization. What is clear is that her new hometown offered ample opportunity for temperance reform. Denver was in the midst of the great Western mining boom, and in 1880 the city's 35,000 inhabitants were served by 98 saloons; by the next year the population had nearly doubled, and the consumption of alcohol increased accordingly.[86] Known for its "saloons, prostitution, and urban vice," Denver had earned a reputation as a "[center] of moral libertinism"; as a city where men significantly out-numbered women, Denver "seemed to Victorian women to exemplify the dangers of men's living without the moral guidance of women."[87] Hardly a setting conducive to the self-restraint that Victorians celebrated, it was rather a place where "even a normally self-controlled man might lose his hold on self-restraint and abandon his commitment to Victorian moral-ity."[88] Local government officials only exacerbated the situation. "Reluctant citizens," the city's leaders were intent upon pursuing wealth; they often tolerated or even supported saloons and prostitution, and sought to impose only a "minimum of order."[89] Indeed, the Colorado legislature not only appeared "indifferent" to the work of female reformers, but "flaunted its masculinity by holding its deliberations in saloons."[90]

For middle-class women like Bushnell who arrived in Western cities during this unrestrained time, conventional benevolent work became a way to oppose "the male-dominated social order" they encountered.[91] Just as they felt called to foreign mission fields on behalf of "heathen" women, many Victorian women looked for ways to answer that call closer to home, finding local opportunities to engage in "woman's work for woman." A women's "home mission" movement thus emerged alongside foreign missions and thrived in Western cities like Denver, where women found vast opportunities for their endeavors.[92] As historian Peggy Pascoe explains, Protestant women soon "invested the phrase home mission with ideological significance," designating it not only with a sense of location, but also tapping into the rhetoric of the Christian home, the centerpiece of Victorian culture. But home mission women employed this rhetoric in a different way than did many Victorian men. Rather than as a bastion of male patriarchy, Protestant women put forth an image of the home as "a symbol of female moral authority," one "pruned of patriarchal power." In doing so, they abandoned the idea of female submission as "a mark of true womanhood," and instead identified patriarchal behavior as an intrinsic threat to the Christian home.[93]

It was in the context of this contested "masculine milieu" that Bushnell took up temperance work.[94] She soon established a state newsletter, and in 1884 served as head of the Colorado WCTU.[95] In connection with her temperance work, Bushnell also turned her attention to the city's prostitutes.[96] Her work at the Chicago Hospital for Women and Children had already acquainted her with the plight of destitute women, and Denver's saloons introduced her to the close connections between alcohol and prostitution. Around the time Bushnell arrived in Denver, the city's tenderloin district was one of the most notorious in the nation. Demand for prostitutes was high among miners streaming through the city on their way to the Leadville mines, and distressingly low wages for other forms of women's work kept up the supply.[97] For a time the city permitted open solicitation, raising the profile of the city's nearly 500 prostitutes, but once solicitation was prohibited, officers routinely created public spectacles by raiding the red light district to round up and arrest "depraved women."[98] Bushnell soon began to organize efforts to provide the city's prostitutes with opportunities for reform, and since a small number of Denver's prostitutes were Chinese women who plied their trade in the city's seventeen opium dens, she began working as an "evangelist" to the Chinese as well. Before long she was asked to take charge of the WCTU's Chinese Departments of the West, and though she had not yet fully recovered her strength, she began making ambitious plans to open a temperance school focusing on the abolition of opium.[99] Before she could carry out these plans, however, Willard tapped her to serve as national evangelist for the WCTU's new department of social purity.[100]

The Social Purity Movement

With roots in moral reform campaigns dating back to the 1820s,[101] the social purity movement brought together a diverse group of activists, including evangelicals and holiness advocates, suffragists, socialists, former abolitionists, and temperance workers. "Social purity" can be difficult to define; a dynamic movement that could be both repressive and subversive, it at various times entailed efforts to rescue and reform prostitutes, combat the government regulation of prostitution, raise age of consent laws, address family violence, rape, and incest, eliminate red light districts, promote sex education, oppose contraception and abortion, and censor "obscene literature."[102] But at the crux of social purity was a critique of the sexual double standard, the Victorian convention that held women to far higher standards of sexual purity than men.

Purity reformers sought to rectify this imbalance not by freeing women from strict standards of purity, but rather by raising expectations of male sexual restraint. In a culture where women were circumscribed politically, economically, and socially—where women could be held culpable for crimes perpetrated against them, and where women's reputations and livelihoods could be jeopardized by sexual activity—sexual restraint seemed to best serve women's interest.[103] To social purity reformers, evangelicals and women's rights activists alike, sexual reform was a means to social change.[104] By controlling sexuality, reformers sought to empower women within their families, and within the larger social realm. In essence, by championing sexual restraint, purity reformers hoped to transform Victorian women's powerlessness into a positive identity.[105] In this way, many evangelicals and women's rights activists could join together in a common effort, even if only for a time.

The centrality of sex to late-Victorian evangelical reform, then, should not be characterized simply as a "prudish" backlash against evolving social mores. Rather, the purity movement exemplifies a complex engagement with larger social and economic transformations in a rapidly industrializing nation. Scholars have noted, for example, how "the allegedly private world of sexuality" blurs the unstable boundaries between male and female, between the public and the private—categories crucial to the organization of Victorian society. The management of sexuality, then, has as much to do with these social instabilities as with "religious proscriptions and prescriptions."[106]

The decades after the Civil War were a time of particular fluidity in terms of public and private, male and female. Not only did growing numbers of women expand their activities beyond a narrowly defined domestic sphere, but within the home itself women's roles were shifting in dramatic ways. As historian Phillida Bunkle elaborates, industrialization brought about the waning of an era of domestic production, and as urban middle-class women lost claim to the status of producer, they not only became consumers, but also commodities—objects of consumption. In asserting control over their own bodies, however, "women were resisting objectification, refusing to be consumed."[107] Much like alcohol, then, male sexuality needed to be contained for the sake of women, and for the good of society. Indeed, for many women, temperance and purity reform went hand in hand. But by insisting on holding men to high standards of behavior, temperance and purity reformers alike would be disappointed, time and again, by men's moral shortcomings. Consequently, many of the most devoted reformers developed increasingly antagonistic views of men, and would come to understand their work primarily in terms of protecting vulnerable women from the failings of licentious and predatory men.[108]

The Feminization of Virtue

Even as reformers concerned themselves with the moral failings of Victorian men, they contested as well the elevation of female virtue, which they located at the root of the sexual double standard. Victorians not only idealized female virtue, but they had come to consider virtue itself a feminine trait, exemplified by women's purity, tenderness, delicacy, emotionalism, passivity, and self-sacrifice. As the figure who most clearly exemplified such virtue, the Victorian mother inhabited a hallowed position in Victorian society. Through her purity, love, and self-sacrifice, she ensured the perpetuation of a virtuous society. To many Victorians, this feminine conception of virtue appeared both natural and God-ordained; that virtue was a feminine trait and that women were virtuous had assumed the status of common sense. In fact, however, the feminization of virtue amounted to a substantial departure from earlier political and religious conceptions of virtue.

Among American Puritans, for example, personal virtue in the form of self-control, charity, faith, and temperance had been expected of women and men alike. Public virtue, however, possessed a decidedly masculine character, as Puritans looked to patriarchal authority to ensure civil and religious order.[109] This patriarchal notion of public virtue coincided nicely with classical republican thought, which entrusted virtue to (male) property owners, whose independent means purportedly freed them to pursue the common good, rather than their own self-interest. Women, due to their dependent status, were deemed incapable of exercising such public virtue. But by the eighteenth century, popular conceptions of masculine virtue had begun to wane.

On the religious scene, American Protestants began to emphasize the emotional and experiential aspects of their faith. Within this context, women's alleged emotionalism suggested a heightened receptivity to grace; accordingly, female piety became an increasingly popular theme in Protestant sermons. As Protestants embraced the spiritual role of sentiment and affections, many also began to question the Calvinist doctrine of original sin, diminishing women's centuries-long association with the temptress Eve.[110] At the same time, with the rise of entrepreneurial capitalism, the economic basis of the classical republican model began to falter. As time-honored notions of independent property ownership proved less tenable, traditional republican conceptions of virtue could no longer be sustained. Since the new market economy depended upon men openly pursuing self-interest rather than the common good, a new source of social virtue needed to be found, and American women seemed perfectly situated to meet this need. Positioned in the private sphere and insulated from the self-interest of the public marketplace, women became the new guarantors of social virtue. Reflecting larger economic and social transformations, then, virtue itself was transformed; it was effectively relocated from the public to the private realm, and it was secured not through masculine independence, but through female dependence.[111]

As the epitome of feminine restraint and self-sacrifice, sexual purity emerged as the chief measure of virtue.[112] Although sexual purity had been associated with virtue as far back as ancient times, its significance had receded with the rise of Protestantism, as Protestants tended to place greater emphasis on other virtues, such as piety and frugality. During the Victorian era, however, sexual purity resurfaced as a uniquely feminine trait, and one with profound social and spiritual significance. It was during this time that words like "modesty," "decency," and "purity" gradually narrowed from their more general meanings to connote female sexual morality almost exclusively.[113] Some women, particularly members of the middle class, found in this elevation of female purity a new source of public authority and social empowerment.[114] Indeed, female missionaries, temperance workers, and purity reformers alike all drew upon the social and moral authority derived from this construction of virtuous womanhood.[115] But for many women the Victorian ideal of feminine virtue demanded a level of purity that was difficult, if not impossible, to attain.

Purportedly a model for an all-inclusive "womanhood," the ideal was in fact accessible only to those white middle-class women who properly exhibited the requisite gentility, purity, and domesticity. Women who by choice or circumstance failed to attain the ideal of "true womanhood" felt the weight of the cultural expectations they were unable to meet.[116] Such "fallen women" seemed to be everything that the "true woman" was not: coarse and assertive rather than delicate and self-sacrificing, sensual and tainted rather than innocent and pure. Indeed, for many Victorians there seemed to be no gradations in a woman's character; women were either "madonnas or magdalens, Marys or Eves, angels or whores."[117] Evolutionary theorists later bolstered such distinctions by linking female purity with the advance of human civilization, and promiscuity with a primitive type of womanhood. "Fallen women" thus represented human sinfulness, abnormal femininity, and a reversion to primitive practices. In fact, to many Victorians they were hardly women at all.[118] Many respectable Protestants concurred, and considered such women beyond reform.

Social Purity Feminism

By placing unchaste women beyond the reaches of grace, however, such stringent conceptions of female purity contradicted traditional evangelical notions of redemption, and by the 1870s a new generation of reformers, many of whom had been influenced by holiness teachings and were active in temperance work, began to resist this characterization.[119] Not only did they refuse to consider "fallen women" beyond reform, but they also approached social purity not so much as a subject of individual moral reform, but rather as a symptom of the immoral underpinnings of Victorian society. In doing so, they helped align purity with the movement for women's rights.[120] To purity reformers, the injustice of the sexual double standard was nowhere more visible than in the institution of prostitution in Victorian society. Commonly reviled as social outcasts, prostitutes represented the antithesis of "true womanhood," and yet the men who employed their services were generally accepted into respectable society. For social purity feminists, then, prostitution epitomized the sexual double standard, and served as a poignant symbol of women's victimization and powerlessness.[121]

Although in ensuing years social purity would become a mobilizing force in the American women's movement, and would eventually come to rival temperance as the principal task of the WCTU, at the time that

Bushnell took up purity work it was still a controversial endeavor. In their efforts to build a national movement, American purity activists turned to British reformers, particularly to the pioneering work of Josephine Butler. Hailed by British suffragists as the "great founding mother of modern feminism,"[122] Butler, an evangelical reformer with ties to the holiness movement, was convinced that the sexual double standard lay at the root of women's oppression, and in 1869 she initiated a bold campaign to challenge it.[123] She was aware, however, that opposition to prostitution often ended up further vilifying prostitutes, an outcome she wished to avoid at all costs, and so rather than attacking the practice of prostitution itself, she took aim instead at the government regulation of prostitution.

In 1864, in an attempt to curb the spread of venereal diseases among soldiers, the British government had introduced the Contagious Diseases Acts, a set of laws dictating the compulsory examination of prostitutes in port towns, and allowing for the forced confinement of diseased women in Lock Hospitals for up to three months, or until they were "cured"; these laws were soon expanded to other areas and to the civilian population, and the length of time a woman could be confined extended to one year. To Butler, the laws exemplified the double standard at its worst. Starkly revealing the power that men wielded over women in British society, the regulations effectively sanctioned prostitution as a social necessity, while demonstrating the state's willingness to sacrifice the rights of women over their own bodies in order to enable soldiers to do as they pleased, without physical consequence. Butler made opposition to the Acts the focal point of her campaign for women's rights.[124]

By the 1880s, Butler and fellow purity reformers in England had made some headway in mobilizing opposition to the double standard, but they were still looking for a dramatic event to help counter the "conspiracy of silence" that shrouded public discussions of sexuality. In 1885, Butler's friend and supporter, the muckraking journalist William T. Stead, supplied the spark to ignite the movement with his "Maiden Tribute of Modern Babylon," the first exposé of the modern vice trade. Filled with sordid tales of young girls forced, sold, or seduced into prostitution, Stead's narrative succeeded in awakening the British public to the injustices of the double standard, and helped galvanize social purity forces in Britain and beyond.[125]

When Willard read Stead's account, she was immediately convicted. A few WCTU women like Bushnell had already been active in purity efforts; as early as 1877, the WCTU had formed a Committee of Work with

Fallen Women and had established homes for "penitent, erring women," and by 1883, the WCTU had adopted a larger plan for "Social Evil Reform," which involved holding men accountable for engaging with prostitutes, bolstering and better enforcing laws against rape, and raising age of consent laws (at that time twenty states considered ten years to be the age of legal consent, and one state set the age as low as seven). But Willard had not yet embraced purity as central to the WCTU's mission, and many women found the cause repulsive.[126] Stead's account, by drawing attention to the suffering of women and girls in such stark terms, and by compellingly linking intemperance with impurity, convinced Willard that the WCTU "should be as earnestly at work for fallen women as we were then for fallen men."[127]

Only a few weeks after the publication of the "Maiden Tribute," Willard made social purity the centerpiece of her annual address at the WCTU's 1885 Convention. Following Butler's and Stead's lead, Willard sought to break the conspiracy of silence and awaken in her audience both sympathy and outrage: "It is a marvel not to be explained," she admonished her audience, "that we go on the even tenor of our way, too delicate, too refined, too prudish to make any allusion to these awful facts, much less to take up arms against these awful crimes." She urged the women of the WCTU to cease being "victims of conventional cowardice," and instead to take up the work of social purity "by the inculcation of right principles and the serious demand for more equitable laws."[128] As a part of her address, Willard issued a call for a woman to serve as superintendent of a new Department for Suppression of the Social Evil, "a lady who combines the rare qualities of a delicate perception of propriety with practical ability and leisure." The specific task of the new superintendency would be "to trace the relation between the drink habit and the nameless practices, outrages and crimes which disgrace so-called modern 'civilization'; especially the brutalizing influence of malt liquors upon the sexual nature." She was convinced that men would never pass the necessary legislation on their own, but felt that with "the right woman in this place of unequaled need and opportunity," the WCTU might influence men to curb the outrage perpetrated against "defenseless girls and women."[129] Willard concluded her speech with the hope that "some clear brain, true heart and winsome spirit in our great fraternity [might] cry out under the baptism of the Heavenly Spirit, 'Here am I, Lord, send me!'"[130] Despite her eloquent appeal, however, no one stepped forward, and some members remained resolutely opposed to this controversial new direction. Undaunted, Willard resolved to lead the effort herself, and she asked Bushnell to serve as national evangelist for the new Purity Department.[131]

Bushnell was a logical choice. A physician with experience working with "fallen women" dating back to her days as a medical student, Bushnell also had the pluck necessary to broach the indelicate subject of purity. Happy to abandon her medical practice, Bushnell accepted Willard's invitation and moved to Chicago to take up her new responsibilities.[132] Though her friend Ella Gilchrest had succumbed to her chronic illness the previous year, Gilchrest's faithful deathbed witness had led to the conversion of Bertha Lyons, a "reformed fallen woman," and Lyons accompanied Bushnell to Chicago.[133] There the two women set up reading rooms for women and opened up the Anchorage Mission, described in *Good Housekeeping* magazine as "one of the most beautiful benevolent enterprises yet established by the women of Chicago." The mission soon became "the most populous refuge for degraded women in the West," serving more than five thousand women a year.[134]

Although inspired by a desire to change the behavior of men, along with the broader social context that left women vulnerable to male aggression and social stigmatization, rescue homes ultimately ended up placing "more emphasis on changing the lives of the women who entered them than on challenging the power of men."[135] Bushnell's position as a national evangelist for purity, however, enabled her to turn her attention from the behavior of individual women to a sustained critique of the underlying societal issues that constrained women's choices. Traveling the country, Bushnell lectured to female and mixed audiences, sometimes to standing-room-only crowds. Many members of her audience had never before heard a public talk on sexuality, but "Bushnell's words were brave and fearless,"[136] and earned her a reputation as a "graceful, eloquent, and earnest public speaker."[137] (Three years later, a reporter provided a detailed description of Bushnell's appearance as she spoke: "An abundance of dark hair, turning prematurely gray, surrounded and set off a finely-cut face that kept one's eyes fixed upon it constantly. The eyes were big and brown and looked sleepy until the fire of enthusiasm flushed in them.")[138]

The Woman Condemned

A sense of Bushnell's purity message can be gleaned from a fifteen-page booklet she published in December 1886, as part of a series whose authors included Willard, Butler, and Stead. Written to introduce readers to the

cause of purity, *The Woman Condemned* revealed how Bushnell's interactions with prostitutes had deepened her suspicion of men and had
helped her to formulate a critique of the conventional morality espoused
by "respectable" Christians. It also demonstrated the extent to which she
drew upon her missionary experience as she developed her critique of
Western Christian values.[139]

Bushnell opened her narrative with a dramatic first-person account of
her work in "half-civilized China," in which she vividly recounted her visit
to the family of a young Chinese girl who had been killed by lightning.[140]
She described coming across the girl's abandoned corpse along the road
as she approached the village, and explained how Chinese superstition
held that only murderers could be struck down by lightning, and thus
required victims' families to show abhorrence to the corpse or risk being
accused of the same crime. Though Bushnell claimed to have surveyed the
bloated corpse with detachment, she reported taking in the surrounding
scene with dismay, as neighbors gathered around to denounce the girl
and turned against a lone man who refused to condemn the child. Upon
entering the victim's home, Bushnell glimpsed a metal scythe hanging
on the wall near where the girl had been seated. Quickly ascertaining the
nature of the tragedy, she explained to the girl's family how the lightning
had struck the scythe and caused the child's death, and she assured them
that the girl deserved no condemnation. But in *The Woman Condemned*
she did not hesitate to condemn the community, whom she accused of
"sadly confusing misfortune with immorality, and mistaking a calam-
ity for a crime," an error she attributed to false doctrine, to ridiculous
Chinese superstition.[141]

But then Bushnell added a surprising twist: "You smile," she addressed
her readers, at the "obtuse impracticability" of the Chinese superstition.
"You characterize it as heathenish, barbarous. But may we not find here a
remarkable analogy to the common method of civilized nations in dealing
with sexual crime?" In Christian countries, she insisted, there existed an
equally erroneous belief system that allowed men to freely visit houses of
prostitution, seduce young girls, and even boast of their exploits, while
the girls they disgraced faced ruthless consequences. Condemned by their
communities, the fate of these girls differed little from the fate of those
whose corpses were left to rot along the road. Bushnell described how
such women were often driven to houses of ill-fame "by hunger and poor
health," and were soon entrapped in lives of shame. And though she conceded that some girls "of innate base propensities" might seek out such

work, she reminded her readers that even so, "no woman ever yet went down into the cavern except a man dropped her over the brink." Yet these very men were "standing on our street-corners, sitting on our medical benches, even kneeling among the worshippers in the house of God," while the women with whom they had consorted were condemned to lives of disgrace. The law, however, did nothing to "stamp out of existence this nameless crime"—indeed, instead of punishing men's crimes, it "shield[ed] his secrets by the perversion of the blackmail law," enabled the ruin of young girls through absurdly low age-of-consent laws, and licensed and disinfected houses of shame with Contagious Diseases Acts. And the myth of female virtue only exacerbated the hostile legal environment. Emboldened by the false doctrine that taught that "a woman holds the moral character of her male associates in her own hand," she explained, a man could lead a woman astray, safe in the knowledge that society would blame her, not him.[142]

No different from "heathen superstition," then, modern Western civilization reinforced the notion that the "sinner upon whom misfortune falls is the worst sinner of all." And women's misfortune was indeed grave, Bushnell attested. Illicit activity took a far greater toll on women's health than on men's, and threatened women with "enforced motherhood," a fate that seemed to many a "lightning shaft" of God's judgment. To Bushnell, it was clear that the double standard was at the root of the problem: "Down through the ages has ever rung that saying, which has been looked upon as so complimentary to female chastity, 'Woman stands so much higher than man, that when she falls she falls lower than he.'" But drawing on evangelical and holiness teachings, Bushnell countered this assertion: "Is there any higher elevation upon which woman can plant her feet than the Rock of Ages? and can man stand securely on any other plane of living?" The Son of God modeled perfect purity for women, she maintained, but also for men: "Dare man pretend to be Christian at all and pattern his life after a less perfect model?"[143]

But Bushnell knew that few shared this conviction. She had never once encountered a mother who refused to take a wayward son back into her home, she noted, yet she knew only one woman willing to shelter her own disgraced daughter. "Oh, shame to faithless motherhood that sacrifices its motherly instincts to the dictates of custom! For once it is to be found fault with," she lamented. She denounced as well customs requiring "pure" women to remain aloof from their disgraced sisters in order to maintain their own purity, claiming that women who believed the myth that "woman is naturally so much purer than man" lacked sympathy for the fallen. The Christian church only perpetuated this injustice, Bushnell insisted: "What a shame that we are so ready to pervert intolerance of sin into hatred for sinners! Heaven is full of those who abhor sin, but hell is teeming with those who hate sinners."[144] She recommended that the church instead follow Christ's own example. Just as Christ refused to throw the first stone at the woman taken in the act of adultery, so, too, ought society to respond to the fallen, with compassion and tenderness.[145]

As a national evangelist for purity, Bushnell helped establish the foundation for a national movement by persuading women in town after town to take up the cause of purity as their Christian duty. One woman who attended Bushnell's talk attested to her "peculiar power" as a speaker: "In order to do good work in this channel we need to be instructed concerning the evil to be combated, and through her lectures one gains a deep, quick and *safe* insight into the needs of fallen women. She is consecrated to helping these, and when she speaks upon the theme a power not human is infused into her face and words." The writer recommended that other unions, too, send for Bushnell, for "they will be stirred and strengthened for the work beyond their expectation."[146]

Before leaving a community, Bushnell would meet with members of local WCTU chapters to instruct them on how to organize their own social purity efforts. She emphasized the importance of offering assistance to disadvantaged women in the form of lodging houses, employment agencies, and reading rooms, and she addressed as well the need to alter underlying attitudes. For example, she not only countered the notion that "fallen women" were beyond reform, but she challenged the very use of the term "fallen women," and instead championed "women who have reformed, been converted and are striving by God's help and in His strength to live new and blameless lives."[147] She also recommended that reformed women be counseled to keep their former lives secret if possible, advancing the radical concept that "their liberty in regard to marriage with pure men should be the same as that accorded reformed men in regard to marriage with pure women."[148] Bushnell was soon "in constant demand" as a purity lecturer, and was instrumental in introducing purity to WCTU women across the nation. Already by the beginning of 1887, "nearly every state in the Union [had] appointed a superintendent of work for the promotion of social purity, and thousands of local unions began the study of arguments and methods."[149]

The Wisconsin Crusade: 1888

Despite significant advances within the WCTU, however, American social purity forces still awaited a spark that would ignite a nationwide movement, as Stead's exposé had done for the British. In February 1887, the WCTU had attempted to generate that spark with an article on the "white slave trade" found in northern Wisconsin and Michigan lumber camps. But the article, revealingly titled "Another Maiden Tribute," failed to provoke the desired response. With newspapers continuing to print lurid accounts of underage girls being ensnared under false pretenses and held against their will in dens of vice, however, the WCTU issued a call for a full investigation into the alleged vice trade. When no one stepped forward, Bushnell decided to do so herself.[150]

Bushnell was not the first investigator to take up the task. The previous year, Wisconsin Governor Jeremiah Rusk had commissioned a man named James Fielding to determine if there was any truth to newspaper accounts, and in February 1887 the *Milwaukee Journal* had published a report of his investigation, titled "Where Satan Rules."[151] But the headline was deceptive, for Fielding had found little of note to report. He claimed to have uncovered no evidence "of any girl ever having gone north from Milwaukee to lead a life of shame, unless she had been a street walker or an inmate of a house of ill-fame before, and knew exactly where she was going." He told how the women he met had come to the brothels "in a spirit of adventure and in the hope of making money having grown tired of leading a similar life in the city," and insisted he had found no "young girls pining for home," but only " 'old timers,' who felt more at home there than they could possibly feel in a respectable place." Countering reports of women having been coerced or inveigled into the life, he insisted that the women he encountered, even supposed victims he had tracked down, had known full well what they were getting themselves into. He had located one purported victim, for example, "living a fast life" in Milwaukee, and reported that she had told him how she "always had plenty of fun and made a boodle." Though he did acknowledge that many women became trapped in situations by inescapable debt to their "land ladies," he denied that any women were held by physical force. The den keepers had no need to resort to kidnapping, he explained, since the houses of ill fame enjoyed a steady flow of women, and effectively functioned as "sewers which drained off some of the social miasma which was engendered in the large cities."[152] In short, he assured his readers, tales of atrocities had been grossly exaggerated.

Since many people deemed further investigation into these matters unnecessary in light of Fielding's report, Bushnell began her own inquiry with a thorough examination of Fielding himself. She first disputed his credentials. Rather than "a man who has had years of experience both as a sheriff's officer and a detective," she contended that he was "not a professional detective by any means," but rather "an elderly man who is employed to sweep, dust and do a little writing." She reported that in conversation with Fielding she had learned that he had in fact visited only one town, Marinette, where he entered only one den, and interviewed only one set of inmates. In essence, he confessed to fabricating his entire report. Bushnell did not condemn Fielding for his deceit, however, but reserved her ire for Governor Rusk, whom she accused of having no intention of addressing these injustices, and for whom Fielding was merely serving as a mouthpiece.[153]

Having discredited the state inquiry, Bushnell commenced her own investigation in the summer of 1888. Funded by the national and Wisconsin WCTU, her planned one-month foray quickly extended into four months as she visited fifty-nine "vice dens" and interviewed "some 575 degraded women." After concluding her meticulous and carefully documented investigation, she submitted a full report of her investigations to the WCTU that fall.[154]

In her report Bushnell took pains to counter claims that all of the women housed in the brothels were there of their own free will. Though she acknowledged that some of the women were "criminals (for women can be criminal as well as men)," she insisted that the hardness of the "old stagers" only revealed the "comparative innocence" of others who found themselves trapped in a life of prostitution. She described cases where girls "of good character, both before and since," had been rescued just before falling victim to ruses that would have ensnared them in lives of shame—of girls duped into thinking they were going north to work in a hotel or were being hired as domestic help, only to be saved at the last moment when someone recognized their new "employers." And yet, despite the fact that "there was every reason to believe the victims were innocent," Bushnell knew of no prosecutions brought against these procurers.[155]

Bushnell did not limit her report to accounts of "innocent" girls, but insisted that even those who might have been guilty of improper sexual conduct before their procurement nevertheless deserved public sympathy. These girls, too, had often been tricked into a life of servitude under promises of respectable work, but because of the "previous chaste character" loophole in Wisconsin law they had been stripped of all legal protection. According to this statute, anyone who procured a girl of questionable chastity could be held guiltless, not only in her procurement, even if done under false pretenses, but also of any injustices committed against the girl, such as the withholding of pay or physical beatings. In this way, procurers could defend themselves against charges of fraud or cruelty simply by "proving a past sin in the victim." Indeed, in her report Bushnell cited several examples of den keepers who abused women mercilessly, but with impunity, simply by claiming that the women had been previously unchaste.[156]

Although Bushnell claimed to have observed the rumored "stockades," she noted that it was not clear to her whether the fences and guard dogs were meant to keep women in, or "officers of the law and indignant citizens" out. But, she countered, more effective than fences in confining women to the brothels were the perpetual debts they owed their proprietors, who charged frequent fines for real or imagined infringements. And since most brothels were both dance halls and saloons, many women succumbed to the temptations of alcohol, further contributing to their debt and degradation. When women did try to escape, she reported, they were often caught and returned, either by local law enforcement officials or by their "husbands," local men who enjoyed certain privileges in return for keeping their girls in check.[157]

In her report Bushnell made clear that the dens were nothing like "the 'gilded' place of tinsel" people imagined them to be. Rather, the brothels catered "to a class of customers who are largely foreigners of the lowest type, whose crude sensees [sic] can appreciate nothing but unvarnished filth in its most concentrated form." The men running the dens, too, were "all either foreigners or of foreign extraction," she attested, while their victims were "largely young American girls who, if in times previous guilty, are of a higher grade of civilization." Bushnell was right in that a large number of the lumbermen were foreign-born, hailing from French Canada, Germany, and Poland, but so, too, were the majority of the prostitutes, a fact that Bushnell overlooked.[158]

Despite playing to nativist fears, however, Bushnell reserved her greatest disdain for representatives of this "higher civilization," for seemingly upstanding citizens who profited from and perpetuated the vice. Detailing a "system controlled by trade capitalism," she described how den keepers made fortunes off the slavery and degradation of young women, and then used the great wealth they amassed, estimated to be not less than $1,000 a week, to bring "to their feet" other members of the community.

She accused "a certain class of newspapers," for example, of whitewashing their accounts of the dens, and described a number of instances where local and state officials either turned a blind eye to prostitution in their own jurisdictions, or, more disturbingly, sanctioned and regulated the trade. Meanwhile, local businessmen often favored the brothels, considering them beneficial to the local economy, and—much to Bushnell's personal dismay—many physicians not only tolerated, but even encouraged "the spread of this iniquity" for the additional business it brought them. In fact, Bushnell discovered that many communities had developed their own Contagious Diseases Acts, based upon British models, stipulating the compulsory examination of local women. Though she refrained from reprinting the certificates, which contained "wording too indecent for public print," Bushnell made clear that the ordinances were fashioned in order to allow men to sin "with all immunity from physical danger." Doctors who conducted these examinations did so out of concern for personal profit rather than for public health, she insisted, and in this way medical professionals had developed a personal stake in the continuance of prostitution in their districts.[159]

Appalled to find so many upstanding citizens coming to the defense of local brothels, Bushnell was particularly distressed to find that some "*virtuous* (God forbid the misnomer!) women" considered "the degradation of young girls" necessary for the protection of their own virtue, having embraced the belief that such girls provided an outlet for men's natural iniquity.[160] It was this erroneous ideology, Bushnell contended, that bore the greatest responsibility for the entrapment of women in a life of prostitution. Indeed, although she uncovered some evidence of girls having been tricked into a life of prostitution and held against their will, she was glad to report that "that sensational picture of a den with a stockade as high as its roof, a whole pack of trained hounds and an armed doorkeeper,—is an exaggeration." But "more formidable obstructions to a girl's escape from a life of shame" existed than these, she maintained. It was the "total lack of sympathy" on the part of "men, women, and officers of the law," together with a common belief in the necessity of the dens for public order and for the protection of other women's virtue, that ensured the futility of escape for girls ensnared in the system.[161]

That fall Bushnell presented her findings at the annual meeting of the WCTU in New York City, and accounts of her investigation were published in Wisconsin and Chicago newspapers, and were reprinted in newspapers across the nation.[162] To the delight of purity activists, her exposé succeeded in provoking a public outcry, accomplishing in the United States what Stead's investigations had achieved in Britain. Her account was not accepted without controversy, however. Some newspapers neglected her nuanced analysis of the social factors behind prostitution in favor of sensational stories depicting girls imprisoned in stockaded dens, and other papers then lambasted Bushnell for concocting such stories. The frequency with which her statements had been distorted or exaggerated led Bushnell to suspect a willful and malicious plot to undermine her credibility, and she instructed readers to remain skeptical of any accounts of her talks and to instead turn to her official report published in the Wisconsin W.C.T.U. State Work and the Chicago Herald.[163]

Critics not only challenged the accuracy of Bushnell's reports, but also the purity of her own character. Despite the growing popularity of the social purity movement, a woman discussing disreputable subjects publicly was not immune to slander. No true lady, it seemed to some observers, would place herself in such situations, or dedicate her life to such an unseemly preoccupation. In the face of such aspersions, Willard publicly vouched for Bushnell's integrity, and "brave, unflinching" WCTU members across Wisconsin met regularly to defend her work and pursue legislative action. As one supporter explained, "Where unblushing sin abounds, there do women of grace, grit and gumption much more abound."[164] Local ministers, too, lent their support, though not without risk to their own reputations. (One Wausau minister who vouched for Bushnell ended up being arrested and tried for libel, though he was ultimately acquitted.)[165] Her credibility was further bolstered when journalists investigating her reports substantiated the majority of her claims.[166]

When Bushnell presented her carefully documented evidence to Wisconsin authorities, however, the governor summarily dismissed her report, and the state judiciary committee ignored her. But the Wisconsin state legislature invited her to give an address on the situation, and Bushnell eagerly accepted their invitation.[167] Due to the high level of interest and passionate opposition that her investigation had provoked, she required police protection when she arrived at the capital to give her testimony. Later recalling the dramatic scene, she remembered feeling very much alone as she ascended the platform to address the body; "trembling inwardly," she looked around at the crowded and not particularly friendly room, and, realizing she was the only woman present, she lifted "her heart to God." As she did so, the door opened quietly and "about fifty ladies of the highest social position at the State Capital filed in" and surrounded her, remaining by her side for the duration of her address.[168] Emboldened, she gave a compelling account of her investigations. Impressed with her evidence and stirred by her pleas, the legislature responded by enacting stiffer penalties for those involved in the "white slave trade"—legislation that purity reformers christened "the Kate Bushnell Bill."[169]

In the wake of her Wisconsin investigations, Bushnell became a celebrity of sorts: "the whole country was agitated on the White Slave question," and people clamored to hear Bushnell speak on the topic.[170] Due in part to Bushnell's work, municipal vice commissions appeared in nearly every major American city, and together with Stead's writings, Bushnell's disclosures convinced many physicians to change their own attitudes toward prostitution and regulation. Rather than seeing prostitution as a necessary evil or even as a social good, many medical doctors began to consider it a dangerous vice that needed to be eliminated, rather than regulated. Bushnell had succeeded in shattering the conspiracy of silence, and she had helped establish purity as "the latest and greatest" domain of moral reform.[171]

3

Heathen Slaves, Christian Rulers

AS A LEADING purity activist, Bushnell was both a respected advocate for women's rights and an influential evangelical reformer. Her Christian faith inspired her activism, driving her quest for moral purity for men and justice for women. Over time, however, her reform work led her to adopt an increasingly critical view of traditional Christianity. After repeated encounters with seemingly upstanding Christian women and men who thought nothing of inflicting appalling cruelties upon society's most vulnerable women, Bushnell began to suspect that Christianity itself might be to blame. But it was not until she took her purity activism overseas that she became fully convinced of Christianity's role in propping up a corrupt moral system. It was her international activism, then, that ultimately inspired her to fashion a new gospel for women.

In the aftermath of her notorious Wisconsin investigations, Bushnell discovered that her very success had begun to undermine her credibility as a reformer and imperil her career as a national evangelist for the WCTU. Although people crowded to hear her speak wherever she went, they now listened "impatiently to plain moral instruction in the principles of purity," and instead clamored for more "sensational stories."[1] Already in the winter of 1889, the WCTU began to advise unions that had engaged Bushnell's services not to advertise that she would speak on her investigation: "The people there have been aroused, and it is believed they will do their duty regarding the matter, and it is not wise to be always talking about it. If it is advertised, there will be a disappointment, that is all, for Dr. Bushnell does not believe she is called upon to be forever stirring up this matter, and simply will not do it."[2] Though Bushnell continued to fill speaking engagements over the next several months, the following fall

Willard decided to leave Bushnell off the program of the WCTU's annual convention. Bushnell conceded that Willard's decision was "reasonable enough," as "the main object of the Union was Temperance, and its interests must not be diverted." Claiming no desire "to keep an unhealthy sensation alive," she agreed it would be best to keep a low profile for a while.[3]

It was around this time that Willard invited Bushnell to take up a position as "World evangelist" for the WCTU, to travel the world for the cause of purity and temperance.[4] Upon later reflection, Bushnell realized that Willard probably offered her the position in order to allow her to conduct her purity work in a less sensational manner. If this was in fact Willard's intent, however, she had seriously miscalculated, for Bushnell's new position would enable her to recreate on a global stage what she had just accomplished in the United States. At the time, however, none of this was apparent. Willard may indeed have been motivated by a desire to remove Bushnell from the American purity scene until things quieted down, but she was also genuinely invested in the global expansion of the WCTU. Ever since she had traveled abroad as a young woman, Willard had taken an interest in the international facets of "the woman question," and in 1888 she had inaugurated the WCTU's efforts to work for women in "every land" by commissioning the organization's first "round-the-world missionary."[5] Modeled on the Methodist itinerant ministry, the WCTU's "World evangelists" traversed the globe in the name of temperance and purity. Through their efforts the WCTU established a significant presence in Britain, Scandinavia, Canada, Australia, New Zealand, South Africa, Hawaii, Japan, China, and India, and through regular correspondences published in the *Union Signal*, they helped orient WCTU members to global concerns.[6]

From the time she first encountered the foreign missionary movement as a young woman in Evanston, Bushnell had been an active participant in a global evangelicalism. She and Willard were not unusual in their global outlook; to a degree often unrecognized today, Victorian women participated in a globally oriented faith. The women's missionary movement had not only provided women with unprecedented opportunities to serve abroad, but it had also mobilized and empowered their supporters back home, and oriented Protestant women outwardly to an imagined "global sisterhood." It was not long before temperance and purity reformers followed suit, as they endeavored to bring the benefits of Christian society to women around the globe.

In many ways, the efforts of the World's WCTU, like the women's foreign missionary movement, can be seen as an expression of Western cultural imperialism, as part of the late nineteenth-century expansion of American power through the imposition of cultural institutions and social values upon peoples of the world.[7] As British journalist and reformer William T. Stead wrote in 1902 in *The Americanization of the World*, the World's WCTU's "direct influence in compelling women at once to realize their responsibility and to recognize their capacity to serve the State in the promotion of all that tends to preserve the purity and sanctity of the home, has been by no means one of the least contributions which America has made to the betterment of the world."[8] Historian Ian Tyrrell notes that the World's WCTU exemplified "a new kind of empire," one that "provided an early blueprint for a deterritorialized form of American empire, centered around the networks of nongovernmental organizations conveying American values."[9]

And yet, to a far greater extent than their denominational missionary counterparts, World's WCTU women tended to become critics of Western values. What made the World's WCTU different, according to Tyrrell, "was the fact that their own missionaries were above both nationality and church denomination and that their message of temperance and female emancipation was explicitly critical of Western churches and European missionaries."[10] As "critics of Christianity" even before they took up their missionary travels, WCTU women were far more likely than denominational missionaries to critique their own culture in light of their foreign travels. Indeed, the WCTU's round-the-world missionaries gained a reputation for challenging their own organization's leadership—a tendency that a perturbed Willard once attributed to the extended time the women spent in hot climates. World missionaries were indeed altered by their time abroad, though not primarily by their exposure to tropical climes. As Tyrrell explains, "women who went out to shape the world in the image of Christian temperance were in turn affected by that world, intellectually, culturally, and spiritually."[11] This would certainly be the case for Bushnell.

When approached by Willard to become one of the WCTU's first round-the-world missionaries, the thirty-five-year-old Bushnell accepted the offer, despite the fact that the position came without a salary; it was made clear to her that she could expect no money for travel, or even "for so much as a postage stamp."[12] Confident in her ability to raise funds on the lecture circuit, Bushnell was undaunted. But before she could depart on her round-the-world journey, she was incapacitated by a foot injury, and after being laid up for the better part of four months she began to doubt the wisdom of her plans. Had it not been for a visit from her old friend Elizabeth Wheeler Andrew, she might have abandoned them entirely. Ten years Bushnell's senior, Andrew was the widow of a Methodist minister and the co-editor of the WCTU's *Union Signal,* and years earlier she and Bushnell had attended Evanston's holiness meetings and ministered to college girls together. Upon seeing Bushnell's condition, Andrew feared that her friend would become crippled for life, and she earnestly prayed for healing. Bushnell's recovery was "nearly instantaneous," but she remained uncertain about her future.[13]

As was her custom in such situations, Bushnell sought divine intervention. One warm summer afternoon she opened her Bible and, impatiently flipping through the pages, turned to prayer. She first came upon the story of Joseph's dreams, but found little inspiration there. Next she stumbled upon the New Testament account of Peter's vision, but here, too, she lacked clear direction. Setting her Bible aside, she began to doze off, wondering if she, too, might not be guided by a dream. Much to her surprise, she later recounted, her prayers were indeed answered in the form of a dream directing her to contact Josephine Butler, the renowned British purity activist, to inquire as to what she should do next.[14] Trusting this guidance, Bushnell sat down to write a letter in which she described her previous work and told Butler of her dream. When Butler received the four "rather closely written pages," however, she hastily skimmed the opening lines before setting it aside "with a feeling something between impatience and despair." Butler routinely received letters from women "asking advice on all kinds of subjects," and assumed this to be another of the sort. But a few hours later she happened to pick up the letter once more, and as she read further, her interest grew.[15]

It occurred to Butler that Bushnell might be well-suited to conduct an investigation in India similar to the work she had recently undertaken in Wisconsin. In 1886, after over a decade of petitioning, Butler and other antiregulationist reformers had succeeded in bringing about the repeal of the Contagious Diseases Acts in Britain and the colonies, but they soon began to suspect that the government repeal was disingenuous, and that the compulsory examinations and forced confinement of women continued in the colonies under new Cantonment Acts.[16] They were particularly disturbed to learn of a military order sent in the name of Lord Roberts, Commander-in-Chief of the British army in India, calling for a "sufficient number" of "sufficiently attractive" women to be supplied to the regimental bazaars, or brothels, in the military cantonments. Dubbing the order the "Infamous Memorandum," purity reformers were incensed that rather than instructing soldiers to be moral, the army instead sought to provide soldiers with a safer way to practice immorality, and they were outraged at the abuses committed against Indian women in order to enable representatives of a Christian government to do so.[17] As far as they could tell, the repeal of the Contagious Diseases Acts had done nothing but lull reformers into inaction, with the regulation of prostitution and the procurement of Indian women continuing unabated. But in attempting to verify these suspicions through fact-finding missions to India, British commissioners had made little headway. Butler reasoned that an American woman like Bushnell might be better able to go about this work without arousing suspicion, and that as a female physician she might have the opportunity to gain information where previous male investigators had failed.[18]

Butler communicated her plan to Bushnell, who eagerly agreed to undertake this new mission in conjunction with her round-the-world travels for the WCTU. Before leaving for England, she told her friend Andrew of Butler's offer. Like Willard, Andrew had been deeply moved by Stead's "Maiden Tribute," and through her editorial position at the *Union Signal* she had begun issuing leaflets and pamphlets on social purity. Despite her growing interest in purity work, however, Andrew struggled to shed her prejudice against "fallen women," and often conferred with Bushnell about what it was like to work with such women—how, for instance, one went about talking with "a degraded woman." Bushnell's answer, "Just as I would to any other sinner," touched Andrew deeply,[19] and after hearing of Bushnell's new opportunity, Andrew resolved to accompany her on her investigations. This marked the beginning of a long and fruitful partnership; Andrew would remain Bushnell's faithful companion until her death, nearly three decades later.

Bushnell had found a new cause and an able coworker, but she still lacked the requisite financial resources to embark on her next crusade. With no independent source of income or wealth on which to draw, she frequently found it necessary to fund her own work. "All my lifetime I have been poor," she later recalled, "and had I waited for money and time to do what I saw was needed, what God has accomplished through me would never have come to pass." She had taken for her "life motto" Philippians 4:13: "I can do all things THROUGH CHRIST, who strengtheneth me," and over the course of her career she would often find that "it is He and His strengthening that are needed, and the time and money is supplied to those who will go out with faith and courage." It took both faith and courage for Bushnell to set out nearly empty-handed from Illinois to New York City, earning along the way barely enough to reach her destination, with nothing left for her journey to England. But upon her arrival in New York, money from several unexpected sources awaited her, convincing her of the divine purpose of her voyage and reassuring her of God's provision for her life.[20]

After a brief time in Germany, she continued on to England, where she and Andrew consulted together with Butler. Both Bushnell and Andrew were stirred by "the sacred influences of that interview"; they perceived Butler to be "one who lived near to God, in holy converse with Him," and they left that first meeting filled with "a sense of the Divine Presence." Butler, for her own part, was "much struck" with the two women; they impressed her as "gentle and quiet" souls, filled with "deep and strong convictions." Knowing of Bushnell's "remarkably good work among the terrible lumber camps of Wisconsin," she considered the fact that they were now willing to work for her cause, at their own expense, proof of "the hand of God" at work.[21]

The Indian Investigations: 1891–1893

Butler characterized their assignment as "one of the most difficult and even perilous missions ever undertaken"[22] for the purity movement, but Bushnell and Andrew started off firm in the knowledge that they "were sent for the purpose."[23] The specific task before them in 1891 was to investigate whether the British government was abiding by the repeal of all measures authorizing "the compulsory examination of women and the licensing and regulation of prostitution," and if not, to secure clear evidence to meet official demands for proof.[24] Because of the sensitive nature of their mission they were directed to "enter the country as quietly as possible," to hold no public meetings, and to undertake their investigations "as cautiously as possible."[25]

Upon arriving in Calcutta, they met with one of Butler's contacts, who in turn sent them to a missionary who was to advise them on how to begin. When they met with the man, however, they noticed that he "could not hide his impatience at two women who would undertake (to his mind) so unseemly a task." He attempted to dissuade them of their mission, arguing that it was "only fit work for men, and anyway was a 'wild goose chase.'" At this, Bushnell was moved to "righteous indignation," and retorted that it was certainly appropriate for Christian women to investigate "what pagan women had to suffer at the hands of men from a Christian country," and that God would help them in their cause if he would not.[26] Incensed, she and Andrew set off on their own. But they achieved nothing by inquiring among European officials, and for the next five weeks made no inroads into their investigation. With the winter season slipping away, they began to despair, and, after spending a day in fasting and prayer, they decided to contact a friend in a neighboring city. That friend, too, was "exceedingly hopeless" about their prospects, but she did offer to teach them a number of colloquial phrases and instruct them in local customs. Equipped in a rudimentary way, Bushnell and Andrew resolved to circumvent official channels, and instead seek out "native physicians and the women themselves."[27]

Because commanding officers had the authority to exclude any person from their cantonments, with or without cause, Bushnell and Andrew needed to proceed extremely carefully. They devised a strategy wherein they would hire a local cabman to bring them to a cantonment *chakla*, or brothel, explaining that they were Christian missionaries seeking "the most despised and disreputable women" in order to "tell them of God's care for them and to see what we could do for them." Though not forthright about the primary purpose of their work, they had "promised God" that if directly questioned they would not lie to cover up their intentions: "We were not ordinary detectives, playing a part," they agreed, "but Christian women, and the difference was not to be lost sight of."[28] On several occasions they believed it was only divine intervention that allowed them to proceed undetected. Sometimes they were assisted by a local translator, but often they communicated directly through gestures and the broken English that some Indian women had picked up from their interactions with soldiers; on occasion, they encountered women quite fluent in English.[29]

Upon arriving at a *chakla*, Bushnell and Andrew would present a "simple gospel message," telling of Jesus, "the Friend of the oppressed." Then, after a time of singing and prayer, they would ask the women to share their stories.[30] What they heard affected them profoundly. One woman described how she had been deceived by a woman under promise of employment, while another told how she had been orphaned at the age of six, taken as the mistress of an Englishman at the age of eleven, and then abandoned, with no place to go but to the *chakla*. Another recounted how, nearing starvation, she had come to the British soldiers only as "her last courage gave way"—leaving Bushnell and Andrew to reflect on how the military proved "willing to feed her starving body for the sake of its worth as an instrument of self-indulgence," which appeared to be "the only right to existence accorded to many women, even in so-called Christian countries."[31]

The women's abject poverty was not lost on Bushnell and Andrew, who recognized that Indian women, like their counterparts in the West, were often held to their "wretched life" through debt and fines so that even if they escaped, they could be returned to their servitude on account of their debts. They understood, too, that wages in India were so low "as to constitute the native the virtual slave of the Anglo-Saxon," and noted that "the worst feature of all in slavery is the appropriation of women by their masters." They observed as well that "this form of villainy is always excusing itself by slandering the oppressed women,"[32] and pointed to a shameful tendency among British officials to defend the *chakla* system by dehumanizing and maligning Indian women. For example, British officials excused the forcible examination and detainment of prostitutes by claiming that such women "had no sensitiveness and no deep sense of the degradation of her position"—a premise that Bushnell and Andrew "utterly denied," on behalf of the "scores of women" they encountered during their investigations.

To counter such assertions, Bushnell and Andrew repeatedly emphasized Indian women's "shame and humiliation." Disputing the notion that "the whole nature of a woman was changed by her sinful life," they insisted that prostitutes "spoke almost universally of their hatred of the life." Regardless of a woman's caste, nationality, whether she had been "brought up in virtue and afterwards betrayed, or brought up from infancy in vicious surroundings," they insisted that *chakla* women retained a sense of womanhood that could still be violated. They accused regulationists, however, of seeing only the *prostitute*, and losing all sight of the *woman*.[33]

Bushnell and Andrew emphasized the prostitutes' shame and humiliation particularly when it came to compulsory examinations, the centerpiece of government regulation. They contended that the women they met were remarkably patient "in regard to the various inconveniences and hardships" placed upon them, but "the fire of their hatred and indignation all centered upon *the heart of the regulations, the examinations,* and the violation of womanhood which these examinations were felt to be." When Bushnell and Andrew told the women how they lamented that "those who called themselves Christians should do such things," one woman replied, "Yes; the Commander-in-chief, the Colonel, and all of them, all the way down—your Christian men!—they all favour these things." But the woman maintained that the Queen herself must not approve of the measures, "for she has daughters of her own; and she cares for her daughters in India also." When Bushnell and Andrew published a report of their investigations, they pointedly titled it *The Queen's Daughters in India*.[34]

In their report Bushnell and Andrew also countered claims that government regulations reduced cases of venereal disease, providing statistics of their own to contend that by encouraging vice, regulations actually increased the number of infections. Of far greater significance than statistics, however, was the moral weight of the issue. They unreservedly rejected regulationists' claims that the rules were for the purpose of protecting the health of the women, insisting that "every interest in the woman's character, happiness, health, life itself, is made subservient to the health and convenience of the British soldier."[35] For example, they pointed out that they observed no cases of secondary stages of disease among women in Lock Hospitals, and noted that they had learned from Indian physicians that this was due to the fact that diseased women were frequently turned out of the cantonments. But in exiling these women who had broken caste by living with foreigners, British officials had not only abandoned them to a desperate fate, but also exhibited no concern for the spread of disease among Indian populations.[36] Since only those women who showed promise of returning to the *chakla* were treated for any length of time, Bushnell and Andrew concluded that Lock Hospitals existed for the "treatment of prostitution rather than for the treatment of disease."[37] The regulations did not promote healing "as Christ would have us heal," they made clear, but rather ensured that men could "sin without bodily injury."[38]

Although British officials showed no concern for the spread of disease among local populations, they justified the regulations in terms of protecting soldiers' "innocent wives and children" back home. Bushnell and Andrew, however, shrewdly inquired as to *which* wives and children the officials referred—"those that already exist in India, or those that have not yet materialized in England." They described how hundreds of Indian wives and children—a virtual "nation of Eurasians"—had been abandoned by British husbands and fathers, and insisted that most of these women fully believed they had been "honestly married" and never dreamed that their husbands would abandon them to return to England and start new families. They were the "real wives and the real children in the sight of a just God," Bushnell and Andrew contended, and "to them

should England's attention be first turned."[39] They made their case compellingly: "Weigh the soul of that one dark-skinned heathen girl against
the diseased bodies of a standing army of men, and God knows which has
most weight in his sight, even if a whole materialistic nation may have
forgotten."[40]

Altogether, Bushnell and Andrew traveled 3,597 miles, visited ten
military stations (some two or three times), investigated 637 cases of
cantonment prostitutes, and interviewed 395 individuals, including 6
physicians, 18 *mahaldarnis* (Indian madams), and 34 patients confined
to Lock Hospitals.[41] After completing their investigations, they sent their
detailed report back to London, and then continued on to Australia and
New Zealand as part of their round-the-world missionary tour. It was not
long, however, before they were called back to England to give evidence
before a governmental committee drawn up by Prime Minister Gladstone,
who had been "simply horrified" by their report.[42]

Bushnell and Andrew appeared before the Departmental Committee
in April 1893, and over the course of several days they shared with members of Parliament and other high-ranking officials their extensive evidence documenting the ongoing regulation of prostitution in the colonies,
in defiance of the repeal of the Contagious Diseases Acts. Although the
proceedings were closed to the public, Bushnell and Andrew offered a
summary of their findings to a sympathetic reporter, who, in an attempt
to substantiate their startling allegations, then arranged an interview
with Lord Roberts, who himself had recently returned to England. The
General, however, flatly denied the truth of their allegations, insisting that
"registration and compulsory examination no longer exist," and claiming
to have personally verified this fact through a recent tour of the cantonments. The reporter informed him that Bushnell and Andrew had spoken with utmost confidence and had exhibited clear outrage on behalf of
Indian women, and suggested that the women had taken up their task
"at great personal sacrifice" and with no motive to mislead. Lord Roberts,
however, complained that they ought to have approached him if they had
concerns about the regulations, and he dismissed their report as unreliable. "Well, my lord," the reporter concluded, "the issue is narrowed down
to a plain matter of fact. The Committee is sitting, and we must await its
report." Lord Roberts concurred, and expressed his eagerness to address
the Committee when that time should come.[43]

But the Committee had adjourned until August, leaving Bushnell and
Andrew to confront Lord Roberts's "open charges of falsehood," which

"were heralded throughout the Empire, and freely discussed by the Press," over the duration of the summer. Other officials, too, sought to undermine their credibility, dismissing them as naïve and suggesting that their Indian informants had simply told them what they wanted to hear. Unwavering, Bushnell and Andrew used the interim to hold a series of public talks throughout Great Britain, rallying support for their cause among religious groups and members of the working class.[44]

When August arrived, they appeared again before the Committee, finally coming face to face with Lord Roberts and his Quartermaster-General, Edward Chapman. Openly contradicting Bushnell's and Andrew's earlier statements, Lord Roberts testified that he had fully complied with the Resolution abolishing the regulation of prostitution in the colonies. He declared that "he knew nothing of the Infamous Memorandum which had been issued in his name," and insisted that he "entirely disapproved" of some of its contents, particularly the portion detailing efforts to provide soldiers "with pretty young women." It appeared to be his word against theirs. But then an unexpected turn of events caught Lord Roberts by surprise. Over the summer, additional documents had arrived from India, corroborating "nearly every statement" that Bushnell and Andrew had made. Upon learning of the documents, and realizing that General Chapman was ready to implicate him in the Infamous Memorandum, Lord Roberts hastily departed for Scotland, unwilling to endure such public humiliation.[45]

Once in Scotland, Lord Roberts penned an apology and submitted it to the Committee, and asked that it be included in the report sent to Parliament: "I frankly admit that the statements of the two American missionary ladies . . . are in the main correct," he wrote. And though he claimed to have "hoped and believed" that the repeal had been effectively carried out, he acknowledged that this had "not been completely the case." Professing deep regret, Lord Roberts apologized "unreservedly" to Bushnell and Andrew—yet he nevertheless maintained that they ought to have undertaken their investigation under the watchful eye of his government's authority: "We could have assisted them to carry out the work on which they were engaged; omissions and shortcomings would have been avoided; the ladies themselves would have found their task considerably lightened; and there would have been less chance of their drawing wrong deductions from some of the circumstances which came under their notice, as in sundry instances they would seem . . . to have done." Despite his prevarication, Lord Roberts's apology "made a sensational ripple around the whole world," Bushnell remembered. Their friends found his admonishment that they might have "found their task considerably lightened" had they pursued their work under his authority particularly amusing, as did the press: "As Lord Roberts freely admitted that he did not know these things," one account read, "certainly had the ladies appealed to him they need not have come back so loaded with information; this would have greatly lightened their task." Another echoed this sentiment: "As there was a regulation which allowed any suspicious characters to be expelled from the Cantonments without assigning a reason therefore, the application of this regulation would greatly have 'lightened their task.'"[46]

While Bushnell and Andrew were relishing their "sweeping victory," Lord Roberts's ordeal was not yet over. The time had come for his Quartermaster-General's testimony. As author of the "Infamous Memorandum," Chapman had initially shielded his commander from culpability, but he was now prepared to reveal Lord Roberts's full complicity, directly contradicting statements the General had made "on his honour as a man & a Military Commander!" Upon hearing Chapman's devastating testimony, Committee members "leaned back in silence, shocked & as it were sickened by the strangeness of the situation," according to Butler's version of events.[47] At this point, even those who had initially sided against Bushnell and Andrew came over to their side, furious with Lord Roberts's behavior, and that of the military. Not only did the Committee vindicate Bushnell and Andrew and restore their reputation, but the government also agreed to pay between 700 and 800 pounds to cover the expenses the women had incurred. "So we have fought them with their own money!" Butler exulted.[48] Though the battle against regulationism was not in fact over, antiregulationists did indeed have reason to celebrate. For the moment they had unquestionably prevailed in the court of public opinion.

The Stronghold of Satan: Race, Gender, and Christianity

With British purity reformers basking in their victory, Bushnell and Andrew departed for the United States. Though eager to continue their world tour, they had been asked to address the annual convention of the WCTU taking place that fall in Chicago, in conjunction with the 1893 World's Columbian Exposition. Arriving in the crowded city must have been a jarring experience for Bushnell and Andrew; even as they interrupted their world tour to return home, they found the world had come to Chicago, with 27 million visitors streaming into the city over the course of the summer.

Commemorating the 400th anniversary of Columbus's journey to the new world, the exposition stood as a paean to Western imperialism. Indeed, the very landscape of the fair testified to the inexorable advance of the West. Reflecting the beauty, order, and purity of Western civilization, an imposing neoclassical "White City" rose dramatically along the shores of Lake Michigan, its great halls housing exhibitions testifying to the West's unrelenting progress. In stark contrast and off to the side stood the Midway Plaisance, a corridor constructed by the exposition's Department of Ethnology, where fairgoers could glimpse exhibits representing the nations of the world, carefully arranged along ascending degrees of civilization. In this way, the very architecture of the fair served to reassure Victorians that despite the "unfathomable multiplicity" of the universe, their own society represented the irrefutable pinnacle of progress.[49] The racialized subtext of this visual lesson in evolutionary development was unmistakable, with dark-skinned African Dahomey villagers representing the most primitive form of savagery, in stark contrast to the achievements of white (predominantly male) Westerners displayed in the dazzling White City.[50]

This presumed supremacy of Western culture made perfect sense to most Victorian Christians, who attributed Western superiority in large part to the centuries-long influence of Christianity in the West. Furthermore, by adopting a progressive understanding of social evolution—one that situated Christianity at the height of human development—many Victorians found a way to reconcile their faith with Darwinian theory, without abandoning a world of purpose and order.[51] But to accept the racist and ethnocentric implications of this evolutionary model of civilization, Christians needed to ignore the cosmopolitan and egalitarian impulses of the gospel message. Many Victorians proved willing to do so, having thoroughly imbued Victorian Protestantism with notions of racial and cultural superiority.

As Bushnell's reflections from the mission field and reports from the Wisconsin lumber camps made clear, she, too, was not immune to the prejudices of her day. She was passionately concerned about the condition of women, and responded with sympathy and outrage when she witnessed appalling abuses of women. When perpetrators happened to be Chinese men and women binding the feet of young girls, or foreign-born brothel owners in Wisconsin towns, her indignation reinforced conventional prejudices. Increasingly, however, her investigative work brought her into contact with "respectable" Anglo-Saxon Christians guilty of abusing and exploiting women, in America and around the world. Having witnessed Christian men committing abhorrent wrongs against women, Christian women condoning these abuses, and a "civilized" nation stooping to levels of immorality far beneath that of "savage" peoples, Bushnell found that she could no longer maintain the fiction of Western moral superiority, and she began to dismantle the discourse of civilization that had elevated both Christianity and Western culture above all other traditions. Reflecting her evangelical and holiness convictions, she perceived an antithesis not between the civilized and the savage, but between obedient and disobedient societal responses to God's will for humanity, and in this respect "civilized" societies could be as backward as "savage" ones. Having witnessed empire close at hand, she and Andrew could no longer abide Christian justifications for Western imperialism, and in light of their Indian investigations they minced few words when it came to "so-called" Christian civilization.[52]

On the bright and frosty morning of October 16, just two weeks before the fair was to close, Bushnell and Andrew prepared to share this critique of Western civilization with a global audience. It was the opening session of the World's WCTU, and the great hall of the Memorial Art Palace was festively adorned with flowers, international flags, and a banner depicting the world Union's motto: "Christ for the world." As Bushnell and Andrew ascended the platform, they were accompanied by the officers of the WCTU and other dignitaries, including Susan B. Anthony. To the deep disappointment of many of the women gathered there, however—particularly those who had traveled thousands of miles from WCTU outposts around the globe—Willard herself was too ill to attend. In her stead, Lady Henry Somerset, president of the British Woman's Temperance Association and vice president of the World's WCTU, presided. After dispensing with opening formalities, Somerset read Willard's address to the convention, an overview of the activities of the World's WCTU that gave ample attention to Bushnell's and Andrew's recent work in India.[53]

That evening the time came for Bushnell and Andrew to address the convention. Andrew spoke first, recounting the "journey of faith" they had undertaken since becoming round-the-world missionaries, a three-year sojourn of nearly 100,000 miles, funded entirely by local unions and collections taken at their talks. Andrew then provided a stirring account of their Indian investigations, which she concluded by testifying to the "world-wide sisterhood of women" that the World's WCTU represented. Speaking in the shadow of the White City, she rejected the notion that a "vast gulf" existed between Anglo-Saxons and all other races, and instead insisted that Western women were now learning "better things than in the old days of narrowness and prejudice," that women the world over were one with them in Christ Jesus, "free in the blessed liberty of the gospel."[54]

Bushnell then picked up where Andrew left off. Christ's work on earth was "a scheme of salvation which takes in the whole world," she informed her audience, and Christians were mistaken to think they could be faithful working in their own little corners, without attention to the larger project. Such work would come to nothing, she contended, for God's plan "takes in every nation and every language."[55] She added that "what there is of impotency in connection with Christianity . . . seems to be greatly due to the fact that we have ignored the architect's great plan for the whole universe. We have not been universal in our sympathies." Bushnell then continued forcefully, "Why do I say this? Because the stronghold of Satan at the present day and hour is in the international hatred,—race prejudice." She described the situation they had encountered in India, where "a few men representing the military power of that empire, representing a Christian government and calling themselves before the natives Christian men," had concocted a scheme to enslave Indian women inside houses of shame.[56] She then demanded:

> How is it possible that men could do such a work as this? That men calling themselves Christians; that men representing what they call a Christian and benign government could have done such a thing as this in a heathen country seems incomprehensible excepting for one fact and I want to lay that before you. . . . It was simply because the Anglo-Saxon in India had the hatred for the native race that we see exhibited everywhere where one race comes to close contact with another race. Go to our western states, you will find men there who declare unblushingly that the one human creature who has no soul to save is the Chinaman. Go to . . . [the] frontier states and the people who call themselves Christians will tell you that the only good Indian is the dead Indian. Go to Australia and they will tell you there without hesitation that the native of Australia is the most degraded creature that God ever brought into existence, and that he is absolutely incapable of any moral reformation or any moral

improvement whatever. Go to India and they will tell you that if they were dealing with Chinese, if they were dealing with American Indians, or if they were dealing with negroes or any other class they might do something, but never with the natives of India. Go to our southern states and they will tell you that the colored man cannot be improved, that he only lives to occupy his place as inferior to the white man, and I say to you to-night that race hatred is the stronghold of Satan, and the crime of the age to be rebuked in every place and in every land under every circumstance.[57]

Against the backdrop of the Columbian Exposition, and indeed within the milieu of Victorian Protestantism, Bushnell's and Andrew's speeches were remarkable. Rather than confirming the superiority of their own culture, their international encounters had revealed to them the moral shortcomings at the heart of their own religious and cultural traditions.

And yet the egalitarian vocabulary of sisterhood that they and other WCTU women employed must be closely interrogated. On the one hand, such rhetoric empathetically connoted "a worldwide sorority rooted in a common sense of gender oppression,"[58] and testified to "a distinct kind of gendered, Christian internationalism" that Victorian women had forged.[59] The language of sisterhood, however, should not be accepted as an uncomplicated emblem of internationalism without attention to the imperial context in which such imaginings of sisterhood took place.[60] Upon close examination, it becomes clear that talk of sisterhood often shifted almost imperceptibly into the rhetoric of motherhood; by framing their mission as one of "mothering" other cultures, Anglo-American reformers disclosed the hierarchical orientation of their cross-national relationships that their vocabulary of sisterhood obscured. Indeed, less than a year after her speech at the World's Columbian Exposition, Bushnell herself proposed "a new departure" in the pages of the *Union Signal*, recommending that "every union in a distant country might have its fellow in either 'Mother' England or 'Mother' America."[61] While her proposal met with some support, it also elicited sharp criticism. A woman from South Australia, for example, questioned how a Union "on the opposite side of the globe" might possibly understand a situation better than "those on the spot," and cautioned that "to give 'help and counsel' one must be able to understand the position of those to be helped or advised." While conceding that "'mutual information' is always beneficial," she warned that attempts to guide and direct from great distances were unnecessary and unwelcome.[62] It is not clear how Bushnell responded to this criticism, but her proposal does not seem to have been implemented. The incident does reveal, however, that even one deeply devoted to the concept of a global sisterhood could persist in evincing the imperialistic attitudes so prevalent during that time.

And yet, though Bushnell was in some ways complicit in the cultural imperialism that characterized Victorian reform, her talk of global sisterhood amounted to more than mere rhetoric.[63] To a far greater extent than many of her contemporaries in the American women's movement, Bushnell resisted the temptation to employ a racialized discourse that elevated white women at the expense of non-Western women and men. She and Andrew also took a clear stand against American imperial expansion, opposing the acquisition of Hawaii already in 1893, and arguing that the expansionist policy exhibited by the United States and Britain manifested the advent of "evil times."[64] Perhaps most significant, unlike most other white Christians of her day, she identified racial prejudice as sin. Her global travels had introduced her to women from all walks of life, and their experiences had attuned her to the hypocrisies of her own culture and faith. It was quite possibly the memory of Bushnell's convention speech that led Lucy Thurman, one and a half years later, to ask Bushnell to serve as associate superintendent in the WCTU's Department of Colored Work.[65] Although Bushnell reportedly consented, she does not seem to have taken up this role, possibly due to a falling-out she would have with WCTU leadership. But her powerful critique of racism of all kinds took on a prophetic ring at a time when race, religion, and cultural prejudice were intricately intertwined.[66]

Heathen Slaves and Christian Rulers: 1894–1895, 1904–1907

As the convention came to an end and the fair closed down, Bushnell and Andrew resumed their global travels as round-the-world missionaries. They first returned to India, where their notoriety compelled them to keep a low profile and to work privately with WCTU groups, and from there they traveled to Burma, Singapore, China, and Japan, where they met with Western missionaries and encouraged local Unions.[67] Following on the heels of their highly publicized Indian investigations, their reputations often preceded them, and although they were generally favorably received, they did encounter occasional resistance. In the spring of 1894, for example, Bushnell came upon a hostile audience in Tien-Tsin, China, composed not of local Chinese but rather of Westerners, "chiefly . . . educated men who have come to this lawless country and given rein to the worst that is in them." Knowing that Bushnell was to speak on purity, they came expecting "to hear some coarse low fun." Bushnell, however, had faced more daunting challenges in the past, and she was up to the task. She "looked them calmly in the face and with that deep, spiritual power, before which all base things cower, talked directly to them of God's punishment until they must have felt that the judgment day had come." The missionary reporting the incident declared it impossible to describe "the magnetism of Dr. Bushnell's womanly strength, and her intense exhortation to purity of heart and life."[68]

As they continued on their round-the-world missionary tour, Bushnell and Andrew once again agreed to take up investigative work. While in India they had been approached by a British anti-opium organization and asked to examine the effects of the opium trade on local populations. Though reluctant to launch yet another inquiry, they knew that their travels would bring them through the regions most affected by the trade, and so after careful consideration, they assented. They were well equipped for this new task. As a missionary in China and as a temperance reformer in Denver, Bushnell had witnessed the destructive nature of the drug, and she and Andrew had both observed its devastating effects upon Indian communities. Perhaps more important, their investigations in British India had sensitized them to the plight of non-Western peoples at the hands of imperial capitalists, and had emboldened them to critique the immoral practices of the British Empire.

Around this same time, Bushnell and Andrew also agreed to undertake "a quiet investigation into the slave trade in Chinese girls for immoral purposes" in Singapore and Hong Kong, at the request of the Colonial Office in London. Conducting both investigations simultaneously, they soon identified close links between intemperance and impurity; during this trip and a subsequent one, they gathered an "abundance of evidence that opium fed the social vice, and that the two went hand in hand."[69] And in both cases, they concluded, Westerners bore the chief responsibility for the perpetuation of vice. They insisted that they knew no "man, woman or child in India, Burmah or China" who supported the opium trade." Rather, it "persisted only at the behest of British and American businessmen reaping substantial profits."[70] And their investigations into the trafficking of women yielded similar results. They concluded that the appalling system of public prostitution that they observed in Singapore and Hong Kong was entirely "the product of Western civilization," introduced by Europeans and "utterly unknown in China except in the treaty ports.[71]

They found, however, that the nature of prostitution in the East differed from what they had encountered elsewhere. Chinese prostitutes, they explained, tended to be neither victims of seduction nor women "of base propensities," since as women they lacked the basic freedom to make such choices. In a society in which women could be given temporarily to pay off a debt or trained from a young age to be sold into prostitution, Bushnell and Andrew judged them akin to slaves.[72] And yet they made abundantly clear that despite the virtually unrestrained power that Chinese men exercised over their wives and children, the thriving trade in women in the port cities had no precedent in traditional Chinese culture. So although the precise circumstances of prostitution in the East differed from what they had observed in Wisconsin and British India, one theme remained constant: the culpability of *Christian* men.

The book they would later publish on these investigations, *Heathen Slaves and Christian Rulers*, was filled with stories condemning the uncivilized, unchristian practices of Westerners. Perhaps their most poignant example involved the case of Sir John Bowring, the former British consul in China and governor of Hong Kong, and an esteemed Christian hymn-writer. Bushnell and Andrew charged that as governor Bowring had overseen the virtual enslavement of countless women for the purposes of prostitution; even when the Secretary of State for the Colonies had written Bowring to express concern for the women, reminding him that they had no choice in their subjection and in fact had "an urgent claim on the active protection of Government," Bowering had taken no action to liberate them.[73] Instead, he had issued an ordinance requiring all "immoral houses" to be registered, confined to specific areas, and required to pay fees to the government, and he stipulated as well the compulsory examination of women.[74]

Once again, Bushnell and Andrew were at a loss to explain how a seemingly exemplary Christian man could craft such a loathsome policy. Reflecting on Bowring's famous hymn, "In the Cross of Christ I Glory," they observed: "One is tempted to ask, in which Cross?—the kind made of gilded tin which holds itself aloft in pride on the top of the church steeple, or the Cross proclaimed in the challenge of the great Cross-bearer, 'Whosoever doth not bear his Cross, and come after Me, cannot be my disciple'? The Cross is the emblem of self-sacrifice for the salvation of the world. Oh, that men really gloried in such self-sacrifice. . . ." It was far more important for right moral conceptions to shape "the enactments by which one's fellow-beings are governed," they averred, than to find eloquent expression in hymnbooks.[75]

And Bowring's enactments, Bushnell and Andrew made clear, had wrought tragic consequences. They recounted how government inspectors had secured paid "informers" to ferret out unregistered houses in an effort to enforce Bowring's ordinance. Enticed by lucrative rewards, these informers often used coercive tactics to ensnare "unlicensed" women in the act of prostitution—they might, for example, offer substantial money to tempt a "poor half-starved creature" to succumb, or to a woman's husband, to compel him to turn her in for the reward.[76] Some informers were known to have entrapped innocent women by planting marked money in their homes, or even to have resorted to rape to "prove" their case. In some instances, government inspectors "gathered their evidence" themselves, as was the case of at least one inspector who recounted his activities in an audacious report: "I took the marked money from the Registrar general's office, and followed a woman, and consorted with her, and gave her the money; and the moment I had done so, I put my hand in my pocket and pulled out the badge of office, and pointed to the Crown, and arrested the woman."[77]

Bushnell and Andrew described how ensnared women, and frequently young girls—many innocent of the accused crime—would then be taken away, forcibly examined at the Lock Hospital, and charged fines so substantial that they often had no choice but to engage in prostitution in order to pay them. The entire system was rife with corruption; inspectors exercised tyrannical authority, "vile informers" were rewarded for false reports, and respectable families often fell victim to extortion in order to protect the women and girls in their care. "Imagine the terror that respectable Chinese women suffered," Bushnell and Andrew wrote, "knowing that any man might denounce them, out of malice, and thereby reduce them to the very worst conceivable form of slavery!"[78] They could only conclude that the government seemed "bent on encouraging and developing immoral women and driving decent women either into prostitution, or, by the reign of terror, out of the Colony."[79] And even if, on occasion, an informer might enter an unregistered brothel and encounter a "woman of loose character there," they challenged, "What business have Governments hounding down these women, tearing away their last shred of decency and obliging them if inclining to go wrong to sink at once to the lowest depths of infamy?"[80]

Bushnell and Andrew denounced as well the custom of "protection" that had developed under the British to meet the Western demand for Chinese women, a system in which Chinese women were rented out by their owners to European men, known as "Protectors." "What charm this word 'protection,' and the title 'Protector' has held for certain persons, as applied to the male sex!" Bushnell and Andrew opined. Yes, man was known as the "natural protector of woman," they agreed, but "to protect her from what?" From men, of course: "Man is, then, woman's natural protector to protect her from man, her natural protector. He is to set himself the task of defending her from his injury of her, and he is charmed with the avocation."[81] Not surprisingly, they pointed out, it was men who perpetuated this myth.

Upon bringing their investigations to a close, Bushnell and Andrew submitted a report to the Colonial Secretary. As a result of their work, they recounted, at least one official of high standing "was retired," and "went into business in London more in keeping with his station—he opened a cigar stand."[82] They then returned to England to hold a series of large meetings on the British role in the opium trade and "closely related vices of other kinds," in which they drew attention to "how deeply the questions treated are *women's questions*, in the fullest and most wide-reaching sense." By bringing these painful topics into public view, Bushnell and Andrew once again encountered criticism, but they also garnered popular support; as one of their defenders noted, "if the story has been painful to hear, it must have been infinitely more painful to recite, and immeasurably more painful still to the victims of the system, who had to suffer the horrors which have made the story possible."[83] For her part, Bushnell insisted that the distressing stories must be told, for it was only in "dragging into the light of public intelligence the details of the wrongs committed" that people would be stirred to sympathy and moved to bring an end to such misdeeds.[84]

Much to their dismay, however, only a few years later Bushnell and Andrew would discover that the system of public prostitution they had uncovered in the East had taken root in the United States as well. When they published *Heathen Slaves and Christian Rulers* in 1907, they devoted the second half of the book to their subsequent investigation of the flourishing trade in Chinese women between Hong Kong, Singapore, and the West Coast of America. They had learned of this trade after settling in Oakland, California, from missionaries working to rescue Chinese prostitutes in the area, and they hoped that by exposing the roots of the problem they could inspire someone to organize a crusade to banish "Oriental slavery" from America.[85]

In their book they reminded Christians that the faith was judged "by the moral character of the men who are called Christian," and though they lamented the oppression of women in "heathen" societies, they again refused to attribute the traffic in Chinese women to "heathen" practices, or to allow readers to dismiss the atrocities committed in West Coast Chinatowns merely as Chinese problems, imported and contained among the foreign population. It was the influence of Western Christian "civilization," they insisted, that exploited Chinese practices and fashioned the system of sexual slavery that had taken hold wherever the two cultures intermingled. If it were not for white Christian men—British and American—there would be no slave trade between Hong Kong and California, they contended. To begin with, as their earlier investigations had demonstrated, the European presence in the port cities fostered the conditions for public prostitution that ensured a steady supply of Chinese prostitutes. Then white American men crossed the Pacific to procure the prostitutes, white seamen helped transport them to the West Coast, and white immigration officials granted these virtual slaves entry into the country. In America, white property owners built the brothels and profited enormously from the trade, white policemen protected these brothels, and white men served as Chinatown "guides" and "watch dogs," keeping mission workers and rescuers at bay. White lawyers defended traffickers in court and, together with complicit judges, facilitated the return of women who had managed to escape. And finally, white men frequented the brothels, fueling the demand for Chinese women.[86]

Because Bushnell and Andrew believed that few Americans were likely to take interest in the plight of Chinese women, they employed a variety of tactics to prevail upon their readers. Though they clearly sympathized with the Chinese women, whom they considered victims both of their own culture and of abusive white men, they also contended that the wrongs perpetrated against Chinese women affected all Americans. "Have we spent hundreds of millions of dollars, and shed the blood of thousands of young men, and widowed and orphaned tens of thousands besides, in a civil war to put down African slavery, introduced from the Atlantic Coast, merely to turn about and welcome Chinese slavery from the Pacific Coast?" they demanded.[87] They warned that the slavery of Chinese women would not remain isolated; by fostering "a debased American manhood," it would infect the country's moral system and threaten the freedom of American women, too. "Men cannot live in the midst of such slavery as this, tolerate it, defend it, make gain through it, patronize it, without losing all respect for woman and regard for her rights," they insisted.[88] In alarmist tones, they foretold of ominous dangers ahead, when the Chinese and Japanese would be able to force their way past immigration restrictions. And in racially charged language uncharacteristic of the rest of the book, they warned "the Christian public of America" that the "trickling stream of brothel slaves" currently entering the country threatened to become a "yellow flood," and they asked their readers to consider what might happen to American women "if almond-eyed citizens, bent on exploiting women for gain, obtain the ballot in advance of educated American women."[89]

Taking such rhetoric in isolation, however, obscures the complexity of their argument. For unlike others who employed similarly racist terminology, Bushnell and Andrew did not advocate the restriction of Chinese immigration. They insisted that the real problem was not the presence of the Chinese in America, but rather the slavery of Chinese women, at home and abroad, which persisted due to Western governments' mistaken belief in the "necessity of vice." If Americans wanted to stamp out the enslavement of Chinese women in America, they needed to enforce laws without regard to race, and make a serious attempt to eliminate the enslavement of women in overseas port cities as well. Though Bushnell and Andrew employed racially charged rhetoric in reference to the trafficking of women, they abandoned such terminology when referring to the Chinese more generally. Instead, they insisted that on the whole, "no class of people . . . are possessed of a greater moral sense or can be reached more readily by moral suasion, than the Chinese." And they maintained that upstanding Chinese citizens—those who lived in terror of the "slave-traders and women-stealers"—would be delighted with a proper enforcement of laws that would allow "respectable Chinese family life" to flourish. Testifying to the "real worth of the sort of Chinese character" that one encountered in areas of the country not "vitiated by familiar contact with foreign profligates," they assured their readers that the presence of such people "could not but be a benefit to us, and would afford peaceable, thrifty, useful Chinese settlements in our midst, of which we would feel justly proud."[90]

Heathen Slaves and Christian Rulers provided an important record of the trade in Chinese women in America, but it reached a far smaller audience than had *The Queen's Daughters in India* only a few years earlier, and it failed to elicit a notable response. By 1907, much had changed for Bushnell and Andrew. They had severed their ties to the WCTU, and both Frances Willard and Josephine Butler, their once-beloved mentors, were dead. The years leading up to their Oakland investigations had been tumultuous ones for the two women, and had left them increasingly ostracized from the communities in which they had once enjoyed widespread respect. In the coming years, Bushnell and Andrew would lack the apparatus of an international organization that could provide them with opportunities to advance their critique of Western racism, and the institutional backing that could position them to offer their prophetic vision to the wider Christian church. But the events of those turbulent years would set Bushnell on a new path, leading her to embark on an investigation of a different kind—one that she would pursue, with few interruptions, for the remainder of her life.

4

The Crime Is the Fruit of the Theology

IT WAS AS a young missionary to China that Bushnell had first entertained the possibility that the Christian Scriptures, which she had always assumed to contain the word of God, might in fact be unreliable when it came to revealing God's word to women. Her initial work in temperance and purity reform had deepened her suspicions of the trustworthiness of Christian men, even those who seemed most "respectable," but it was her encounters with non-Western women that ultimately convinced her of the need for radical theological revision. After witnessing repeated instances of Christian men perpetrating acts of alarming cruelty against women, Bushnell could only conclude that Christianity itself, as it had been handed down from generation to generation, must be to blame. The pervasiveness and egregiousness of the abuse she witnessed at the hands of Christian men, together with the lack of outrage exhibited on the part of so many of her fellow Christians, convinced her that the problem was not simply one of weak or corrupt individuals failing to live up to the ideals of the Christian faith. Rather, the problem must lie within the teachings of the faith itself—teachings that depicted women as weak and subservient, and men as masters with God-given authority to rule over women. Yet Bushnell refused to accept that such patriarchal Christian doctrines reflected God's will for humanity. Instead, she set out to examine the Scriptures, from beginning to end, to discern how God's original intent for women and men had been distorted by centuries of faulty translation and skewed interpretation.

Bushnell's turn to biblical study was not only motivated by a deep desire to reveal God's will for women, but it was also prompted by her abrupt departure from the world of reform. Her crusading spirit, unwillingness to compromise, and courage in the face of adversity suited her well for the controversial investigations she undertook in the name of purity, but these attributes could create difficulties when it came to her relationships with individuals or organizations whose ideas differed from her own, particularly when it came to seeing the occasional wisdom in compromise.

Already in 1895 there had been signs of tension between Bushnell and Andrew, on the one hand, and the WCTU, on the other. In the wake of their anti-opium campaign, Bushnell and Andrew were spending the summer in Switzerland, praying, studying, and consulting daily with Josephine Butler, who was vacationing nearby.[1] Butler, a staunch antiregulationist, shared with them at that time her discouragement over what seemed to be a growing ambivalence toward government regulation among certain members of the WCTU, most notably Frances Willard and Lady Henry Somerset. With regulationist forces once again gaining strength in Britain, Butler feared that the Contagious Diseases Acts could be reinstated if purity reformers failed to present a united opposition, and she had written a public "Letter of Warning" to her fellow reformers, insisting that there were "no two sides to this issue." Bushnell and Andrew were thoroughly convinced of the rightness of her position, and they determined to "give their lives" to the cause. Butler, for her own part, found "great encouragement" in their support, and reflected that while there were many women willing to take up temperance work, few were "so fitted for repeal work" as Bushnell and Andrew. She considered them "really *valuable* women," and hoped they would receive permission for future work in the purity movement from their "Chief," Willard, since "they do nothing without her word of command."[2]

Apparently, Bushnell and Andrew were not only seeking Willard's consent, but also anticipating an official appointment within the WCTU's European purity movement that would provide them with financial support for their work. Later that summer, however, they were shocked to learn that Willard and Somerset had selected another woman for the position. Butler, too, was at a loss to account for this unexpected act: "Lady H. Somerset and Miss Willard have done a thing wh[ich] I cannot explain except that they were under some bad spiritual influence," Butler wrote, lamenting that they had passed over Bushnell and Andrew in favor of "a lady who knows nothing of our federation work, and is not even a Christian woman, nor clear headed, but a clever, pushing, ambitious woman." Butler felt that Willard and Somerset had "overlooked and . . . shamefully

slighted our good Mrs. Andrew and Dr. Bushnell," who were "fully qualified and fully equipped" for the work, and eager to take up the position as
her "special fellow workers." Butler reported that the two women "feel this
slight bitterly," and worried that they might choose to leave the World's
WCTU, despite being "dependent in the matter of funds."[3] After growing frustrations with the organization, Bushnell and Andrew did indeed
resign from the World's WCTU, in June 1896.[4]

Fearful that the WCTU was poised to undermine the cause for which
they had long toiled, Butler penned a second "Letter of Appeal and
Warning" against the regulation of prostitution. "Perhaps some people will
think it a little stern," she noted, "but Dr. Kate Bushnell and others have
told me how evil men are, in so many parts of the world," and of the power
such men wielded in influencing well-intentioned but ignorant women
to do their bidding.[5] In the spring of 1897, however, Butler's fears were
realized: Lady Henry Somerset, vice president of the World's WCTU, publicly came out in support of the Contagious Diseases Acts.[6] In a stunning
about-face, the long-time supporter of Bushnell's and Andrew's investigative work now condoned compulsory examination—with the stipulation
that it apply to women and men equally. Many men had their own reasons
to resist this recommendation, but among WCTU women on both sides
of the Atlantic, Somerset's change of heart unleashed a furor. Many of her
fellow reformers considered her act a horrific betrayal of their cause. As
one of her critics bluntly demanded, "does Lady H think she will ever get
men to do their fornications like going to a concert, with a ticket, price,
date and place? Fool! fool!"[7] Bushnell and Andrew, for whom this betrayal
was particularly bitter, were among Somerset's most vocal detractors.
Charging that "the high standard of the early days of the Womens' CTU,
as it took its rise in America are [sic] not being maintained," they took
the dramatic step of resigning from the national WCTU as well. Willard
regretted their decision but repudiated their allegations, insisting that the
WCTU's commitment to "total abstinence and prohibition" remained as
strong as ever.[8]

In her annual address to the WCTU that fall, Willard publicly scolded
Bushnell and Andrew for their condemnation of Somerset, suggesting
that such "bitter denunciation of any co-worker implies a condition of
heart that is not sweet toward God."[9] Undeterred, Bushnell and Andrew
started work on another leaflet criticizing the WCTU.[10] With their life's
work seeming to crumble before their eyes, they prayed "daily, hourly,"
that God would hear their prayers, and trusted that it would not be long

before "that miserable woman's [Somerset's] public career will be ended." They felt betrayed and infuriated by Willard in particular, who, despite disagreeing with Somerset, refused to condemn her influential friend. Bushnell informed Willard that neither God nor the women of America would hold her guiltless for her silence.[11] Even Butler, who had resigned her position as superintendent of the purity department of the World's WCTU out of protest, found Bushnell's and Andrew's bitterness excessive. When Somerset once again reversed her decision in February 1898, in part out of concern for the toll her actions were taking on Willard's health, Butler was willing to forgive past differences and look to the future. Bushnell and Andrew, however, could not bring themselves to do likewise.

In America, Willard, who had long suffered ill health, was relieved to hear of Somerset's return to the fold. But only two weeks after Somerset's retraction, she succumbed to pernicious anemia. Bushnell and Andrew, who saw in Somerset's retraction only a conspiracy to undercut the overwhelming opposition rising up against her, remained so embittered that they welcomed the death of their former friend and mentor.[12] They lamented that one who "was once so great a blessing, has of late wrought only injury to the many causes which she had laboured so many years to build up," and grieved over "a once glorious life crowded with noble activities, *gone out in eclipse!*" Indeed, they saw "the hand of God" in her timely death.[13]

Willard's death, however, meant that Somerset assumed the presidency of the World's WCTU, a fact that roused Bushnell and Andrew to action. Circulating letters and press releases disparaging Somerset, they attempted to mobilize opposition among American women.[14] To further protest Somerset's leadership, they withdrew their local WCTU membership as well, completely severing their relationship with the organization.[15] Butler strongly disapproved of their extended resentment, and "in a very serious and solemn letter" she "freely scolded" them for their bitterness and told them "they could not have real blessing on their work unless they could to the bottom of their hearts forgive Lady Henry, and love her." Butler evinced a grace that Bushnell and Andrew found hard to muster, but they answered Butler's "rather bitter pill" humbly, and obediently refrained from their vitriolic public attacks on Somerset.[16] Despite their restraint, however, Bushnell and Andrew discovered that they were no longer enthusiastically received in British temperance and purity circles. They found it difficult to schedule public talks—long their primary means of support—and that summer Bushnell was unable to secure a British publisher for her book on purity, *A Clean Life*.[17] Without the backing of a powerful organization, and hamstrung in their efforts to raise their own financial support, Bushnell and Andrew faced trying circumstances.[18]

The "Rangoon Horror"

Realizing that they could accomplish little in England for a time, Bushnell and Andrew decided to return to India to fight the reinstitution of government regulation from afar. They departed for India in early 1899, without a specific course of action but hopeful that their work would become clear upon their arrival.[19] Once in India they began by retracing the steps of their earlier investigation, whereupon they soon encountered evidence that the regulation of prostitution continued unabated. Discouraged by the apparent erosion of their earlier efforts and dismayed by the ongoing abuse of Indian women, Bushnell spent the long, hot summer pouring over her Bible for direction.

It was while "prayerfully seeking light as to what the Word teaches of the duty of one sex towards another" that Bushnell came across a startling article Butler had written in the July issue of the *Storm-Bell*, the journal of the Ladies' National Association for the Abolition of State Regulation of Vice. In it Butler recounted the story of the brutal rape of a Burmese woman perpetrated by a dozen British soldiers. The brazen attack, which had been reported in several British newspapers, had occurred in broad daylight near a public highway in Rangoon, within sight of around thirty additional soldiers—all of whom had failed to intervene. The victim, described in the press as an "elderly and respectable" woman, was first reported to have died as a result of injuries she sustained, though later accounts suggested she had survived, only to have been driven to insanity by the assault. No soldier involved in the attack had been brought to justice. Butler was outraged, and insisted that while proponents of the "necessity of vice" argued that providing soldiers with officially sanctioned "means of gratifying their appetites" would deter such violence, the very opposite was in fact the case. Sanctioned prostitution instilled in men "contempt for the natives of India," she explained, particularly for native women, whom soldiers came to regard as "mere tools, as degraded, helpless, purchasable slaves, soulless, worthless creatures, fit only to be food for their shameful appetites." At the same time, the myth encouraged men to believe in the "impossibility for themselves of a decent self-restraint."[20]

Despite Bushnell's familiarity with the many atrocities that Christian men had committed against non-Western women, Butler's report of this "Rangoon horror" affected her profoundly. With a new intensity she searched the Scriptures to comprehend how Christian men could perpetrate such deplorable acts against women, and with immunity. Beginning with Genesis 3:16, she then examined "all that the Apostles, particularly Paul, have to say of the relation between man and woman." Already in her 1896 book, *A Clean Life*, she had attributed some of the obstacles purity activists faced to a faulty understanding of the book of Genesis, noting how men had concocted "the theory that God ordained woman to be a scapegoat of her husband's self-indulgence, as a permanently adjusted penalty for Eve's sin at the beginning," and she pointed out that in doing so they had neglected the efficacy of Christ's atonement for all women.[21]

By the end of the summer, "after a calm prayerful study" of key passages regarding the status of women, Bushnell had outlined a comprehensive critique of traditional interpretations. In a letter to Butler she described how she had come to reject "the theological conception that they form collectively the doctrine that the sexual abuse of wife by husband was ordained by God at the fall of Eve." She defended her use of the term "abuse," insisting that subordination *was* abuse: "Man would feel *abused* if enslaved to a fellow man," she argued, and the same was true of women, even if theologians liked to consider women's subjugation "the happiest state in which a woman can exist." (She noted, too, that it was "the *male* theologian and not the *female* victim who pronounces the state a happy one.") And yet by deeming that "happy state" the result of sin and the source of woman's sorrow, theologians revealed the contradictory nature of their own teachings. Instead, she asserted that what theologians taught to be "the God-ordained marriage relation between man and woman" in fact robbed women of their "will and wishes," and amounted to nothing less than "the sexual abuse of the wife by the husband." She marveled that theologians had long championed a teaching "in essence contrary to good morals and defiant of the Lord's law 'whatsoever ye would that men should do unto you, even so do ye also to them.' "[22]

Reflecting on the "Rangoon horror" that Butler had recounted, Bushnell wondered how people might respond if each of the perpetrators had stated clearly their "*Christian* (?)" beliefs, that "solely because 'Adam was created first, then Eve' and because Eve 'being beguiled hath fallen into transgression,' " woman had been "cursed in the subordination of her sexual appetite to man's whim and caprice in the marriage relation." That it was a wife's place " 'to manifest the glory of her husband'—the glory of such husbands as these!—with *no* qualification, mind you, as to whether that husband is a saint; a heathen, a blasphemer, a lunatic, a drunkard, or an adulterer," struck Bushnell as ridiculous. If male theologians were to be believed, the "God of truth and justice" put "all this honor upon the male *simply because he is a male*," and placed "humiliation and abuse and sorrow in the compulsory bearing of children upon the female, *simply because she is a female*." Bushnell, however, declared her "utter and entire dissent and apostasy from such monstrous conceptions." [23]

In her letter to Butler, she took issue as well with conventional notions of male headship, under which men assumed for themselves "manifold functions," including "unusual and unique spiritual enlightenment on sexual relations," and granted themselves "a thousand-and-one privileges and prerogatives" over women, effectively giving free reign to their own egotism under cover of "headship."[24] She went on:

> Yet it is by such traditional "reading between the lines" and teachings wrought out by masculine egotism in the Dark Ages, that at last we have at hand a whole fossilized system of theology, which makes of one half the human family some resplendent glory which the other half is appointed to reflect and manifest forth . . . —and this glorified and spiritualized half of humanity is so glorified and spiritualized—and appointed to teach theology and the love of God to the other half—not because of the nature of his moral or spiritual character at all; but merely by the nature of his physical body,— solely because he *is* a male!
>
> One calm, steady gaze at such a scene as this Rangoon horror is quite sufficient to spoil all such theology as that. And the only way to keep women from repudiating utterly such theology, is by binding them down to ignorance and superstition.
>
> In fact, *such* theology and the Rangoon horror are not far removed from each other. The crime is indirectly the fruit of the theology, since if theology teaches the enslavement of woman to man *inside* the marriage relation; that law of sin which forbids its regulation by law at all—causes this abuse and injustice to leap the bounds which a mistaken theology would throw around it to keep it *within* marriage relations, and the single man claims that *because he cannot marry* he has the right to abandon himself to the same

irresponsible incontinence outside the pale of marriage law. Men cannot make unquestioning, obedient slaves of *wives only*—sooner or later the iniquity of slavery will be visited upon the head of *unmarried* women also; for iniquity knows not the name of restriction.

Hence this question of the subordination of the wife, virtually concerns the unmarried woman as well as the wife.[25]

A Bird Set Free

Bushnell had long worked on behalf of women who failed to achieve the Victorian ideal of "true womanhood," but over the course of that summer she had come to recognize the enslavement of *all* women in a patriarchal society. And she had begun to identify the theological roots of women's subordination to men. Armed with these new convictions, Bushnell returned with Andrew to England. Once again, they began to hold a series of public talks on their Indian investigations, until Butler summoned them to London. Claiming to have a "message of God" for them, Butler shared with Bushnell that the time had come for them to "turn away from the painful details of your Oriental investigations, and refuse to talk of them," since "the public will keep you on them forever." Instead, she recommended that Bushnell "hold some Christian meetings of a general sort," adding that Bushnell's Bible studies had equipped her well for such work. Butler had often discussed the significance of theology with Bushnell, and she now counseled her friend to think of this shift in purpose not as an abandonment of purity work, but simply as a turn in a different direction.[26]

Bushnell was "unable to describe with what joy [she] welcomed this advice." She eagerly shared with Butler her desire to "give Bible instruction on the lines of purity, and to show the importance of the freedom of women for the purification of society," and Butler "entered most heartily into the plan." They prayed together and discussed how "the social evil would never be got rid of so long as the subordination of woman to man was taught within the body of Christians," and they agreed that the cause of purity could not succeed "until men—Christian men—came to understand that a woman is of as much value as a man; and they will not believe this until they see it plainly taught in the Bible." Feeling like "a bird set free from long imprisonment," Bushnell finished her few remaining public meetings, and in 1901 returned with Andrew to America.[27] Settling in Oakland, she began to devote herself to her biblical studies.

Feminist Theology in Victorian America

Over a century ago, Bushnell's contemporary, the systematic theologian Martin Kähler, characterized mission as "the mother of theology." Theology began as "an accompanying manifestation of the Christian mission," Kähler explained, and not as "a luxury of the world-dominating church."[28] More recently, missiologists have reflected further on this observation. As Andrew Walls notes, theology "springs out of practical situations," and is always addressed to specific cultural settings.[29] For this reason, the "cross-cultural diffusion of Christian faith invariably makes creative theological activity a necessity."[30]

While theological creativity is perhaps most evident in indigenous adaptations of the gospel, cross-cultural engagement often compels fresh theological inquiry among members of the sending culture as well.[31] In the case of Bushnell, cross-cultural experiences on the mission field in China first revealed to her the enculturation of the gospel within Western cultural systems, introducing her to the possibility of its distortion in traditional biblical translation and interpretation. Indeed, ever since discovering the "sex-biased" Chinese translation of the Scriptures, Bushnell had scanned her English translations for evidence of bias, spending "nearly every moment" of her "many sea voyages and railway journeys . . . in these studies."[32] But it was her encounters with women in India and East Asia that ultimately compelled her to pen her exhaustive theological investigation.

Traveling the globe for purity, Bushnell time and again encountered the pressing question: "How can officials of high standing as Christian gentlemen, be so indifferent to the wrongs of women and girls, and so complacent in dealing with the sensuality of men; so ready to condone their offences against decency?" How could men like Lord Roberts and Sir John Bowring be esteemed as honorable Christian gentlemen, while helping to ensnare countless women in virtual slavery? That men could do such things was bad enough, Bushnell reflected, but that a man could be "given public recognition as a Christian brother," even after his shameful conduct had been publicly exposed and believed, ". . . this is what puzzled one."[33] The widespread acceptance of what to Bushnell appeared to be unmitigated evil led her to conclude that the problem must stem from the faith itself. In light of this reality, Bushnell concluded that laws and regulations alone would do little to protect or emancipate women.[34] Rather, a new theology was needed—one that could form the basis of a new moral system. Having repeatedly clashed with Christian men who had attempted to undermine her purity work at every turn, Bushnell now set out to challenge the theology handed down by generations of Christian men as she took up her theological investigation in earnest.

In believing that Christianity was not only essential to reform, but also that Christianity needed to be reformed, Bushnell was not alone. From the earliest days of the women's movement, women like Angelina and Sarah Grimké, Elizabeth Wilson, and Elizabeth Cady Stanton had advanced feminist readings of the Scriptures in the defense of women's rights.[35] As historian Timothy Larsen has demonstrated, "the Bible loomed uniquely large in Victorian culture," even among those who placed themselves outside the Christian faith.[36] In addition, the public authority that churches wielded, together with the vocal opposition that activists perennially faced from Christian ministers, made Scriptural interpretation a necessary battleground in the early years of the women's rights movement.[37] In fact, to a degree often unrecognized today, the nineteenth-century women's rights movement was a religious movement. With roots in a millennial perfectionism forged in the religious awakenings of the late eighteenth and early nineteenth centuries, women's rights advocates understood their task as an expansive moral mission.[38] Participating in a larger societal rejection of patriarchal Calvinism, reformers for women's rights pitted moral women against immoral men, and combated the "dangerous split between public governance and private morality" by seeking to integrate the two.[39] Early women's rights advocates had discovered that women's suffering at the hands of intemperate men proved "fertile ground for rights consciousness," and that obedience to God was a powerful motivating factor, inspiring many women to take up the feminist cause.[40] Although over the course of the nineteenth century the mainstream women's movement would develop a more individualistic and pluralistic orientation than would Christian women's organizations such as the WCTU, many of the movement's organizing principles continued to resonate with women across the religious spectrum, and with evangelical Protestant women in particular.[41]

By the time Bushnell came of age in the 1870s, then, a vibrant Christian women's culture with strong connections to the broader women's movement had established itself across Protestant denominations. Like their predecessors in the early women's rights movement, members of this Protestant women's culture remained convinced that Christ was woman's "great emancipator,"[42] and that Christianity, rightly understood, was not only compatible with women's rights, but in fact demanded the political and social emancipation of women. They would find, however, that while this emancipatory interpretation of Christianity was widely embraced among Christian women, particularly among those active in reform circles, it continued to face entrenched opposition among many churchmen.

Even as women asserted significant religious and cultural authority, in their efforts to work for the advancement of women they frequently encountered resistance from men within their own churches. Indeed, despite significant areas of collaboration, the coalescing alliance between Protestantism and feminism was far from universal, both on the part of women's rights activists, and on the part of Protestant churchmen.[43] Eventually, this persistent antagonism would lead some women to abandon their commitment to the compatibility of traditional Christianity and the advancement of women. Elizabeth Cady Stanton was one such woman, as her *Woman's Bible* plainly attests. Women like Bushnell, Willard, and other activist Protestant women would also come to conclude that the Christianity preached from many pulpits did in fact work against their emancipatory aims. However, rather than abandoning the Christian faith altogether, they continued to uphold Christianity as essential to the advancement of women, even as they increasingly came to believe that Christianity itself required a feminist corrective. Equipped by enhanced educational opportunities and bolstered by the close networks that churchwomen had established, women of Bushnell's generation were ideally situated to fashion a feminist Christianity.

In order to bring about religious reform, Protestant women sought both institutional and theological change,[44] and the WCTU, under the direction of Frances Willard, was at the forefront of these efforts. During national conventions of the WCTU, members filled local pulpits, and the organization's journal, the *Union Signal*, delighted in reporting how their eloquence and power succeeded in winning over even their most stalwart critics. The WCTU also worked to provide resources for women struggling to secure ecclesiastical rights within their own denominations, and the *Union Signal* routinely published articles and promoted books defending churchwomen's authority and spiritual empowerment. In 1888, Willard herself published *Woman in the Pulpit*, a powerful defense of female preaching, and of the authority of women within Protestant churches and Christian tradition. "When will blind eyes be opened to see the immeasurable losses that the church sustains by not claiming for her altars these loyal, earnest-hearted daughters, who . . . are going into other lines of work or taking their commission from the evangelistic department of the

Woman's Christian Temperance Union?" Willard demanded. "Are they willing that woman should go to the lowly and forgotten, but not to the affluent and powerful? Are they willing that women should baptize and administer the sacrament in the zenanas of India, but not at the elegant altars of Christendom?"[45] She reminded her readers that the WCTU had "a department of evangelistic work, of Bible Readings, of Gospel work," which together employed "several thousands of women who are regularly studying and expounding God's Word to the multitude," and that this number was over and above those women who ministered in home and foreign missions, and in church evangelism. Yet nearly all of this "great host" who "publish the glad tidings" had been excluded from doing so within the bounds of the institutional church.[46]

Willard was not only concerned with women's ecclesiastical rights, but also with the pressing need for women to have a hand in interpreting the Scriptures. She considered biblical exegesis, given human predilections, "one of the most time-serving and man-made of all sciences, and one of the most misleading of all arts";[47] in the case of spiritual authority, she concluded, "it is not good for man to be alone."[48] Under her leadership, the WCTU's Evangelistic Department sought to equip ordinary women to read and interpret the Bible independent of men, distributing Bible readings to local unions and dispatching speakers around the country to advance progressive interpretations of Scripture. As early as 1887, the WCTU began offering New Testament Greek lessons at its national convention in order to bolster women's theological expertise,[49] and before long the Evangelistic Department developed a four-year correspondence training course that included a comprehensive study of the Revised English Bible, elementary lessons in New Testament Greek, and lessons on the history of Christianity; the courses were demanding, requiring an hour's study each day.[50] Independent courses in Greek, evangelism, and Bible reading were later added, and by 1890 over two hundred WCTU women from around the country were enrolled in the classes.[51] Some women studied with the intent of serving as evangelists or deaconesses, others merely for personal enrichment. As an update in the *Union Signal* noted, they were "of every degree of capability: women zealous to the verge of fanaticism: women distracted with the cares of home and church and society, yet filled with holy enthusiasm . . . women old, and with the conservatism and the understanding that years bring: women young and fiery in ambition . . . ; women of scholastic culture; women cultured or uncultured; queens of the salon, queens of the prairies. . . ."[52]

Already equipped by her background in classical languages, Bushnell did not enroll in the courses, but she did independently pursue an intensive study of the Greek and Hebrew Scriptures. Even before Willard had published *Woman in the Pulpit*, the two women had been in conversation over questions related to women's religious authority and gendered biblical interpretation.[53] It is probable that these conversations, together with Willard's book, helped prompt Bushnell's further work in this area, for it was the very next year, 1889, that Bushnell published the first of her theological reflections in the pages of the *Union Signal*.

Early Writings

In her initial reflections Bushnell turned her attention to key texts that had long been used to silence and subordinate women. She began with 1 Corinthians 14:31–40, a passage in which the Apostle Paul appeared to command women to "keep silence" in the churches. Bushnell, however, accused the male commentator who achieved this interpretation of "plunging right into the middle" of the text, of "making chaos of everything else, that he may, by sheer masculine force, keep the verses plumb to his ideas of womanly uprightness."[54] In a detailed explication of the passage, she argued that, shorn of masculine prejudice, the text in fact taught the exact opposite, authorizing women to prophesy in the Spirit.

Three years later, at the request of the editors of the *Union Signal*, she penned a lengthy, three-part rebuttal to the prominent Congregational minister Lyman Abbott's interpretation of Ephesians 5:21–24, a passage that seemed to dictate wives' submission to their husbands. Writing from Shanghai in the midst of her round-the-world tour, she contended that the bulk of evidence establishing man's "final authority" in the household could be traced not to the Greek Testament, but rather to the English translation, and she painstakingly contested traditional interpretations of the passage by arguing that no *Christian* man would seek such exaltation; only a heathen man might be expected to do so.[55] The following year, she addressed 1 Corinthians 11:1–16, a rather obscure passage on women veiling in public that similarly seemed to institute male headship. Here, too, she discovered that traditional interpretations contradicted the true meaning of the passage. Rightly translated, she insisted, Paul's words empowered women in the freedom of Christ.[56] In future publications she would further develop her analysis of each of these passages, but already in these early writings her methods were well established, as she combined a vast knowledge of the Scriptures and meticulous attention to detail with an entrenched suspicion of men.

In addition to contesting familiar passages on female authority, Bushnell examined a number of other instances "where sex affects the English translation." She discussed, for instance, the account of the "dukes of Edom" in Genesis 36, where in verse 14 Anah was introduced as the daughter of Zibeon, but ten verses later, and again in 1 Chronicles, translators had depicted Anah as a male. "We illiterate women are able to spell out the fact that several of these dukes were women!" Bushnell asserted, "Yet we are called upon to prove that women have ever ruled to any extent, or can rule, or were meant to rule, according to Bible teaching or history; and I answer that when woman's sex is snowed under without protest between the beginning and end of a single chapter, by careless translators who take it for granted that men are doing almost everything that is done, the case is singularly hard to prove."[57]

In a similar vein, Bushnell pointed to the Greek word *diakonos* (διάκονος), which was translated as "minister" or "deacon" in each instance where it referred "to an office held by a man in the church," but was rendered "servant" in the single instance where it referred to a woman (Romans 16:1), despite the fact that it was "distinctly [stated] that this is her rank in the church—an ecclesiastical order." Bushnell also drew attention to Romans 16:7, where Paul mentions Junia as being "of note among the apostles," a fact that both Chrysostom and Origen accepted as clear evidence of the existence of female apostles in the early church. To Bushnell's dismay, however, modern commentators had "found themselves able to master the difficulty with one masculine flourish," arguing that "if Junia is a woman she cannot be an apostle, and if Junia *is* an apostle he [she] cannot be a woman!" Bushnell also pointed to 1 Timothy 5:1, where the word *presbyteros* (πρεσβύτερος) was translated as "elder," in reference to an office in the church, when it referred to a man, but in the very next verses its feminine form, *presbytera* (πρεσβυτέρα), was rendered as "elder woman"—despite being "masculine and feminine forms of one and the same word."[58] To Bushnell these discrepancies typified the destructive legacy of an enduring male monopoly on biblical translation and interpretation.

In her public addresses for the WCTU, Bushnell generally focused on her purity work, but there is evidence to suggest that she occasionally discussed some of these exegetical themes. In a letter published in the *Union Signal* in the summer of 1890, one woman described how Bushnell had emphatically asserted "women's equal footing with men on this earth of ours; how God made man and He made woman, each a complete human being before Him, each equally endowed, each with the same rights." The woman testified to the awakening that Bushnell's words had stirred in her: "I saw very clearly that woman's place is in this life of conflict between the powers of good and evil, between God's design for His children and the devil's plots to sink those children lower than hell: her place is right to the front of the battle, side by side, shoulder to shoulder with her brother, ahead of him if he fall, but *never for any reason whatever, one-half step behind*. Wherever Christ's cause needs supporters . . . it is woman's grand and God-given privilege to go, it is moreover, her duty, and she dare not disobey."[59] The letter writer concluded fervently: "We bore the curse as long as we could, we tried to believe we must be keepers at home, silent, non-aggressive, but the enemy visited the very cradles which we rocked, and left the blight of sin and death there, he came and drank of our life-blood, until, God-awakened, we went out in His strength to fight this demon, and never shall we lay down arms until he lies slain forever at our feet."[60]

Over the course of the 1890s, Bushnell's theological reflections began to focus more explicitly on the intersections of the Christian faith and social purity, and when Butler invited her to devote herself to her biblical studies, she was eager to plumb the depths of the Scriptures in order to undo this "monstrous" theology.

God's Word to Women

Upon returning to America, Bushnell immersed herself in her studies. Although she was for a time drawn away from her work as she investigated the traffic in Chinese women on the West Coast of the United States, in 1908, after the publication of *Heathen Slaves, Christian Rulers*, she and Andrew once again departed for Britain in order for Bushnell to continue her studies. Though Butler had died two years earlier, they settled near her Liverpool home—first in Hawarden, Wales, and then in Southport, Lancashire. With access to materials at the British Museum and the Gladstone Library at Hawarden, Bushnell spent her days researching and writing, and before long she began disseminating her ideas through a correspondence course for women. Women who subscribed to "The Women's Correspondence Bible Class" received three lessons at a time, along with a "self-binder" to secure the lessons into a book, and though it is not clear how many women did so, the fees Bushnell charged—10 shillings and 6 pence per year—contributed to her support. She also received vital encouragement from her subscribers, and she attributed the physical, mental, and spiritual strength that sustained her efforts to the "constant prayers of an inner circle of 'upholders.' "[61] She continued updating and revising her lessons until the course consisted of hundreds of numbered paragraphs arranged in three series of forty-eight lessons each, meant to be studied over the span of three years. Going far beyond her initial analysis of key texts on women, the course amounted to a comprehensive revision of the Scriptures. She hoped that her studies might liberate the gospel from the monopoly of men, free women from seeing themselves as "condemned and accursed creatures of God," and ultimately provide them with "a better understanding of their God."[62]

While she was issuing her correspondence course, Bushnell also published *God's Word to Women. 101 Questions Answered. A Woman's Catechism.* Containing 101 questions and answers succinctly outlining her key theological arguments, the booklet, first published in 1910, was reprinted a number of times, and according to Bushnell it "had an extensive sale" and was of some influence among British suffragettes in the 1910s.[63] In 1911 and again in 1913 she compiled and bound the lessons in her "Women's Correspondence Bible Class," even as she continued to edit the work.[64] In 1916 she first published the correspondence course lessons as *God's Word to Women*,[65] but in ensuing years she continued to revise and edit her work, and it was not until 1923 that she published the edition of *God's Word to Women* most commonly reprinted today. (She issued the final edition of her book in 1930.) *God's Word to Women* was a notable achievement. While scrupulously adhering to Scriptural authority, the book nonetheless contained radical revisions of the Scriptures, from Genesis through Revelation, and offered a dramatically new interpretation of God's will for women and men.

While remarkable in its depth and originality, *God's Word to Women* in many ways reflected the tenor of its times. To begin with, Bushnell shared with many women's rights advocates a deep disenchantment with traditional Christianity. Rather than rejecting orthodox Christianity in its entirety, however, she remained committed to the historic faith, and to the authority of the Scriptures. But the Christianity to which she was devoted was not the faith practiced and professed by contemporary Christians, and the Bible she upheld was neither the King James nor the Revised Version. By offering new translations and interpretations of the Scriptures, she sought to provide a foundation for a new Christianity, a faith that more accurately reflected God's will for women.

In her quest for more accurate translations, Bushnell was very much in step with her fellow Victorian Protestants. Although the King James Bible had long reigned supreme in the English-speaking world, by the 1870s modern scholarship had convinced many Christians of the need for a more accurate Bible, one that more closely mirrored the "original" Hebrew and Greek texts and more precisely revealed the true word of God. In 1879 a group of biblical scholars had come together to replace the King James Bible with "King Truth"; confident in their own abilities and in their scholarly credentials, and believing that a more accurate text would bolster the authority of the Scriptures in the modern age, they set out to produce the most perfect Bible the world had ever seen.[66] Upon its completion in the 1880s, the Revised Version met with enthusiastic responses from liberals and conservatives alike, and the American public rushed to possess the "unadulterated" Word of God.[67] In time, however, conservatives came to question the disinterested, "scientific" work of the revisers. Increasingly suspicious of translators' liberal intentions, a growing number of conservatives began to reject the Revised Version, and along with it even the lower critical methods its translators had employed.[68] By the 1920s, faced with the troubling possibility of an "unholy scriptures," some conservatives would re-enshrine the King James Version as the only acceptable word of God.[69]

Bushnell, too, was highly skeptical of the revisers' optimism that they could, through scientific methods, achieve an unbiased translation of the Scriptures. But she remained critical of the King James Version as well. As far as she was concerned, neither the authority of Christian tradition encapsulated in the King James Bible nor the "scientific" work of modern translation committees could be trusted, since both were marked by a profound male bias. "Turn to the Title Page of your Bible," she instructed her readers in God's Word to Women: "If you have an Authorised [King James] Version, you will read the assurance given to the reader, that the Book has been 'Translated out of the original tongues; and with the former translations diligently compared and revised.' If you have a Revised Version, of 1884, it will claim to be 'the version set forth A.D. 1611 compared with the most ancient authorities and revised.'" But, she contended, "[t]hese assurances do not hold good"—at least not "in this case where the status and welfare of one-half the human race is directly and vitally concerned."[70]

An avid reader of theology, Bushnell found that she could exploit the growing awareness of the subjectivity of biblical interpretation to formulate a gendered critique of biblical scholarship. "Few are the translators, fewer the exegetes . . . to abstain from finding in the Bible thoughts which it does not contain, and rejecting or unjustly modifying the thoughts which are indeed there," she wrote, quoting popular theologian F. W. Farrar, Dean of Canterbury.[71] Bushnell seemed to delight in citing theologians who discussed the subjectivity of biblical interpretation using conventional masculine pronouns, which she then employed in a gender-specific sense. "Give men what proof you will," she wrote, quoting biblical scholar Canon Payne Smith, "but seldom do they find more than what it suits them to find. If what is said agrees with their preconceived notions, well; if not, they reject it."[72] Echoing the words of Unitarian Charles Beard, she warned her readers that "[m]en only need to bring to the Bible sufficiently strong prepossessions, sufficiently fixed opinions to have them reflected back in all the glamour of infallible authority."[73] And, citing British evangelist G. Campbell Morgan, she urged readers to "interpret your Bible by what the Bible says, and not by what men say that it says."[74]

The more Bushnell compared the English Scriptures to ancient texts, the more she appreciated the considerable potential for revision. "All translation implies some, if only a slight, alteration of the sense of the original," she explained, and thus what might first seem to be the "scientific" or neutral task of translation was in fact a far more fluid and value-laden "art" in which the translator used his or her judgment to determine the correct rendition of the original language.[75] Due to the nature of the ancient Hebrew language, this subjectivity was particularly evident when it came to translations of the Old Testament. Bushnell described how the original Hebrew of the Old Testament contained no spaces between words and did not distinguish between capital and lower-case letters, and double letters were often written only once. More important, the original Hebrew contained no vowels. It was only after the Israelites were taken into Babylonian captivity, she explained, that scribes selected four consonants to serve as vowel sounds; due to continuing ambiguity between these vowel signs and original consonants, later scribes added interlinear vowel-signs to clarify pronunciation. All of these scribes, Bushnell pointed out, were *uninspired*, and all happened to be men, who, according to her reading of the Talmud, "held women in utter contempt."[76] For these reasons, Bushnell insisted that only the original Hebrew consonants could be considered the true and infallible word of God. As translators worked to render the Hebrew Scriptures into modern languages, then, there was ample opportunity for preconceived notions to shape their translations. Again citing Farrar, she agreed that "a translator has the need of invincible honesty if he would avoid the misleading influences of his own a priori convictions." She found little evidence of such honesty, however, when it came to men abandoning their preconceived notions about women.[77]

For centuries, men had claimed the sole right to translate and interpret the Word of God, to the detriment of women, and of the Christian faith, Bushnell explained. And without knowledge of the biblical languages, even intelligent and spiritually mature women could do little to combat this masculine distortion.[78] But armed with authoritative opinion that religious truth was neither disinterested nor neutral, Bushnell made a powerful case for women's theological reflection; if religious truth was inseparable from an individual's experience of the truth, then the experiences of women *as women* might bring them to a different truth than the teachings that had been handed down through male theological tradition. The time had come, Bushnell believed, for modern, educated women to translate and interpret the Scriptures for themselves. Sufficiently trained, women would then be empowered to challenge the authority of the early church fathers, medieval scholastics, Protestant reformers, Puritan divines, and even their own ministers.

At times, Bushnell went so far as to accuse men of conspiring to suppress women through willful misinterpretation and faulty translation. At one point, Bushnell even intimated that men, through their misrepresentations of Scripture, had allied themselves with the devil, in the devil's enmity with women.[79] Generally, however, she took a less conspiratorial view, concluding that many—though not all—of the existing errors had proceeded unintentionally from a long line of exclusively male expositors. Granting that these men may have "done the best they could alone," she nevertheless asserted that they had not done *"the best that could have been done."*[80]

To illustrate this point, Bushnell explained how it was known that a man who lost his way on the prairie would eventually begin to drive his wagon around in circles, as he tended unconsciously to pull with greater strength upon the rein in his dominant hand. So it was with the translator, she suggested: "He pulls unconsciously on the strong side of preconception or self-interest"; though such distortion might be unintended, it was "none the less inevitable to the uninspired hand."[81] She reminded her readers that "no translation can rise much above the character of the translator," and that translators should be known for their honesty as well as their learning. Even then, however, the translator would be bound by his or her cultural presuppositions, and could not "properly render what has not as yet entered in the least into his consciousness as the truth."[82] It was little wonder, then, that "all versions, having for all time been made by men, should disclose the fact that, on the woman question, they all travel more or less in a circle, in accordance with sex bias, hindering the freedom and progress of women." Down through the centuries, man's self-interest had repeatedly "led him to suppose that woman served God best as his own undeveloped subordinate." Thus, every time a passage presented more than one possible translation, "this or that man of learning" took the opportunity "to build up one sex and to depreciate the other." The result of this tendency, "through the ages, has been cumulative," Bushnell explained, and for this reason "no class nor sex should have an exclusive right to set forth the meaning of the original text."[83]

Bushnell was careful not to assert an innate female superiority, though some of her comments might have implied such. She acknowledged that while women's experiences revealed to them different theological insights, there existed "equally in each sex, certain sex prejudices and certain sex limitations that unfit either sex to be the sole custodian of divine truth for the opposite sex."[84] But since theology had for so long been the exclusive domain of men, there was a critical need for women to take their rightful place as translators and expositors. The work of previous translation committees "would have been of a much higher order had they first helped women to learn the sacred languages, (instead of putting obstacles in their way),"[85] she insisted, and added that "had educated women been on the last Revision Committee," some of the errors that plagued the Revised Version might have been avoided.[86] She lamented, however, that even in her own time, an era marked by women's advancement in nearly every realm of activity, women had made only modest inroads into the centers of theological education and citadels of religious power. As a result, the Christian faith remained gravely distorted.

Bushnell repeatedly entreated her female readers to undertake their own study of the biblical languages in order to help rectify the imbalance brought by centuries of male translation and interpretation. She counseled women to "learn to read and judge of the original" for themselves if at all possible, and, admitting that not all women could accomplish this feat, urged readers not to rest until they had "seen to it that a sufficiently large number of young women are kept in training in the sacred languages."[87] "The world, the Church and women are suffering sadly from woman's lack of ability to read the Word of God in its original languages," she insisted,[88] for only when women had a voice in interpreting the Bible, particularly passages relating especially to the interests of women, would "women's temporal and spiritual interests receive their due consideration."[89] And for those women who were unable to interpret the original biblical texts, Bushnell had further words of advice: "if we find even in the Bible anything which confuses our sense of right and wrong, that seems to us less exalted and pure than the character of God should be: if after the most patient thought and prayerful pondering it still retains that aspect, *then we must not bow down to it as God's revelation to us*, since it does not meet the need of the earlier and more sacred revelation He has given us in our spirit and conscience which testify of Him."[90] Reflecting her holiness upbringing, Bushnell advised women that if, after serious deliberation, they were unable to reconcile the biblical text they read with their innermost convictions, they ought to reject the passage as a faulty exposition, for "the Holy Spirit invariably refuses to seal to us as *truth* that which is *error*." Women should trust the Spirit to warn them "against accepting the error, even though it appears on the page of our Bible translation."[91] Bushnell, however, found little occasion to follow this advice. In her hands, even the most troubling passages yielded to fresh translation and interpretation.

Though Bushnell seized upon modern notions of subjectivity, she pointedly eschewed the aid of higher critical methods. Denouncing the efforts of "destructive higher critics" who manipulated the text beyond what was acceptable, she insisted that her own work "assumes that the Bible is all that it claims for itself"—that it is "inspired," "infallible," and "inviolable."[92] Though she found higher criticism "both tempting and fascinating," allowing for "brilliant guesses" as to the meaning of particular passages, she preferred to leave the text unaltered, even if at times the meaning must remain obscure. Comparing the higher critical method to cut glass and her own lower method to uncut diamond, she concluded that she preferred the unaltered text "to a pretty setting forth of mere sentiment."[93]

She rejected higher criticism in part due to her theological convictions, but also for pragmatic reasons. Though some historians have suggested that "radical feminists received the higher criticism from Europe 'as a gift from heaven,'"[94] Bushnell insisted that the Bible was far too valuable to women to subject it to the vagaries of higher criticism, particularly a criticism developed and applied by men. "However freely certain male scholars of the present day manipulate the text," Bushnell warned her readers, "no confidence would be placed in the results thus obtained by a woman," who would "at once" be accused of manipulating the text to suit her argument. And "even if we thought it lawful under any circumstances," Bushnell added, higher critical methods were unnecessary.[95] Equipped with a knowledge of the biblical languages, she would demonstrate how a radical re-reading of the text could be accomplished without the tools of higher criticism. She was confident that the Bible, shorn of its rhetoric of male supremacy and freed from the fallacies of male interpretation, would accomplish immense good for women, and for the Christian church.[96]

5

Leaving Eden

IN HER EFFORTS to provide a new theological foundation for the Christian faith, one that would protect women by placing them on equal footing with men, Bushnell began with the book of Genesis. For centuries, Christians had looked to Eden to discover and defend foundational values, and even as higher criticism and evolutionary theory had begun to call into question the historicity of the Genesis account, its cultural significance endured. At a time when traditional notions of gender, sexuality, and morality were increasingly in flux, the Genesis narrative seemed to offer universal truths that could be rediscovered or reaffirmed.[1] Though Bushnell was aware that many people no longer believed in the literal truth of the Genesis account, she refused to dismiss the early chapters of the Bible as "mere 'folk-lore'": "We are convinced that they are history, and to women very valuable history," she asserted. Even if she were to doubt the historicity of the events depicted in the Bible, she added, as a woman she could not afford to ignore them, for their false interpretation had caused women very real suffering.[2] By devoting a significant portion of *God's Word to Women* to the first chapters of Genesis, Bushnell hoped to offer a new narrative of creation, sin, and salvation, and ultimately provide the basis for religious and social revolution.

To change the world for women, Bushnell began by rewriting the story of the first woman, Eve. According to Christian tradition, Eve had been cursed by God as a punishment for tasting the forbidden fruit, and for inviting Adam into her sin. Blamed for humanity's fall into sin, Eve had come to symbolize human frailty, representing both a pathetic vulnerability and a dangerous capacity for seduction. Bushnell knew that this dual legacy constituted a formidable barrier to women's emancipation, but she was convinced that the inspired Scriptures told a very different story, and she set out to prove that it had been false exegesis and the fallibility of human (male) understanding, not the word of God, that had condemned Eve, and through Eve all women, to her disastrous fate. "The false teaching that God is in some way punishing women for the sin of Eve," Bushnell explained, had "throughout past ages, and up to the present hour" robbed women of sympathy, "furnished a cloak for sensuality," and sanctioned "much unnecessary cruelty to women." By depriving women of self-respect and self-confidence and stunting their development, it had caused "the entire Church of Jesus Christ" to suffer grave "moral and spiritual loss."[3] But such teaching amounted to "wicked and cruel superstition," Bushnell contended, and she dismissed it as "unworthy the intelligence of Christians."[4]

Bushnell was optimistic that much could be accomplished by "clearing the reputation of one so remote in history as Eve,"[5] but she knew she faced a daunting task. Men's defamation of Eve had begun "so early in the world's history" and had "prevailed so persistently" that it had become thoroughly entrenched in Christian thought.[6] Already in A.D. 177, Bushnell pointed out, Irenaeus, Bishop of Lyons, had ascribed devastating consequences to Eve's disobedience, portraying her behavior as "the cause of death, both to herself and to the entire human race."[7] Writing only a few years later, Tertullian of Carthage had visited this guilt upon all women. Bushnell quoted Tertullian at length: "Do you not know that you are an Eve?" he demanded of women. "God's verdict on the sex still holds good, and the sex's guilt must still hold also. YOU ARE THE DEVIL'S GATEWAY, you are the avenue to the forbidden tree. You are the first deserter from the law divine. It was you who persuaded him [Adam] who the devil himself had not strength to assail. . . . For your deceit, for death, the very Son of God had to perish."[8] Other prominent Christian theologians, from Jerome to Augustine, had followed suit, echoing Tertullian in blaming Eve for the sin of the world, and passing this teaching down through the centuries.

Time and again, Eve had served as a convenient symbol to bolster negative views of womanhood. Indeed, even as nineteenth-century Protestants emphasized women's innate virtue and well-tuned religious sensibilities, the specter of Eve lurked just beneath the surface. Although women were idealized as paragons of moral perfection, those who fell short of this ideal suffered the consequences. Women's rights leaders on both sides of the Atlantic recognized the enduring significance of the "curse of Eve," and whatever their personal beliefs regarding the authority of the biblical text, they considered Eve a powerful cultural symbol to be reckoned with.[9] Stanton and her co-authors had understood well the need to disrupt the traditional narrative that cast Eve as "the author of all our woes"; approaching the text in an "unprejudiced" manner, they found Eve's behavior above reproach. Co-author Lillie Deverreux Blake, for instance, praised Eve for her "courage," "dignity," "lofty ambition," and "intense thirst for knowledge," and deemed Eve's conduct, from beginning to end, "so superior to that of the whining Adam"—who behaved "to the last degree dastardly"— that she found it hard to believe that men based their "dogma of the inferiority of woman" upon those chapters.[10]

Bushnell may well have agreed with this interpretation of Adam's character, but she employed markedly different methods in her own efforts to dismantle the traditional narrative. She began by taking pains to demonstrate that the negative portrayal of Eve did not in fact stretch from the beginnings of time. It had been invented at a particular moment in history, and was therefore "man-made," not God-ordained. She pinpointed the emergence of Eve's identity as "the temptress" to around 250 B.C., when one of the books of the Apocrypha—writings deemed by Protestants as non-canonical due to their spurious origin or authority, she reminded her readers—first contained the assertion: "From woman a beginning of sin, and because of her all die."[11] Bushnell surmised that in the "days of mingling," the time between the writing of the Old and New Testaments, the "pagan Greek myth" of Pandora had become intertwined with the story of Eve, and as the mythical Pandora shaped interpretations of the biblical Eve, the true meaning of Genesis had been lost. Through "uninspired" Apocryphal writings, the story then infiltrated Jewish Talmudic teaching on the Fall, and from there it entered into the writings of the early church fathers, who, like Irenaeus and Tertullian, blamed Eve for humanity's fall into sin.[12] Over the centuries, this Pandora-Eve had infiltrated Jewish and Christian tradition, she explained.[13] It is important to note that in locating the origins of the temptress in the pre-Christian writings of the Jewish faith, Bushnell reflected anti-Semitic sentiment popular among late nineteenth- and early twentieth-century Protestants. Even as she was quick to condemn Jewish influences on Christian thought, however, her chief opponents remained men of her own faith. It was by undoing centuries of *Christian* men's manipulation of the biblical text that she hoped to provide a new template for womanhood, and to reframe the course of human history.

Establishing Equality

Bushnell began her exposition of Genesis with a biblical argument for the original, God-ordained equality of the sexes. Rather than commencing her study of women at Genesis 3:16, *after* the fall into sin, as men tended to do, she insisted on beginning with the first two chapters. In Genesis 1:26, she reminded her readers, God had said: "Let US make man [or 'Adam,'—it is the same word] in our likeness . . . male and female made HE THEM." To make sense of this language, Bushnell proposed that the appellation "Adam" initially "belonged equally to male and female," that "man" entailed both "male and female in one person." Rather than understanding this androgynous state figuratively, she offered a literal interpretation, suggesting that Adam may well have been a "bi-sexual organism." Though she conceded that this might sound incredible, she attempted to bolster her argument by drawing on modern scientific evidence of hermaphroditic organisms.[14] But what was most significant to Bushnell was not the mechanism by which "Adam" contained both male and female, but rather the fact that God had created male and female to be equal, and had given both dominion over the earth.

The Bible contains a second account of creation that demanded Bushnell's consideration as well, the more familiar story of Eve's formation out of Adam's rib, found in Genesis 2. Because this account seemed to contradict the first, higher critics had attributed it to a different author. Bushnell, however, rejected this assessment. Instead, she found a way to translate the second chapter in a manner that complemented, rather than contradicted, the first. She noted that after "Adam" had been created in chapter one, "God saw everything that He had made, and, behold, it was very good." But this condition did not last long, for the next chapter describes how God decided that it was "not good that the man [or 'Adam'] should be alone."[15] To understand how the "very good" state of humanity had become "not good," Bushnell explained that the Hebrew expression traditionally translated "alone" could also mean "in-his-separation." And from whom could Adam be separated, but God?[16] This conclusion implied the rather startling suggestion that Adam had been less than perfect before the serpent's tempting.

Although the vast majority of theologians believed that humanity's fall from perfection had occurred when Adam and Eve had eaten the forbidden fruit, a few scholars had in fact drawn attention to the possibility of Adam's earlier "stumbling." Bushnell cited William Law, for instance, an eighteenth-century British clergyman, who had proposed that Adam must have "altered his first state," bringing "some *beginning* of evil into it," in order for it not to have been good for him to be alone; Adam had thus "lost much of his first perfection before his Eve was taken out of him; which was done to prevent worse effects of his fall, and to prepare a means of his recovery when his fall should become total."[17] Bushnell also cited the German philosopher Jacob Behman, who considered that "[t]here must have been something of the nature of a stumble, if not an actual fall, in Adam while yet alone in Eden." Behman surmised that Eve had then been created (or "elaborated," as Bushnell described the process) in order "to 'help' Adam to recover himself, and to establish himself in Paradise, and in the favor, fellowship and service of his Maker."[18] In other words, God had created Eve in order to redeem the stumbling Adam. In this context, Bushnell explained, the traditional interpretation of Eve as Adam's "helpmeet," as an inferior or servile assistant, could not be legitimated. To bolster this contention she noted that the Hebrew word translated as "help" in this passage (עזר) occurred twenty-one times in the Old Testament, and in all but three cases it referred to divine assistance. Thus, God had fashioned Eve in order to bring Adam back into communion with God.[19]

Bushnell understood, however, that conventional translations of Genesis 2:21–22, where God allegedly formed Eve out of Adam's rib, seemed to confirm that Eve had indeed been but an afterthought, an inferior helpmeet, a "weaker vessel." But Bushnell insisted that the "inane fable" of the rib derived from a faulty rendering of the Hebrew text. She explained that the word translated as "rib" (צלע) in both the King James and the Revised Versions occurred forty-two times in the Old Testament, but only in this instance had it been translated in this way.[20] A more apt rendition would be "side," she contended, a term that evoked a process of separation not unlike the fissiparous reproduction scientists observed among the lower organisms. Rather than producing a product of inferior quality, this process connoted mutuality and equality, she maintained, since "each human body retains still abundant traces of a dual nature, in almost every organ and part."[21] Furthermore, this translation corresponded better to Adam's declaration that woman was not only "bone of my bone," but also "flesh of my flesh" (v. 23). She advised her readers that when they heard "a rationalist ridiculing the 'rib' story," they should keep in mind that he was not "in reality ridiculing the Bible, though he may think he is. He is holding up to contempt a stupid mistranslation."[22]

In her efforts to clear up "stupid mistranslations," Bushnell needed to confront centuries of hostile tradition that had interpreted nearly every aspect of the Genesis account as evidence for woman's God-ordained inferiority. The order of creation, for instance, was said to have established the "natural" inferiority of women; since man had been created first, the reasoning went, man must be superior to woman. The Apostle Paul himself seemed to confirm this logic in his epistles (1 Cor. 11:8–9, and 1 Tim. 2:13–14). Bushnell, however, was dubious of this claim. Indeed, even theologians who agreed with Paul's conclusions faulted his reasoning. John Calvin, for example, conceded that the evidence Paul provided from creation order "appears not to be a very strong argument" for the subjection of women, since "John the Baptist was before Christ in order of time, and yet was greatly inferior in rank." Bushnell noted that Calvin might also have observed that "[e]very man has a mother who was made before himself, and yet she is held to be his inferior." And, taking Paul's "logic" to its extreme, she added that since "cows were made before men—even before theologians,—men must be subordinated to cows."[23]

Whereas some commentators had attributed Paul's nonsensical argument to his "indulg[ing] freely in frivolous Jewish sophistries," as "a quaint example of the way in which the Jews were wont to derive arguments from Scripture, and to twist and torture its words in order to support the opinions which they were stating," Bushnell demurred.[24] Although she shared such commentators' anti-Jewish inclinations, as did many Christian theologians of her day, she insisted that the Apostle Paul rigorously combated such "Jewish fables," and thus it would make no sense if he here employed the very sophistry he otherwise denounced. "A grave responsibility rests upon those who subject Paul to ridicule, and the Bible to suspicion as to its worth," she warned, by offering "lame apologies" for Paul's "far-fetched" reasoning. She refused to "admit for one moment that either the Apostle or the Bible in general needs any apology."[25] Rather, she maintained that "the Holy Spirit prompted Paul's writing; and we do not believe the Spirit needed to study rabbinical rubbish to suggest a reason for silencing and subordinating women."[26]

Instead, Bushnell claimed that the "flimsy arguments" were not Paul's at all, but rather were "the work of manipulators of Paul's language." Paul had not "twisted Scripture; rather, men have twisted Paul's arguments out of conformity with Scripture."[27] She again blamed "the Judaizers" of the early church—those who promoted Jewish customs and against whom Paul himself contended—of distorting God's word, along with "masculine interpreters, who for (perhaps unconscious) self-interested reasons, have adopted that ready-made tortuous special pleading of the 'Judaizers.' "[28] For her part, she would rather believe "that the expositor is mistaken, than that the very term 'Gospel'—'Good News,'—proclaims oppression to women."[29] As would later feminist theologians, Bushnell rejected patriarchal readings of the Scriptures as relics of misogynistic Jewish tradition and contended that, shorn of such influences, the gospel presented a clear message of liberation for women. In her own New Testament exegesis, she insisted on interpreting Paul's words in terms of the larger story of Scripture, which in her hands had become a story of women's redemption: "Man's dominion over woman is a piece of property vested in a faulty title-deed," she explained, "and woman has God on her side of the contest."[30]

Bushnell also took issue with generations of male theologians who had based their defense of male supremacy on the supposed fact that God had given Adam the power to name the animals, and, significantly, to name woman as well. Since Bushnell had theorized that "Adam" initially consisted of both male and female together, the first point was moot, since it was this "Adam" who had been given the authority to name. And as for Adam naming Eve, Bushnell contended that although the man called his companion "Woman," closer examination of the text revealed that "it was not Adam, but the Word of God itself" that declared woman the "mother of all living" (Gen. 3:15). Adam simply affirmed this fact when he called his wife "Eve" (Gen. 3:20), which in the Hebrew resembles the word "living."[31] Moreover, Bushnell pointed out that Christ, who was "born of a woman," was also "fittingly named by woman." Eve herself "bestowed upon Him the title 'Lord' ";[32] Hannah "first called Him 'The Anointed,' that is, 'Christ' " (1 Sam 2:10); and the Virgin Mary "was instructed to name Him, before He was born, 'Jesus' " (Luke 1:31). Thus, Bushnell concluded, "that name which is above every name, THE LORD JESUS CHRIST, at which *every knee shall bow, of things in heaven, and things in earth, and things under the earth,*' " was in fact bestowed upon the redeemer by three individual women, three "prophetesses of God."[33]

Contending with the Curse

And the LORD God said unto the serpent, Because thou hast done this, cursed art thou above all cattle, and above every beast of the field; upon thy belly shalt thou go, and dust shalt thou eat all the days of thy life.

And I will put enmity between thee and the woman, and between thy seed and her seed: it shall bruise thy head, and thou shalt bruise his heel.

Unto the woman he said, I will greatly multiply thy sorrow and thy conception; in sorrow thou shalt bring forth children; and thy desire shall be to thy husband, and he shall rule over thee. (Genesis 3: 14–16, Revised Version)

Bushnell's efforts to establish and defend the equality of woman and man at creation would have mattered little had she not also addressed the third chapter of Genesis, the account of humanity's fall into sin. According to traditional interpretations, after Adam and Eve ate from the forbidden tree, God punished them by afflicting the ground so that Adam could produce food only through painful toil, and by cursing Eve directly, greatly increasing her pains in childbearing, and commanding that her "desire" should be for her husband, and that he should rule over her. This purported "curse of Eve" had profoundly influenced the status of women throughout Christian history, Bushnell lamented, as biblical expositors had sought in Genesis 3:16 the key to understanding "womanhood," and therein found justification for women's enduring subjugation to men in the home and in society. But Bushnell identified a theological double standard in this practice, for the verses where God addressed Adam never registered as more than an afterthought.

To discern man's destiny, scholars turned either to man's commissioning before the Fall, or to the redemption from the Fall accomplished through Christ's atonement. Indeed, the atonement was a foundational tenet of Protestantism, Bushnell reminded her readers. Reformers had broken with the Roman Catholic Church over this very issue, rejecting the Catholic system of penance because of God's "inestimable grace." But, Bushnell asserted, Protestant theologians from that time forth had never paused to think that such might be the case for women as well. Instead, they taught women "to keep to penance (seek to satisfy God's justice) for Eve's sin by silence in the Church and obedience to man."[34] By turning to Genesis 3:16 to understand God's will for women, male theologians had effectively denied the efficacy of Christ's atonement for women. "Expositors of the Bible will never be able to understand, or to set forth a clear, consistent, correct interpretation of the Word of God as regards women," Bushnell averred, "until they abandon, once for all, the attempt to found the social, ecclesiastical and spiritual (as far as this life is concerned) status of Christian woman on the Fall." Instead, they must establish woman's status on the atonement of Christ, as they had done for man. Employing a biblical metaphor, she explained that "they cannot, for women, put the 'new wine' of the Gospel into the old wine-skins of 'condemnation' before God's law." It was just this sort of faulty theology, she added, that was to blame for the "free-thought" abounding "among justice-loving persons"; confusing the errant teaching for the actual biblical message, they had mistakenly but understandably denounced the Bible as a whole.[35] By perpetuating such erroneous teaching, then, the church unwittingly contributed to the secularization of the age.

"As Christian women, we refuse to address ourselves to the task of working out Eve's 'curse' for sin," Bushnell contended, but she then added pointedly, ". . . if indeed she ever had one." For as it turns out, Bushnell not only objected to finding women's destiny in the curse, but she also advanced the revolutionary notion that Eve had never in fact been cursed by God. She pointed out that nowhere in the Bible did one encounter a discussion of "the curse" in connection with women. Rather, the teaching came "wholly through tradition."[36] In contesting "the curse," Bushnell knew that she was embarking on innovative theological territory, but she maintained that since traditional theology pointed "no other way for women" but "into a 'curse,'" women needed to "hew a hermeneutical and exegetical road for ourselves."[37]

In an effort to forge a new path, she began by examining the presumed sins of Adam and Eve, respectively. Though popular tradition blamed Eve for humanity's fall into sin, Bushnell pointed out that the New Testament taught that Adam, not Eve, had "brought sin into the world, and death through sin." New Testament passages twice referred to Eve as having been deceived, and thereby brought into the transgression, but eight times the Apostle Paul declared that "one person" alone was accountable for the Fall; twice he named Adam as that person, noting that he had not been deceived. Eve's greater culpability for the Fall was thus thoroughly unbiblical, Bushnell maintained, and *taught by tradition only*."[38]

Paul held Adam, rather than Eve, accountable for the Fall, Bushnell explained, because of the strikingly different ways in which they responded to God after they had eaten the fruit. When God confronted Eve, she had confessed, "The *Serpent* beguiled me, and I did eat"; Adam also confessed, but added, "The woman whom *Thou* gavest to be with me, *she* gave me of the tree, and I did eat."[39] Both admitted that they had eaten of the forbidden tree, Bushnell assessed, and both told truthfully of "the *immediate* influence that led to the eating," and in that they were equal. But rather than assigning the remote cause of his sin to Satan, Adam instead "accuses God to His face of being Himself that remote cause." Bushnell surmised that Satan, who in all likelihood lingered nearby during this interview, "must have rejoiced as much in Adam's attitude towards God in charging Him with folly, as in Adam's attitude towards himself, the tempter, in shielding him from blame."[40]

Bushnell ascribed profound significance to Adam and Eve's contrasting responses. By "becoming a false accuser of God," Adam "advanced to the side of the serpent." But Eve, by exposing "the character of Satan before his very face, created an enmity between herself and him."[41] For Bushnell, this divergence provided a crucial context for understanding the "curses" found in Genesis 3:14–19. If Eve rightly blamed the serpent, considered Bushnell, but Adam blamed God, why then would Adam be "wonderfully rewarded for his part in that Garden fruit-eating?" Why would Adam, "who accused God of unwisdom and sheltered Satan from blame," be "elevated to government over women; and . . . be allowed to dictate, by his own whims, how much or how little physical suffering she is to endure, as the price of his fleshly indulgence!" If anyone caused Eve to suffer through a curse, Bushnell reflected, logic dictated that agent to be Satan, her newly established enemy. Correspondingly, if anyone would reward Adam for shielding Satan, it would not be God, but Satan. The curse that Christians had for centuries understood to be Eve's divine punishment, Bushnell asserted, was in fact *Satan's* handiwork, meted out to punish Eve for rightly blaming the serpent's deceit, rather than her God.[42]

According to Bushnell, the background to Satan's cursing Eve could be found in Genesis 3:15, where God had declared to Satan: "I will put enmity between thee and the woman, and between thy seed and her seed; it shall bruise thy head, and thou shalt bruise His heel." By informing Satan that woman would be both "the progenitor of the coming destroyer of Satan and his power," and also *"in her own person"* an "enemy of Satan," God widened the breach already opened when Eve had blamed the serpent, Bushnell explained.[43] Satan would naturally attempt to cripple woman and inhibit her from carrying out her noble destiny, she added, and since it would be through childbearing that woman would bring into the world the seed that would crush the serpent's head, it should come as no surprise that Satan would choose to strike there.[44] But, she lamented, what "common sense tells us Satan would *most certainly* wish to do," that is, increase woman's pain in childbearing, most theologians ascribed to God. They would have people believe that after God had exalted Eve as the progenitor of Christ and put enmity between her and Satan, so that she was "no longer associated with God's great enemy," God suddenly turned and pronounced several curses upon her. Bushnell rejected this interpretation as incoherent and indefensible: "The idea of God's passing a punitive sentence upon Eve, after the wonderful prophecy regarding her in verse 15," was both inconsistent and illogical, and an unprecedented occasion where God and Satan would be working on the same side, for the same result. This notion that God and Satan were working harmoniously together in their treatment of women, "from the Fall in Eden as long as this world lasts," struck Bushnell as absurd.[45] "Every word of God is tried," she attested, "and if we attempt to insinuate a false interpretation into it, it proves, on close inspection, a misfit all around"; traditional interpretations of Genesis 3:16 were clearly untenable.[46]

To work out an alternative interpretation, one that did not contradict common sense or her sense of God's righteousness, she recommended a different reading of the Hebrew text. Rather than "I will greatly multiply thy sorrow," Bushnell suggested that Genesis 3:16 should instead read: "Unto the woman He said. A snare hath increased thy sorrow." Her version established Satan, not God, as the author of woman's woe, and the difference between the two translations lay wholly with the interlinear vowel-signs, she explained.[47] Bushnell also took issue with the translation of the Hebrew "HRN" (הרן) as "conception" at the end of that phrase; wrongly translated, this passage had "wrought terrible havoc with the health and happiness of wives," she argued, "because, so read, it has been understood to rob woman of the right to determine when she should become a mother, and to place that right outside her will and in abeyance to the will of her husband." But the word in question was actually two letters short of spelling the Hebrew word for conception, Bushnell attested, as "all Hebrew scholars know"; the "highest lexical authorities" considered it "a 'contraction, or erroneous.'"[48] "Indeed!" she exclaimed, "And is one-half the human family to be placed at the mercy of the other half on such a flimsy claim as this!" Turning a commitment to biblical inerrancy to the defense of women, she asserted: "We stand for our rights, as women, on the assurance of our Lord, that *no word* in Divine law has lost any of its consonants, or angles of a consonant; and on our Lord's promise we demand a very different rendering of the word." She offered an alternate reading by turning to the Septuagint, which had translated the word in question as "thy sighing." Accordingly, the sentence reads: "A snare hath increased thy sorrow and thy sighing."[49]

Having cleared up the first part of verse 16, she then turned her attention to the sentence that followed: "Thy desire shall be to thy husband, and he shall rule over thee." This phrase, too, had "been the cause of much degradation, unhappiness and suffering to women," Bushnell contended, having instigated "much immorality among men, in the cruelty and oppression they have inflicted upon their wives."[50] She quoted several examples of male commentators' devastating interpretations of the passage: woman would "desire man's society, notwithstanding the pain and subjection which are the result"; her subjection to her husband's will was a punishment from "which even God's mercy will not exempt her," and since a husband's will was often so capricious, "a sorer punishment no human being can well have."[51] This pattern of interpretation was made worse by the association of sensuality with "desire," Bushnell explained, a connotation she again traced back to early rabbinical texts. She described how these Talmudic teachings had then influenced an Italian Dominican monk named Pagnino, who in his 1528 translation of the Hebrew Bible had rendered the Hebrew word *teshuqa* (תשוקה) in Genesis 3 not as "desire," but as "lust." Due to persecution in England at the time, Bushnell explained, both Tyndale's and Coverdale's English Bibles were published on the Continent, where they came under the influence of Pagnino's translation and likewise rendered *teshuqa* as "lust." With the exception of two earlier Vulgate versions of the Scriptures, every English translation followed this pattern.[52]

This inaccurate translation of *teshuqa* insinuated that God had instilled in women the potential for a "morbidly intense sensuality," Bushnell wrote, a misconception that had wrought tragic consequences for women. She cited commentators, for example, who argued that God had caused woman to "be possessed by passionate desire" for man, or "punished with a desire bordering upon disease"; one theologian described "the special punishment of the woman" as consisting "in the evils by which she is oppressed in her sexual vocation, in the position she occupies in her relation to man." Yet, Bushnell remarked, this man would "scarcely hesitate to pronounce such a relation 'Holy Matrimony!' "[53] To her, the connections between faulty translations and contemporary ideologies were clear. She was all too familiar with "Christian" teachings depicting women as sensuous and morally susceptible, and knew well the fate of "fallen women" who bore the brunt of this misinterpretation. But she understood that "virtuous" women, too, suffered from erroneous readings of this text. It was women's sensuality, so the thinking went, that made all women desire cohabitation with men, exposing them to the pain of childbirth and thereby assigning and confining them to the domestic sphere.[54]

In this way, theologians attributed women's narrowly prescribed roles to God's design. But Bushnell was astounded that the men propounding such misinterpretations failed to see that "if a wife must be under a 'curse' because she is under a husband who exercises the cruelties that constitute that curse, that is equivalent to saying that God has ordained that man and marriage shall be a curse to woman." Not only did this undercut the lofty ideal of Victorian marriage, but it also contradicted biblical teaching by essentially relieving "a husband of the duty to observe nearly the entire Decalogue, if only the person he practices his transgressions upon happens to be the one he has vowed, before the marriage altar, that he will 'love and cherish.' "[55] After studying several ancient texts and scholarly commentaries, Bushnell rejected both "lust" and "desire" as erroneous renditions of the Hebrew *teshuqa*.[56] She recommended "turning away" as a more accurate translation of the term, one that erased any sense of libidinous desire or sensuality. Rather than "Thy *desire* shall be to thy husband," or "Thy lust shall pertayne to thy husband," then, the passage should read: "Thou art turning away to thy husband."[57] A number of ancient texts strongly supported this translation, she contended, yet both the King James and the Revised Versions had perpetuated the mistranslation.[58]

By expunging any hint of female sensuality from Genesis 3:16, Bushnell not only accomplished a crucial step in rehabilitating the legacy of Eve, but she also provided the foundation for a comprehensive reassessment of woman's relation to man, and to God. Before that strategic move can be explored, however, the final phrase of verse 16, ". . . and he shall rule over you," must be addressed. Bushnell insisted that the key to understanding those words lay in determining whether the phrase should be read as prophecy or penalty. Whereas traditional interpretations had construed it in a punitive sense, Bushnell argued for the prophetic. For centuries, however, the passage had been misinterpreted, she explained, in part due to the King James's consistent confusion of "will" and "shall." But in this case the difference between the two was substantial: "shall" indicated God's bidding; "will" allowed for God's dismay at the consequences of sin. "All the stress of teaching woman's supposed obligations to man is in the '*shall be*,' which is *supplied* by the translators," Bushnell asserted. But that "force of the mandatory teaching" rested on an inaccurate translation.

"*Must* man rule woman, whether he will or no?" The answer to this question carried profound implications, theologically and socially.[59]

In Bushnell's hands, the third chapter of Genesis revealed that "the lordship of the husband over the wife, which began when man sinned, was satanic in origin," not mandated by God.[60] This interpretation made far more sense than traditional readings of the text, she argued, for had God dictated that women must desire and be ruled by their husbands, as male expositors suggested, it would logically follow that "the more carnally-minded a man is the better he keeps that sort of 'law!' "[61] God could not be the author of such moral absurdity, she protested. It was not God who had "subordinate[d] Eve to Adam, and all women to their husbands, as has been claimed by the Church throughout many centuries," but rather man, who "gradually brought about that subordination to himself."[62] The effects of women's subordination were undeniable; having rejected the punitive reading of the passage, Bushnell found ample evidence to substantiate the prophetic. "As a prophecy it has been abundantly fulfilled in the manner in which man rules over women."[63] Since Eden, the path of women had led precipitously downward.

Although she accused men everywhere of following in Adam's footsteps, blaming and dominating women throughout history, Bushnell did not hold women altogether guiltless in their fate. Eve had not sinned grievously by blaming God for her own disobedience, as had Adam, but she had committed another grave mistake, with dire consequences. According to Bushnell, God uttered the prophecy in Genesis 3:16 ("Thou art turning away to thy husband, and he will rule over thee") upon seeing that Eve was "inclining to turn away from Himself to her husband," in order to warn her of the appalling consequences her actions would entail.[64] To make sense of the passage, Bushnell again departed from Christian tradition by suggesting that Adam alone had been "thrust out of Eden, with a flaming sword between himself and the tree of life."[65] When God had warned Adam that he "would surely die" if he ate from the tree, God spoke of a *spiritual* death, not a physical one, Bushnell explained. But she reminded her readers that immediately after the woman's confession of guilt, she was called the "mother of all *living*"; and at the very moment Adam was facing his own spiritual death, he addressed her as "Eve"—"*Living*"— marking a spiritual contrast between himself and his wife.[66] If Eve were indeed spiritually living, Bushnell reasoned, then "we see no reason why Eve should have found a 'flaming sword' between herself and the tree of life."[67] And yet further reading finds Eve outside the garden. It is here,

Bushnell explained, that the immediate consequences of the prophecy found in Genesis 3:16 become clear. Eve had made the disastrous choice to turn to her husband, away from her God, and follow him out of Eden.[68]

Bushnell, then, did not exonerate women from all sin, but she did dramatically redefine what constituted sin for women and for men. She recognized that traditional conceptions of sin were unmistakably gendered; women had long been regarded "the weaker sex," considered more prone to sin than men and censured for their inappropriate assertiveness. But Bushnell articulated a markedly different gendered construction of sin.[69] Based on her re-reading of Genesis, she maintained that while conventional associations of sin with pride remained appropriate when applied to men, since the time of the Fall women had been far more likely to commit the sin of inappropriate humility. Both Adam and Eve had wanted to be "as God" when they had eaten from the tree of the knowledge of good and evil, she explained, a sin of pride. But whereas Eve repented, Adam continued in his rebellion, and since that time a dispute had raged between God and man for control of the throne. And what role would God have women play in this dispute? Bushnell inquired. According to a tradition shaped by male expositors—men who, Bushnell claimed, continued to wage this battle for the throne—women were to "show their humility, their willingness to take a lowly place," to "show they owe no allegiance but to MAN ALONE," not even to God's angels.[70] But if women were to obey this injunction, Bushnell challenged, would they not be acting as accomplices in man's rebellion against God? "What madness for women to do this!" she exclaimed, "And call it 'humility!'" For Bushnell, male authority over women contradicted God's will and perpetuated man's original rebellion against God. "Satan knew very well how to clothe an insult to God in the garments of 'humility' and 'womanliness,'" she wrote; when men urged women to be silent, submissive, and "womanly," they followed in Adam's footsteps, in alliance with the devil.[71] Women, on the other hand, continued to commit the sin of Eve when they submitted to men, rather than to God. In a theological coup, then, Bushnell redefined virtue and vice for both women and men, and in so doing upended Victorian understandings of womanhood.

Redefining Virtue

Bushnell considered her biblical studies "vital to the advancement of purity."[72] Rehabilitating Eve was a crucial first step, but she knew that

additional theological work would be necessary to undo widespread cultural misperceptions concerning female virtue. Years earlier, in the pages
of the *Union Signal*, she had identified several cases where translators
had assigned an "unusual meaning" to a word whenever it referred to
a female.[73] Through further research she found this gendered pattern of
mistranslation alarmingly evident when it came to passages concerning
female virtue. The clearest example of this trend could be observed in
connection with the Hebrew word *chayil* (חיל). *Chayil* occurred over two
hundred times in the Hebrew Bible, Bushnell explained, and each time it
had been understood to connote "force, strength, or ability," having been
variously translated as "army," "war," "host," "forces," "might," "power,"
"goods," "riches," "substance," "wealth," or "valiant."[74] But there were
four exceptions to this rule: "In every case where it referred specifically
to a woman," translators had assigned a different meaning: " 'virtue'—i.e.
chastity."[75]

The first of these exceptional cases occurred in the book of Ruth, where
Ruth, who had left her home and family to accompany her mother-in-law
Naomi back to Israel, was described as "a woman of cha-yil." From the list
of available meanings, Bushnell considered "an able woman" or "a woman
of courage" to be suitable translations, in accord with other instances
found in the Old Testament.[76] But it "almost" seemed to Bushnell as if
"our English translators took no care" as to the precise language of the
text when they rendered the phrase, "thou art a virtuous woman." Despite
the fact that *chayil* never once referred to any moral characteristic other
than strength or force, here "man was praising a woman, and 'of course'
here is a reference to her reputation for chastity," Bushnell commented
wryly.[77] She found additional mistranslations of *chayil* in Proverbs 31,
a passage theologians had long turned to for a description of the ideal
wife. But Bushnell pointed out that while the text praised the woman of
Proverbs 31 for her "general goodness and trustworthiness, energy, efficiency, enterprise, far-sightedness, early-rising, business capacity, garden-
ing, muscular strength, weaving, benevolence, fore-thought, embroidery
work, elegant clothes for herself, tailoring for her husband, honour, wisdom, kindness, piety . . . as it happens, no definite reference is made to her
purity, or to her faithfulness to her husband in the marriage relation."[78] Yet
when the text described her as "a woman of *cha-yil*," translators rendered
the term, "a *virtuous* woman."[79]

"We must suppose," Bushnell observed, "that the translators hastily
concluded that they knew, without looking closely at the original, what

sort of a woman" should be held up as an ideal. "Who can find a *virtuous* woman?" undoubtedly represented the sentiments of the translators, she reasoned, "but it *does not represent* the teaching of the original text." Though she conceded that "'Virtue' is of priceless value to woman, to be sure," she insisted that a woman's "duty to her husband is not her *only* duty; all her life cannot be summed up in that *one* moral quality."[80] Reviewing the anomalous translations of *chayil,* she could only conclude that there must have been "an instinctive distaste, disrelish" on the part of the translators in showing that the Bible praised "a 'strong' woman, for doing 'valiantly.'"[81] But, she insisted, "women prefer to know what the Bible *says,* rather than to be merely reminded of a favorite axiom among men."[82]

Bushnell recognized that critics might argue that "virtue" need not refer to sexual purity, that it might in fact connote "a summing up of all moral characteristics," but she countered that the English Bible was translated for "the common folk," the majority of whom would understand "virtue" to refer to a woman's chastity.[83] She also understood that the term "virtue" was rooted in the Latin *vir,* meaning "man," but again pointed to the contemporary use of the word. In English, "virtue" did not connote "manliness," but, among men, "'morality' in general," and with regard to women, "morality of one sort," namely, sexual purity.[84] Though she conceded that sexual purity should indeed be considered "a quality of great importance to women," she contended that women would be better equipped to guard that virtue if properly instructed from the pulpit to be "strong, in body, mind and spirit."[85]

Bushnell found a similar pattern of gendered mistranslation when she turned her attention to the New Testament. The Greek adjective *sophron* (σώφρων), for example, occurred four times; twice it was translated as "sober" and once as "temperate," but when it referred to women only, the King James Version rendered it "discreet" (Titus 2:5).[86] Citing a Greek commentary written by Henry Alford, Dean of Canterbury, Bushnell demonstrated how this "sex-bias" had been purposeful. Having established the meaning of *sophron* in its noun form as "self-restraint," Alford nonetheless insisted that "discreet" "certainly applies better to women," for the latter implies effort, "which destroys the spontaneity, and brushes off, so to speak, the bloom of this best of female graces." Bushnell sardonically thanked Alford "for thinking that women can practice self-restraint without effort," but on behalf of Christian women everywhere she added: "when we are reading our Bibles we prefer to know *precisely* what the Holy Ghost addresses to us, instead of finding between its pages the opinion of even the most excellent uninspired man."[87] In a New Testament lexicon, too, Bushnell found the noun form of *sophron* given a *"female* meaning"— "modesty"—further confirming her suspicion that translators assigned distinct meanings based on gender.[88]

She found additional examples of bias in other New Testament passages. The Greek word *kosmios* (κόσμιος), for example, was translated as "well ordered, in both outward deportment and inner life," except when referring to women's dress, where it was rendered "modest." And *hagnos* (ἀγνός), a term meaning "holy," was translated as "pure" or "clear" five times, but on each occasion where it qualified a noun of the feminine gender, it was rendered as "chaste." Given this pattern, Bushnell wondered why men shouldn't also be taught chastity. "These may be straws," she concluded, "yet they all point in the same direction."[89]

The Pericope de Adultera

Perhaps the most significant New Testament text to which Bushnell turned in her efforts to dismantle the theological foundations of the sexual double standard was the well-known story of a woman caught in adultery. Found in the Gospel of John (7:53–8:11), the story recounts how scribes and Pharisees brought the woman before Jesus to inquire whether she should be stoned, in accordance with the law of Moses. In reply, Jesus uttered, "He that is without sin among you, let him first cast a stone." Upon this, the crowd dispersed, and Jesus then turned to the woman and said, "Neither do I condemn thee: go, and sin no more." Bushnell drew attention to the significance of the Savior's response. "All through the ages" men had persistently applied two different standards of chastity to men and women, but here Christ insisted that "man must first show himself to be chaste before dealing with woman's unchastity."[90] As Bushnell explained, "Christ's blow was aimed at two standards of morality," and at injustice and hypocrisy.[91]

Bushnell was alarmed, however, to discover that higher critics had launched an attack on the canonical legitimacy of the *pericope de adultera,* as the text was commonly known among biblical scholars. "Misinterpretations are bad enough," she lamented, and "mistranslations worse," but worse still were "mutilations." She argued passionately for the legitimacy of the passage.[92] Some critics had disputed the authenticity of the pericope based on the fact that it contained words not found in the rest of the Gospel of John. Bushnell acknowledged the discrepancies, but reasoned that the woman herself might have written the account, only allowing John, "long after the event when none could identify her, to put it in his Gospel, for the encouragement to repentance of other sinning women." Such circumstances would satisfactorily explain the mixed character of the passage.[93]

A more serious challenge to the authenticity of the pericope, however, was its irregular appearance in early New Testament manuscripts. The German scholar Constantin von Tischendorf, for example, had cast doubt on the passage by citing eight uncial manuscripts that omitted the passage,[94] and the Revised Version had reflected this skepticism by bracketing off the passage from the rest of the Gospel and accompanying it with a marginal note explaining that "most of the ancient authorities omit John 7:53–8:11. Those which contain it vary much from each other."[95]

In defense of the passage, Bushnell cited the conservative biblical scholar John Burgon, who had contended that several manuscripts lacked the pericope simply because they were missing those particular pages. Such "evidence," she explained, would be akin to claiming that a certain hymn was not in the church hymnal simply because its page had been torn out of a particular copy. After closely examining the ancient texts, Burgon had concluded that only three of the ancient uncials omitted the passage, and two were copies of a common original. And he found that only around seventy of the thousand or so cursives—the generally more recent biblical manuscripts—lacked the text.[96] According to Burgon, these omissions made sense in light of the liturgy of the early Eastern Church since the passage surrounding the pericope was used in the liturgy for the Festival of Pentecost, while the pericope itself was reserved for St. Pelagia's Day. The early uncials and cursives omitting the pericope, then, were likely to have been manuscripts prepared for church lectionaries.[97] If inauthentic, Burgon had pointed out, the pericope would not have been "so imbedded in the ancient Church readings" that authorities would have found the need to write notations to skip the portion for the purpose of the lectionary readings.[98] Bushnell heartily agreed with Burgon that "no sincere inquirer after truth" could agree with Tischendorf's findings.[99]

Bushnell attributed scholars' repeated attempts to expunge the passage from the canon to the enduring unpopularity of its teachings. Long before modern critics had challenged its authenticity, she pointed out, the majority of Christian leaders had already rejected its message. "No one can pretend that anything more than lip-homage to the teaching of the *pericope* has ever been exhibited in the Church up to the present day, excepting in rare instances," she asserted.[100] The fact that many of the church fathers had failed to mention the pericope in their commentaries made sense given the persisting notion of woman as temptress, she explained, for at a time when men deemed "the very face of the chastest woman" a cause of corruption, the lesson of the pericope simply "was not palatable." "How *could* the leniency of the Lord be accounted for by men who harshly put away from their midst the purest of women as a source of defilement of their imagination?" she demanded. Such men "did not care to teach that a fall in a woman was no worse than a fall in a man,—especially as they believed that every fall in man was due to some woman."[101] In fact, Augustine himself had explained how men, "from fear lest their wives should gain impunity in sin, removed from their manuscripts the Lord's act of indulgence to the adulteress."[102] Other patriarchs, too, had noted "the mischievous tendency of the narrative."[103] Given such resistance to the teaching of the pericope, it was little wonder that some men had thought it prudent to remove the provocative passage from their copies of Scripture.

In Bushnell's opinion, what was remarkable was not that male scholars might question the pericope's authenticity, but rather that it had survived centuries of male bias to be available, in any form, to the present generation. In fact, Bushnell suggested that the persistent opposition to the teaching of the pericope paradoxically provided some of the strongest evidence for its authenticity, for "[w]hat but truth could hold its own and progress through the ages with such adverse winds against it?"[104] To Bushnell, the "amazing vitality" of the passage self-evidently demonstrated that it contained "the living truth of God," for otherwise how could "the ecclesiastical authorities" who lived "so far beneath its principles of justice in dealing with fallen woman" have allowed the story to persist, not daring to "wipe it out of existence"?[105] Moreover, Bushnell reasoned, "[w]here ever has existed the man, in ancient times or modern, so jealous for the rights of women, so skilful in drawing a picture of *absolute justice*, and yet so unscrupulous in character, and so influential, as to have foisted this story upon the credulity of the Church"? She noted that even some of the passage's staunchest critics had conceded that its "own internal character" lent it credibility: "The story itself has justly seemed to vouch for its substantial truth."[106]

For Bushnell, the historicity of the pericope was of paramount importance, since Christ's response to the woman demonstrated his compassion for all women and dismantled the sexual double standard. Dismissing traditional fears that the pericope condoned sin and moral laxity, Bushnell contended the very opposite—that the story cultivated *true* virtue. Though it would not "suit the views of men who are over-careful as to the prudent conduct of their wives, while loose in their own morals," she acknowledged, it brought hope to "the fallen girl," and to "the victim of society's cruel injustices."[107] She insisted that the basic principle of morality ought not to be women's purity, but rather justice, for "there is nothing which destroys morality out of the human heart so effectually and quickly as injustice"; without justice, other moral qualities would be vitiated.[108] "No good was ever done, and no good can ever be done, by legal enactments for the benefit of society, which, for reasons of 'prudence' omit principles of justice," she intoned. In fact, "[h]ere is where the great mistake is being made on the 'woman question.' Is it 'prudent' to allow women to do thus and so?—men ask themselves at every step of woman's progress." But, Bushnell insisted, "[t]he only question that should be asked is, Does justice demand this? If so, 'let justice be done though the heavens fall;' anything short of justice is mere mischief-making."[109]

As far as Bushnell was concerned, the Victorian moral system was fundamentally unjust. Rather than cultivating morality, it encouraged and sanctioned vice. In order for women to be truly virtuous, they needed to be strong and courageous, not weak, submissive, and "feminine."[110] "Servility and weakness are two contemptible vices," she elaborated, but "they have been too often recommended to women clothed in the names of 'humility' and 'meekness,' to which virtues they are as opposed as north is to south."[111] She denounced conventional Victorian characterizations of womanhood as perversions of biblical truth, amounting to nothing less than rebellion against God: "When an expositor and preacher of the Gospel wanders out of his path of duty 'to preach Christ' as woman's one example of conduct, and instead preaches 'womanliness,' he sets up an idol of his own creation for women to worship," she wrote, and "he turns himself to folly." With characteristic impudence, Bushnell added: "we imagine such expositors would have been pleased had God sent into the world, an additional *female* Christ, to set women a *female* example; but since God did not see fit to do so, women are under obligation to endeavor, as best they are able, to follow the 'manly' example of Jesus Christ, and leave the consequences with God." This, she concluded, "is woman's truly humble place. Any other is sham humility."[112]

In theory, Bushnell advocated a common virtue for women and men, but in light of the long history of unbiblical ideals of manhood and

womanhood, she believed that modern men and women required different correctives in order to achieve Christ's "true humility." Through his
incarnation, Christ, "the Second Adam," had emptied himself and become
human, in stark contrast to the first Adam's overwhelming pride.[113] To follow Christ, then, men needed to abandon their pride and become less
domineering. Women, on the other hand, needed to gain confidence and
assertiveness. In effect, Bushnell redefined women's subservience as disobedience, and self-assertion as virtue. Yet even as she effectively inverted
traditional notions of sin and virtue, she insisted that she was not making a case for women's inherent moral superiority, the very construct she
was working to combat.[114] Indeed, she held women culpable in their submission to men. Eve had been the first woman to forsake God for man,
but she would not be the last, and Bushnell held women responsible to
God for the choices they made. God had called women to be followers of
Christ, she reminded her readers, and a woman "must not sell her birth-
right . . . by a vicious self-effacement." As moral beings, women were to
relate directly to God, and she castigated those who renounced their will
for another's as "base by choice."[115]

Bushnell knew that her teaching squarely contradicted the Victorian
ideal of "true womanhood" that defined female virtue in terms of renun-
ciation and self-sacrifice, but she encouraged women to hold their ground
and rebuke men for their pride and egotism; failing to do so in order
to avoid men's displeasure would only nourish "masculine weakness."
She did caution women not to imitate men and "sin their sin" by becoming unduly proud themselves, yet she readily conceded that "we will be
accused of this, at any rate, even if we should do no more than our duty
and administer rebuke."[116] Above all, it was essential that women reject
any imposed "meekness" and subordination forced upon them in the
place of genuine Christian humility. Only then could they be free to follow
Christ. And only then would women's religious, social, and sexual subjugation come to an end.

6

Redeeming Eve

IN ORDER TO free women to take hold of their redemption in Christ, Bushnell worked to dissociate conventional Victorian family arrangements from their presumed Christian roots. By redefining female virtue, Bushnell had undermined the linchpin of the Victorian cult of domesticity: the ideal of self-sacrificing womanhood. She then extended her critique of conventional gender relations by contesting the traditional patriarchal marriage relationship—and with it the doctrines of male headship and female submission—and by altogether dismissing the Victorian idealization of motherhood. And she abandoned the very notion of a separate "woman's sphere." Drawing on history, anthropology, science, and theology, Bushnell crafted innovative and often radical reinterpretations of traditional passages in order to offer women a new gospel, one that redefined virtue and vice, sin and salvation, and one that ultimately established a new social order.

In setting out to liberate women from traditional marriage, Bushnell parted ways with the vast majority of her Protestant contemporaries. Her critique of marriage did not conflict with her understanding of Christianity, however, since she based her critique on her revised creation narrative. Patriarchal marriage was not ordained by God, she insisted, but rather resulted from man's rebellion against God. To make this case, she directed her readers to Genesis 2:24, where, immediately after separating Eve out of Adam, God had declared: "Therefore shall a man leave his father and his mother and cleave to his wife." In this "most interesting" interjection in the account of ancient history, Bushnell explained, God "directly and impressively" addressed humanity, and established the law of marriage. But she contended that by dictating a husband's duty to his wife, not a wife's to her husband, God had clearly ordained a matriarchal society, rather than a patriarchal one.[1]

In making this argument, Bushnell drew liberally on the work of a number of anthropologists who had posited the existence of a prehistoric matriarchy. She cited Johann Jakob Bachofen, for example, whose *Das Mutterrecht* (1861) first brought the notion of a prehistoric matriarchy from the mythical realm into historical and scientific studies, and J. F. McLennan, the leading exponent of matriarchy in the English world, along with E. B. Tylor, Edward Westermarck, James Fraser, John Lubbock, W. Robertson Smith, Herbert Spencer, and Henry Lewis Morgan.[2] In using the term "matriarchate," however, Bushnell made clear that she did not mean to imply the rule of women over men, as men had established over women; such societies occurred rarely, she noted, and only in small communities.[3] Rather, by matriarchy she was referring simply to "the absence of an exclusive government by men,—the existence of that saner, righteous state, in which the governing privilege is invested in the competent, without regard to sex."[4] And she was convinced that the Bible provided ample evidence that God had intended such a state. Genesis 2:24 clearly revealed the divine establishment of both matrilocality (that husbands were to move into their wives' homes upon marriage) and matriliny (laws of female kinship), customs instituted by God to safeguard women against abandonment or maltreatment at the hands of malicious or irresponsible husbands. God had intended for marriage to "disjoint man from his kin" and not woman from hers, she insisted, adding that God's plan had no provision "for that sentimentality which talks of the loveliness of that devotion in a young bride which causes her to forsake her kindred to follow her bridegroom—almost a stranger as yet—to the ends of the earth."[5] As a purity worker, she knew well the perils of such devotion, and maintained that it was for this reason that God had ordained a woman's "natural protectors"—her own family—to protect her until satisfied that the groom was trustworthy.[6]

But by choosing to follow her husband out of Eden, Eve had reversed the fundamental law of marriage, and subsequent history, from biblical times to the present, bore out the consequences of that choice. According to Bushnell, both the Bible and the anthropological record revealed traces of the gradual dismantling of God's intended matriarchate, and she examined each source in light of the other. For instance, a number of anthropological studies had identified wife-capture as a crucial step in the decline of matriarchy, a theory that Bushnell found substantiated in Old Testament narratives. Genesis 6, for example, revealed how the descendants of Cain took wives "from the daughters of Seth," after which the earth became "filled with violence." With no rights of her own, she explained, a captured wife was but "a sexual slave" to her husband, and thus over time the prevalence of wife-capture lowered the status of all women, and ultimately brought about "the degradation of the sex."[7]

Bushnell found further evidence of matriarchal customs in the account of Abraham and Sarah in the book of Genesis. Sarah was Abraham's half-sister on his father's side, in accord with the rules of female kinship,[8] and Bushnell noted that when God called Abraham and Sarah to leave their idolatrous homes to participate in the story of salvation, God gave Sarah her own revelation, "lest she should follow the usual custom and remain with her kin."[9] As Abraham's wife, Bushnell pointed out, Sarah maintained an independent residence and served as "tribal mother," the independent head of her tribe.[10] Indeed, her very name meant "chieftainess," or "female prince."[11]

Sarah exemplified well the early dignity of women in a matriarchal age, Bushnell explained, but her life also revealed the difficulties women encountered in maintaining their power in light of humanity's fall into sin. Indeed, Bushnell framed the entire narrative of Abraham and Sarah in terms of Sarah's need to learn to depend on God, rather than on Abraham, in order to become the woman God intended her to be.[12] Early on, Sarah had remained silent in the face of Abraham's poor decisions, such as when he had passed her off as his sister in the courts of foreign rulers. And in offering Hagar to Abraham as his concubine, she had erred in accommodating cultural practices that contradicted God's will for women. But as she grew in wisdom, Bushnell contended, Sarah began to critique the polygamous customs she had once observed, as reflected in her insistence that Abraham send away Hagar and her son Ishmael. Here, Bushnell paused to reflect how Sarah, in addressing the wrong done her as a childless wife, committed a more serious offense against Hagar, for "women who have superior advantages cannot yield to enactments that are unjust to themselves without bringing greater injustice upon other women in less fortunate circumstances."[13] But she maintained that Sarah was nonetheless right to resist the polygamous conventions of her day. "Doubtless Abraham," she added, "like many another man, wished his wife would stop dwelling upon the injustice of the laws which govern women; and quit accusing him of wrong, if he merely observed them."[14] But she drew attention to the fact that God commanded Abraham to obey his wife, and noted that "[i]f Abraham improved in character and saw the hatefulness of mixed marriage relations in the sight of God, it was under the joint training of God and Sarah."[15]

Although male commentators often criticized Sarah for her "unwomanly imperiousness," Bushnell pointed out that it was God who called Sarah "Mine Anointed," and God who constituted Sarah a ruler in her own right—"not because she was a woman," but because "she had better views on the subject of social purity, and probably on other subjects." In this case, headship or household leadership "turned not upon sex, but upon which one, husband or wife, knew best what to do."[16] Bushnell considered Abraham and Sarah, like Eve, to be "in training to believe in a coming Christ," and for this reason she designated them "the first Christian family," and suggested that God had intended for them to provide "a pattern for Christian homes for all time." But to create this "first household of faith,"[17] God needed to correct man's "oldest and most inveterate faults"— his "love of ruling and sensuality"—by curbing Abraham's sensual tendencies and teaching him the benefits of monogamy and respect for his wife. Sarah's training, meanwhile, "was in dignity, authority and self-respect."[18]

Despite the fact that "God started His theocracy with Sarah in high honour," matriarchal customs declined precipitously among Sarah's descendants. Bushnell speculated that Israelite women must have suffered more grievously than men during their captivity in Egypt, as they were more vulnerable to sexual violence, and were handicapped by the children they bore. Thus, after four hundred years of slavery, Israelite women emerged in very "different relation to their men"; they were, "for the most part, inferior to them."[19] It was due to the "ruin of woman's character by slavery," then, that men emerged "ahead of women," and it was at this point that men, not women, were selected as chiefs.[20] The consequences of women's subjugation would echo through history.

Humanity's rejection of God's will for marriage had resulted not only in calamitous social problems, Bushnell explained, but in theological quandaries as well. The difficulties that conservatives encountered in defending the virgin birth of Christ, for instance, were at least in part due to the overthrow of female kinship.[21] Bushnell considered the virgin birth essential, both to the Christian faith and to the dignity of women. She believed that the first promise of Christ had come in Genesis 3:15, where God had prophesied that the seed of the woman would crush the serpent's head.[22] But by setting aside female kinship, male conventions could no longer account for a redeemer "'made of a woman' (Gal. 4:4), without male agency."[23] "Man did not consider," she explained, "nor did Satan intend he should," that in cutting women from the genealogical records, "he would leave no room for the record in unquestionable terms, of the greatest event that could ever transpire in human history."[24] Instead of tracing Christ's lineage through Mary back to Eve, New Testament genealogies in the Gospels of Matthew and Luke awkwardly included Joseph, "one in no way related to Jesus Christ by ties of blood."[25] This insertion of a "foster father in the place of his only actual parent"[26] fit within patterns of male kinship but obscured the miracle of the virgin birth. To make matters worse, the genealogy of Christ found in the book of Luke went back not to Eve, but to Adam, the only person in the entire human race who could not possibly be a descendant of Eve.[27] Underscoring these inconsistencies, liberal scholars had cast doubt on the very notion of the virgin birth, but Bushnell contended that, had female kinship persisted, it would have been clear that the "seed of woman alone" fulfilled the Old Testament prophecies.[28]

Patriarchy: The "Reform Against Nature"

Bushnell considered her investigations into the prehistoric matriarchate crucial both to her theology and to her social reform. By demonstrating how men had gradually subordinated women to themselves in a process "accomplished so late in human history as to leave traces of its history," Bushnell believed that contemporary anthropology testified to the truth of her interpretation of Genesis.[29] It proved that women's subordination was "*not* the result of God's ordinance," but rather "the fruit of wrong-doing,"[30] accomplished "through the working of ages of custom."[31] And, she asserted, "nothing is of more importance to the Christian woman to-day than to understand that God did not Himself subordinate woman to man."[32] While Bushnell freely mined anthropological studies to support the notion of the matriarchate, however, she parted ways with leading anthropologists on one essential point.

By the late nineteenth century, when Bushnell commenced her research, a sociocultural evolutionary school of thought had come to dominate the field of anthropology. Formulating their ideas in the midst of the Darwinian revolution, evolutionary anthropologists adhered to a developmental framework that characterized human history as a story of progress. Within this framework, the matriarchate represented a "primitive" form of social organization, while contemporary Victorian social arrangements exemplified the very peak of human development.[33] Bushnell, however, deemed Darwinian models of progress incompatible with both her understanding of biblical truth and her critique of contemporary Victorian society, and she staunchly rejected the sociocultural evolutionary framework. Instead, she offered a degenerationist model of human development. Whereas evolutionary anthropologists had assessed the shift from a matriarchal to a patriarchal order as evidence of evolutionary progress, Bushnell insisted that patriarchy was neither an advanced nor a moral condition. It was, rather, the fulfillment of the ominous prophecy given Eve, the culmination of man's rebellion against God. Anthropologists' "highway of progress," Bushnell wrote, "is wet with woman's tears and blood, and strewn with her shackles and prostituted virtues." No woman could accept such regression as the will of God.[34]

Bushnell emphasized that the "immense difference" between her own biblical perspective and that of evolutionists should not be underestimated. Whereas evolutionists had cast aside the early chapters of Genesis, "and would lead women to do the same declaring the Biblical teaching to be degrading to women," she reminded her readers that it was the "theological *perversion* of the real teachings of these early chapters" that had proved injurious to women. Rightly understood, Genesis provided an invaluable foundation for the liberation of women, while the "teachings of the social evolutionists of the present day" would altogether undermine "the progress of womanhood."[35] She, for one, refused to abandon "the light to be found in the early chapters of Genesis,"[36] where the Bible revealed patriarchy to be "a defiant going against God's expressed will" rather than the advanced state claimed by evolutionists.[37] She denounced the patriarchal "reform" that had displaced female kinship as "the greatest 'reform against nature' this world has ever seen," a "systematic defiance of nature's laws and just claims."[38] Accomplished only through the "most cruel, oppressive, and immoral methods,"[39] the transition to patriarchy had wrought "nothing but misery and social degradation."[40]

In asserting that evolutionists erred in depicting "everything of the past as worse than the present," Bushnell was able to fashion a comprehensive critique of Victorian society; contemporary arrangements reflected neither the will of God nor the culmination of naturalistic development.[41] And by rejecting sociocultural evolutionary theory, she continued to rebuff the related discourse of civilization that pervaded late nineteenth- and early twentieth-century social thought. Having witnessed countless wrongs committed by Christian men and "civilized" societies, she remained dubious of any claims of civilization's steady moral advance. Bushnell, then, not only contested the authority of prominent theologians, but she also challenged the other leading arbiters of cultural authority, the practitioners of modern science. Just as "the predominance of male expositors of the Bible" had misled centuries of Christians, she feared "the predominance of male expositors of scientific and archaeological facts" would lead people astray "as to their deductions from plainly demonstrable teachings of nature, ancient history, customs and the Word of God."[42] Having witnessed the harm that centuries of male-dominated theology had accomplished, she was not about to entrust a powerful new truth to male expertise under a different guise.

Male Headship and Christian Marriage

In her efforts to overturn patriarchy, Bushnell needed to grapple as well with a number of New Testament texts that appeared to both affirm and sanctify women's subordination to men. Foremost among these were passages that seemed to establish a husband's "headship" over his wife. Bushnell believed that "[n]o teaching of the New Testament has ever been more cunningly perverted" than the notion of male headship, and she developed an extended critique of the concept. To begin with, she contested the very conception of power upon which traditional understandings of headship were based: "Does Christ jealously keep the Church from rising into His power: or does He say, '*Behold, I give you power?*' Does He say, 'This is *My* throne, keep away!' to the Church; or does He say, '*To him that overcometh will I grant to sit with Me on My throne?*'" Since Christ was not jealous of his own exaltation, but rather secured it that he might share it with his followers, why, then, would men seeking to follow Christ's lead claim power over women?[43] To do so was inconsistent with the gospel message, Bushnell contended, and yet in asserting headship over women, that was precisely what generations of Christian men had been doing.

1 Corinthians 11:1–16

Bushnell then turned her attention to key passages that seemed to institute male headship, beginning with 1 Corinthians 11:1–16, where, according to the King James Version, Paul had asserted that "the head of every man is Christ; and the head of the woman is the man" (v. 3), that man was "the image and glory of God," while "the woman is the glory of the man" (v. 8), and that because woman was created "for the man" (v. 9), woman needed to "have power on her head" (v. 10), traditionally interpreted to mean a veil over her head. Already in 1895, in the pages of the *Union Signal*, Bushnell had called for new translations of this puzzling text, and had expressed her impatience that despite widespread disagreement over the precise meaning of the passage, men nevertheless seemed able to agree that members of their own sex were "the glory of God," whereas women "only get their glory from men."[44] And from this point, she elaborated in *God's Word to Women*, theologians had extrapolated the divine establishment of man's "godlike rule," an exalted position manifested in woman's role as housewife.[45]

But Bushnell had little patience for such theological conjecture. She argued that the Greek word *exousia* (ἐξουσία), interpreted in verse 10 to mean "veil" and to signify man's authority over woman, had never before in Scripture or classical literature been found to have that meaning. The word appeared 103 times in the New Testament; 69 times it was rendered "power," 29 times "authority," 2 times "right," and once each "liberty," "jurisdiction," and "strength." There was "no mystery about the word," she assured her readers, "but in one single instance it happens to be used exclusively of woman's power," and "here at once its sense is called into question."[46] Indeed, in "the longest marginal rendering in the Bible," the King James Version explained how in this case *exousia* meant that a woman ought "to have a covering on her head, in sign that she is under the power of her husband." Unable to accept that women should have power, translators and interpreters had twisted the meaning to explain how "this 'power' must be abdicated by woman, in order that her *husband* may assume it instead." This was not only inaccurate, Bushnell argued, but was in fact "an emphatic denial of the statement of the sacred text itself." Indeed, she considered it "the most audacious handling of the sacred text on record." Plainly and simply, the text ought instead to read: "Therefore ought the woman *to have power* over her head." To "substitute the idea of 'subjection'—no power—for the word 'power' is shameful," she protested.[47]

"That 'power' means a veil, here, but *has never meant that before or since in all human history*, and a veil means subordination to the male sex, is pleasing to ego-centric males, but absurd to the mind of the ordinary man," Bushnell contended.[48] The erroneous interpretation reflected men's foregone conclusions, not God's word, she insisted, and she reminded her readers that it was "*husbands*, not wives," who had "discovered this extraordinary meaning for St. Paul's words."[49] In equally caustic language, she disparaged those who had interpreted verse 7 to suggest that only men were made in the image of God, pointing them to Genesis 1:27: "Any argument drawn from the 'image' idea must apply surely quite as equally to woman, who was created at the same time as man, and by the same act. It is the spirit of phallic worship which contends that this image inheres in physical sex, not the spiritual characteristics."[50]

In order to discover the "real purpose" of the passage, Bushnell insisted that the historical context of Paul's words be taken into account. At that time, Jewish men "veiled as a sign of reverence before God, and of condemnation for sin," she explained; the Romans, too, veiled in worship, and the Corinthian church to which Paul was writing contained a number of Roman converts. But Paul commanded all Christian men to unveil, since "[t]here is now no condemnation to them which are in Christ Jesus."[51] Paul cared so much about veils, Bushnell elucidated, because veils signified a rejection of Christ's atonement. The power of Christ's atonement was central to the Christian faith, and to Bushnell's theology for women, and she believed it must be at the heart of Paul's teaching as well. In light of Christ's redemption, she contended, "*any badge* that signifies guilt or penance for sin is out of place, for women as much as for men."[52] As she explained:

> Poor, fallen, sinful man does not bear God's image and likeness simply because he is a *male!* God is not male or female, so that one *sex* bears His image more than the other. It is the glorified Jesus Christ who bears that image and manifests that glory (Heb. 1:3). It is only *in Him* that our humanity takes that standing before God. He is our Representative, our Head. It is because Christ, the Head of the redeemed man, is in heaven, there '*to appear in the presence of God for us*' (Heb. 9:24), that man is permitted to cast aside all tokens of guilt and condemnation on earth.[53]

Bushnell directed her readers to the historical setting to illustrate why Paul, despite preferring that women unveil "before God, man, and angels," did not insist that they do so.[54] At that time, she explained, Talmudic teaching dictated that a woman cover her hair; if she did not, she might be accused of adultery and have her head shorn, and her husband could then be compelled by synagogue authorities to divorce her, whether or not he approved of her actions.[55] For this reason, Paul refused to command women to unveil, though he insisted that there was "nothing for a woman to be ashamed of in showing her hair, for it is a 'glory' to her," and he clearly preferred that women, like men, worship God free from all signs of guilt and condemnation.[56] Bushnell made clear that Paul only found it necessary to discuss the sexes separately because of common "prejudices of man against woman"—prejudices he renounced as unchristian at the end of the passage (v. 11–12), as well as in Galatians 3:28 ("there can be no male and female: for ye are all one in Christ Jesus").[57] Once again, Bushnell attributed erroneous and even absurd traditions not to the Scriptures themselves, but to centuries of mistranslation and manipulation: "The truth is, had some of these expositors been one-tenth as broad as St. Paul on the 'woman question,' and honest besides," she insisted, "we should never have been taught these pitiful, puerile and ego-centric perversions of Paul's meaning."[58]

Ephesians 5:21–24

Bushnell turned her attention to Ephesians 5 as well, where, in the words of Revised Bible translators, Paul had commanded wives to "be in subjection unto your own husbands, as unto the Lord. For the husband is the head of the wife, as Christ also is the head of the church, being himself the saviour of the body. But as the church is subject to Christ, so let the wives also be to their husbands in everything" (v. 22–24). Years earlier, Bushnell had countered Lyman Abbott's assumption that Paul was here addressing Christian married couples by contending quite simply that no *Christian* husband would seek such authority. God required humility and meekness "in all without regard to sex," she reminded her readers, and she pointed to numerous biblical passages that explicitly forbade Christians from exercising authority over one another, and from "exalt[ing] themselves as chief."[59] She had also taken issue with Abbott's assertion that a husband and wife might recognize each other's "equality," even as he commanded and she submitted; "the wife *cannot* obey while recognizing her equality with her husband, without also realizing his injustice," she insisted, and the husband "cannot command a wife who is his equal without his conscience accusing him of wrong." Bushnell agreed that love leads to a spirit of submission, but not for women alone. Thus, when husbands were commanded in verse 25 to "love their wives," this love ought to evidence itself in submission to their wives. Any "spirit of despotism" came from hate, not love.[60] Bushnell also countered popular claims that "woman's love is different in quality from man's; that when she loves she desires to be submissive," and instead insisted that she knew "a thousand wives in Christendom who are starving for the *same* kind of love they could give." As she explained, "masterfulness between equals starves love, while mutual submission feeds it."[61] Only a sinner would desire "to exalt himself and have dominion over others," she contended, and he would do so "in exact proportion to the degree of selfishness in his heart."[62]

Writing in 1894, Bushnell had suggested that one need only look to the nearly universal subjugation of women in heathen countries to prove beyond doubt that man's desire to subject women was proportional to his own sinfulness, and she surmised that Paul was talking about just such husbands. In the early church, she reminded her readers, many Christian women remained wives of heathen husbands, and they related to their husbands much as slaves did to masters, whom Paul addressed in a similar manner; the wives and slaves whom he addressed were generally "within the fold," while the masters and husbands were largely "beyond his reach."[63] Here, then, Paul was not talking about the mutual "submission of love" between a Christian husband and wife, since given the nature of heathen marriage he could not command husbands to obey their wives any more than he could command masters to obey their slaves. He could, however, advise enslaved wives to "submit," in the spirit of Matthew 5:41, "but with the added precautionary limitation, 'as unto the Lord.' "[64] Interpreting the passage as an endorsement of a husband's authority over his wife made the same hermeneutical error that proponents of slavery had committed in the recent past, she claimed, and she reminded her readers that Christians had since come to see that Christ, who " 'took upon himself the form of a servant' did not at all imply the right to others to take upon themselves the form of masters."[65]

In her 1923 edition of *God's Word to Women*, Bushnell interpreted the passage in light of the decline of matriarchy as well. "When the Word says, 'the husband is the head of the wife,' by the pen of St. Paul, it merely states a fact; those were the conditions under which women lived *at that time*," she explained, noting that after centuries of patriarchal oppression, women had come to occupy a demonstrably degraded position. A husband was head "simply because he held the superior place." In the patriarchal culture of Paul's day, for example, a man could divorce his wife on a whim—a practice that Jesus challenged, Bushnell noted, to the surprise of his own disciples (Matt. 19:3). In this setting "there could be no doubt that women were compelled to be ignorant, inferior and very cheap," and thus Paul instructed men to "'[b]e a head, as Christ is a Head of the Church,—to help your wife upward to your own level,'—for it is only as man imitates Christ in his conduct that he can remain in the Body of which Christ is Head." Just as Christ elevated his church, so, too, could men help to liberate women from their oppression. "This is the headship of the husband that Paul speaks of," Bushnell argued, for "[h]e would never encourage the husband to imitate Adam and antichrist in trying to be '*as God*,' to woman, and to interfere with Christ's authority over His own servant,—woman."[66] Those "willing to justify male rule" had misconstrued Paul's words, while remaining "silent as to Paul's clear utterances elsewhere, as to '*the glorious liberty of the children of God*,'"[67] and in doing so they had disregarded the "revolutionary ethics of a Christ-like love."[68]

In addition, Bushnell distinguished the meaning of "subjection" from both "obedience" and "submission." Though the King James Bible often confused the terms, she suggested that Paul himself made careful distinctions between the two, using "obedience" when addressing children and servants, and "subjection" when addressing wives.[69] The true sense of subjection, she insisted, entailed "the Christian grace of yielding one's preferences to another, where principle is not involved, rather than asserting one's rights."[70] It did not entail unblinking obedience, she contended, pointing out that in Ephesians 5:21, Paul exhorted all believers, "without regard to sex," to subject themselves to one another in the fear of Christ, and elsewhere Paul commanded men to "be in subjection" to other men, or men to women.[71] In none of these cases did commentators interpret this to mean absolute obedience. When it came to the three passages where Paul instructs women to be in subjection to their husbands, however, "one is considered almost heretical who questions whether this exhortation to 'wives' means absolute obedience."[72]

Bushnell also advised interpreting Ephesians 5 in light of the way women in apostolic times would have understood Paul's words. Such women, she reminded her readers, would have had a very different understanding of Genesis 3:16. Rather than finding in it the pernicious curse ("Thy *desire* shall be to thy husband, and he *shall* rule over thee"), they would have been familiar with the verse in the Septuagint, which translated the passage as had Bushnell: "Thou art turning away to thy husband, and he will rule over thee." Bushnell asked her readers to consider what Paul's language might have conveyed "[t]o women who never knew that Genesis taught (?) that God subordinated woman to man at the time of the Fall? To women who had never heard that the Bible taught the wife to obey the husband, because Eve brought sin into the world? Or to a woman who had never heard that, according to the Bible, her 'desire' must be under her husband's control?"[73] Not having the teaching of women's subordination to their husbands from their own Scriptures, early Christian women would have associated the practice with heathen religions, and in place of such teachings the recent words of Christ would have stood out in their minds, "with startling clearness": "No one can serve two masters," and "he that is greatest among you shall be your servant . . . whosoever shall exalt himself shall be abased." In light of these teachings, she remarked, "How differently they must, therefore, have construed Paul's language!"[74]

Bushnell attested that she could find no other New Testament text that might establish "by 'divine law' the husband as 'final authority' for the wife." In 1 Timothy 3:4–12, for example, the father is exhorted "to 'rule' the children and the house, but no mention is made of the wife as being under this rule." And if one wanted to argue that wives were to be subsumed under "the house," Bushnell directed her readers to 1 Timothy 5:14, where Paul instructed younger women to "guide the house," presumably of which husbands were part. Indeed, here the word translated as "guide" shared a root with the English "despot," and in fact denoted "the possession of supreme authority." As she explained, "Had Paul wished to indicate in Greek the 'final authority' in the house he could not possibly have found a stronger word than this one which he applies to the *woman*-head." By contrast, the word Paul used when discussing the husband's role in 1 Timothy 3:5 and 5:17 connoted " 'to stand before' or to maintain or to profess." Thus, Paul may have been merely instructing husbands to support or maintain the household well or honestly, rather than to rule it. Bushnell assured her readers, however, that she was "not interested in showing that the Bible does or not give woman the place of supreme rule over the husband or any one else, for I believe Christ sternly forbids such rule in either husband or wife." She wished only "to point out the extreme unfairness of the English translators."[75] "When 'to stand before' and 'to profess' mean 'to rule' for the *male*, and to 'do the work of a despot' means only to 'guide' for the female," Bushnell mused, "I wonder if sex or intelligence has the determining power in the 'final authority' exercised in the translation of the English Testament from the undefiled original Greek!" Reflecting on the fact that "men were educated and taught ancient languages long before women," she could not help but wonder "how the case might have turned had woman got into the green pastures of learning ahead of man."[76]

Because the Bible made clear that "NO ONE can serve two masters," Bushnell contended that women constrained by patriarchal marriages were not free to follow Christ.[77] "Christian women belong to Christ, who purchased them with His own blood,—not to their husbands," she insisted, citing 1 Corinthians 6:19–20.[78] Thus, "[w]oman can never be matured as a useful instrument in God's hands, or an efficient servant of His church, until she comes to understand that 'she is not her own; she is bought with a price,' and it is neither her duty nor her privilege to give herself away to any human being,—in marriage or in any other way."[79] We are to obey Christ, she attested, "*because he is God*, and because he is *King of kings*; and these a husband *is not*, and he should not usurp Christ's prerogatives."[80] Drawing on Christ's own example, she advised women against trusting men unduly or sacrificing themselves to the point that their surrender to God alone be vitiated.[81] In mock horror, she added: "What! A woman not trust her husband!" She knew well that Victorian convention taught that "every husband *loves* a trusting wife," and that anything short of absolute trust would "bring discord into the family." Though she conceded the potential for discord when wives failed to trust their husbands to an "idolatrous extent," she reminded her readers that Christ himself had come "not to send peace, but a sword." She believed that family concord could be preserved without a wife's idolatry of her husband, "but if not, let discord prevail."[82]

Her life's work had taught her that "to be humble and obey God alone will surely bring tribulation to any human being, sooner or later," for it would only be a question of time before one encountered a human law that contravened God's laws. "We are often told that the days of persecution are past and ended," she noted, but that was only because people had accepted "man's laws as God's whole will." But she insisted that laws and social customs, such as the belief that wives owed husbands unquestioning obedience, should not be confused with the will of God: "It is as true to-day as it ever was that 'traditions,' i.e., man-made laws, ever 'make void the commandments of God' at all inconvenient points, and it ever will be so."[83] Indeed, in her book she twice quoted John Stuart Mill's injunction that "to pretend that Christianity was intended to stereotype existing forms of government and society, and protect them against change" was to distort the faith.[84]

Because marriage had become so far removed from God's original intentions, Bushnell considered divorce a necessity for women. Protestants had long opposed divorce based on Jesus' teaching that "what God hath joined together, let not man put asunder" (Matt. 19:6), and in the light of rising divorce rates that seemed to threaten social stability, many of Bushnell's contemporaries redoubled their opposition to any dissolution of the marriage contract.[85] But Bushnell pointed out that Jesus' prohibition of divorce was premised on the preceding verse, that in marriage "a man shall leave his father and mother...." Traditional, patriarchal marriage had reversed God's law of marriage, and in Bushnell's assessment, until the patriarchal distortion of the marriage relationship was rectified, the prohibition of divorce would only increase suffering. "The Church will never effectually enforce the conclusion of that statute," she attested, "while it defies the premises upon which it rests."[86]

Along with rejecting conventional Protestant views on marriage and divorce, Bushnell cast aside the very notion of a "woman's sphere," a concept she considered utterly unbiblical. She accused male expositors of having convinced themselves that "Nature" had outlined a certain sphere for women (these men would not own up to doing it themselves, she noted), while insisting that men remained at liberty to define their own "sphere." Men then manipulated biblical texts to reinforce this prejudice, exaggerating in the English translation passages that seemed to support their view of "woman's sphere," and toning down in translation those that contradicted their "masculine preconception." Bushnell considered this use of "diverse weights and measures" an "abomination in the sight of God."[87] She lamented that at every step women had been taught to ask themselves: "'How will this look, for a *woman?*' As though woman should do everything with reference to her sex, rather than with reference to her God!"[88] A careful reading of the Scriptures, she was convinced, "would lead to remarkable revisions in the commonly-accepted ideas of woman's 'sphere.'"[89] Though she knew that challenging the very concept of woman's sphere would undoubtedly incur spirited resistance, she again reminded her readers that genuine obedience to God might well contradict what was deemed legal or acceptable by earthly standards. Trouble was sure to brew for a man or woman who determined "to wholly follow the Lord," she conceded, for those who gave "uncompromising testimony, by word and deed, against all sham customs and wicked human legislation."[90]

Female Religious Authority
1 Corinthians 14:31–40

Along with contesting conventional Victorian gender and family arrangements, Bushnell also addressed texts that had long been interpreted to justify women's ecclesiastical subordination. Chief among these was 1 Corinthians 14:31–40, particularly verses 34–35, which in the Revised Version read: "Let your women keep silence in the churches: for it is not permitted unto them to speak; but let them be in subjection, as also saith the law (v. 34). And if they would learn anything, let them ask their own husbands at home: for it is shameful for a woman to speak in the church (v. 35)." In an 1889 *Union Signal* article, Bushnell had noted how male commentators found those two verses "of infinitely more importance . . . than all the rest in the passage put together," but she identified serious problems with traditional interpretations. First, she pointed out that in 1 Corinthians 11:5, Paul himself clearly recognized female prophets. She considered as well whether Paul could have intended Christian women to be subject to "heathen" husbands; if so, "the Divine spirit in a prophetess" would be "controlled and guided by the devilish spirit of a Corinthian heathen." This interpretation contradicted common sense, Bushnell insisted, and treated neither Paul nor Scripture with proper reverence.[91]

In *God's Word to Women*, Bushnell expanded her argument, noting that the Old Testament "says *absolutely nothing* from Genesis to Malachi to forbid women to speak," and thus no such "law" existed anywhere in the Scriptures. Before accepting "the superficial conclusion that St. Paul's one utterance about 'silence' closes the mouth of every Christian woman," she directed her readers to consider biblical accounts of Miriam (Exod. 15:20), Deborah (Judg. 4–5), Huldah (2 Kings 22), Anna (Luke 2:36–38), and the daughters of Zelophehad (Num. 27:1–7) and Philip (Acts 21:9), together with other examples of Old and New Testament women who prophesied (1 Chron. 25, Ezek. 13:17, Acts 2:16–18), and whom "Christ *caused* to speak in public" (Luke 8:47, 13:13).[92] She then challenged readers to consider how this purported "law" silencing women related to "the hundred and one other 'laws' in the O. T. opening the mouths of women,—such as 'Let the redeemed of the Lord say so,' 'Praise ye the Lord' (repeated about a hundred times in the Psalms alone), 'Make a joyful noise unto the Lord,' 'Declare His doings among the people,' 'Let everything that hath breath praise the Lord,' 'Tell of all His wondrous works'?" She insisted that it was "simply impossible" for men to claim that all of these Old Testament "admonitions and exhortations . . . were meant for themselves only," noting that it had not been "so understood or taught for thousands of years." That certain expositors' "over zeal" when it came to interpreting "a *single* sentence" ran counter to "a hundred or two of other Scriptural utterances" should caution against a hasty acceptance of the prohibition, she averred.[93]

Instead, Bushnell argued that the sentiments expressed in verses 34 and 35 ought to be attributed not to Paul, but rather to another person reasoning with the apostle. Indeed, Paul himself ascribes the passage about women keeping silence to "the law." And since "the law" obviously did not come from within Scripture, it must come from without—from the oral law of the Jews.[94] She claimed that Paul made clear that he was challenging one of "those sticklers for *law* who were always contending with [him],"[95] and it was apparent to her that in verses 34 and 35 he was "quoting *what the Judaizers in the Corinthian Church are teaching,*—who themselves say women must 'keep silence' because Jewish law thus taught."[96] Paul then declares his impatience with them by exclaiming: "What! was it from you *men* that the word came? isn't God's authority higher than your law? Remember that the word didn't even come upon you men alone."[97] Here Paul was referring to the day of Pentecost, Bushnell explained, when "the Spirit was poured out upon 'all flesh,'" on young and old, male and female. Of that day Peter had written: "*This is that which hath been spoken by the prophet Joel . . . your daughters shall prophesy . . . and upon my handmaidens . . . will I pour out of my Spirit.*" To signify "the inauguration of the present Gospel dispensation," Bushnell asserted, "the 'word of God' 'came out' from God, not from man, and it '*came unto*' women, and not unto men only."[98] She maintained that her interpretation not only fit with Old Testament examples of women's prophecy, but also with Paul's own words in verse 31: "Ye may all prophesy, one by one, that all may learn, and all may be comforted."[99] She then translated verse 39 to read: "Wherefore, don't forbid these women to speak with tongues. Let everything be done decently and in order." Making Paul "his own interpreter," Bushnell rejected the tradition of male interpretation that had "invented the remarkable theory" that when it comes to souls, "God is no respecter of persons," but when it comes to sexes, God treats women and men discordantly. She had found in Paul's writings a very different word to women.[100]

1 Timothy 2:11–15

Bushnell also contested traditional interpretations of Paul's words to Timothy in 1 Timothy 2:11–15, a critical text for proponents of the ecclesiastical subordination of women. In the Revised Version, the passage reads:

> Let a woman learn quietly with all submissiveness. I do not
> permit a woman to teach or to exercise authority over a man;

rather, she is to remain quiet. For Adam was formed first, then Eve; and Adam was not deceived, but the woman was deceived and became a transgressor. Yet she will be saved through childbearing—if they continue in faith and love and holiness, with self-control.

Bushnell began by asserting that men had greatly exaggerated the significance of the passage. Reminding her readers that Paul was writing a personal letter to Timothy, she maintained that here "Paul merely states his own practice and gives his reasons, as a matter of advice. He does not command or exhort Timothy, or anyone else, to do the same." She noted that in the same letter Paul instructs Timothy to "use a little wine for the stomach's sake" (1 Tim. 5:23), yet she maintained that "no one is so foolish as to believe that all Christians for all time are expected to drink wine." And in another letter Paul asks Timothy to bring him a cloak he left at Troas (2 Tim. 4:13), "yet expositors do not teach that we must all follow Paul's directions to Timothy, and fetch a cloak from Troas."[101] In addition, she pointed out that "men who would be scandalized by women daring to teach or preach, or to exercise authority themselves," ignored Paul's counsel against marrying, and his recommendation that unmarried women and widows remain so (1 Cor. 7:7–8).[102] In fact, "if there is one point on which prejudiced males would give advice to women who wished to preach," Bushnell wrote, it "would be to 'get married,—the home is woman's sphere.'" And yet "strong masculine prejudice" had led these same expositors to find in 1 Timothy a prohibition against women teaching God's word for all time. "All that is claimed by the Bible, for the Epistle to Timothy is that it was meant for Timothy," she insisted. "This all will admit, as to the 'wine' and the 'cloak' question; and we claim it for the 'woman question,' too."[103]

Though she acknowledged that Paul was inspired, and that even in personal letters he might communicate commands that could not be disobeyed "without sin," Bushnell maintained that "Paul was not so *limited* and *hampered* by his inspiration that he could no longer give *individuals advice*, and make *private* requests"; he could still "give advice of *temporary use only*,—advice unsuitable for all individuals to practice under all circumstances." She had no patience for expositors who could see no difference "between God's inexorable laws, or eternal principles of justice and righteousness, as described in personal epistles, and practice or advice suitable for the emergency only," and she castigated such men as "too literal in their mental make-up to be useful teachers for their age and generation."[104]

Here again, Bushnell emphasized the significance of the historical context. Drawing on the work of early church historians, she explained how Paul's advice to Timothy likely dated to around A.D. 67, the period of Nero's ruthless persecution of the Christian church.[105] It was a time of exceptional danger for all Christians, she wrote, but women faced "a peculiar peril"—"not only to life, but, as Church history shows, to virtue also."[106] Bushnell was referring here to New Testament scholar William Ramsay's description of the Roman practice of raping female prisoners before their execution.[107] Despite great risk, however, Christian women occupied highly visible roles in their communities, frequently assuming positions of leadership. Indeed, citing William Lecky's *History of European Morals,* Bushnell contended that what most distinguished Christians from Jews at the time was their treatment of women, which helped to explain the high numbers of female converts that contributed to the remarkable growth of the early church.[108] And again citing Lecky, she attributed the Romans' extreme animosity toward Christians at least in part to "the constant interference with domestic life, arising from the great number of female conversions."[109] To Romans, "who regarded the supreme authority of the head of the family, in all religious matters, as the very foundation of domestic morality," Bushnell asserted, female converts to Christianity could be particularly unsettling, a fact that might explain why the Romans often accused Christian women of scandalous sexual behavior in retaliation for their conversions.[110]

Paul "had intimate first-hand knowledge of all these dangers to women," Bushnell explained, for the church that had gathered around him in Rome only two or three years earlier had been decimated by Nero's ferocity. And during that time, "Christian women, modest maidens, holy matrons" had been forced to "play their parts in torments of shamefulness more intolerable than death."[111] It was quite possible that some of the very women Paul had greeted by name in his letter to the Romans had suffered this tragic fate. "How the tender heart of Paul must have bled when he heard the terrible news of women who had 'laboured with him in the Gospel,' women 'of note among the apostles,' women who had 'succoured' him, or 'bestowed much labour upon him,'" had succumbed to "such a terrible plight . . . !" Paul understandably would have feared the same for "his Christian sisters and female disciples everywhere," Bushnell mused. And yet Christian women themselves did not shrink from the threat of persecution.[112] They continued to be drawn to a religion that offered them unprecedented dignity and opportunity, and for this reason women were frequent martyrs for the faith.[113]

In light of these remarkable circumstances, then, Bushnell again quoted Ramsay to insist that "the advice given by St. Paul as to the relations of the Christians to the society in which they are placed, IS ALWAYS IN ACCORDANCE WITH THE SITUATION WHICH WE HAVE DESCRIBED AS OCCUPIED BY THEM UNDER NERO."[114] Paul's recommendation that the sexes be separated made sense in these "exceptional circumstances" as a way to keep slander at bay, as did his caution against "bringing women into prominence."[115] However willing Christian women might be to embrace martyrdom, Paul did not permit it, and for this reason he insisted that men must take the lead.[116] In accordance with this interpretation, Bushnell offered a metaphorical reading of verses 13 and 14. Just as Adam had been developed before Eve in the natural world, so, too, must man go before woman in the social world; because of woman's vulnerability to the threat of rape, men must go before her in times of peril.[117] And, Bushnell added, because women tended to have less experience than men at that time, due to prevailing social prejudices against women, it was better "in time of tempest" to keep "an inexperienced and immature person" from the "rudder of the ship." She made clear, however, that "Paul does not argue that a *willful sinner*, like Adam, is of more value than a *deceived person*. Paul did not go about ordaining, in the Church, knaves to govern fools."[118]

Though Bushnell again cautioned against carelessly assuming that "anything in the Bible is of exceptional and temporary import only," she insisted that in this case the fact that Paul was writing a personal letter in a time of acute peril "ought to count for a great deal." To her it was clear that his "precautionary advice" to Timothy "was not meant to control all women for all time," and that it made far more sense to interpret his words in light of the perilous events of his own day, rather than to look back to creation, or to a purported "curse."[119] By interpreting Paul's writings to Timothy in their historical context, Bushnell was able to harmonize them with Paul's earlier writings to the Corinthians about women "praying and prophesying" (1 Cor. 11:5), and to his letter to the Galatians (3:28), where he removed all distinctions regarding sex.[120] And in so doing, she also brought them into conformity with her interpretation of Genesis.

Bushnell believed that centuries of theological distortion and abuse had stunted women socially and spiritually, but she remained hopeful that

Christianity could bring about women's "full social development."[121] She based this hope on the final verse of 1 Timothy 2, which had been translated in the King James Version to read ". . . [the woman] shall be saved in childbearing." Generations of male theologians had interpreted this text to establish motherhood as a divine calling or command, suggesting that by bearing and rearing children, women might set aside their rebellious ways, embrace their domestic duties, and thus fulfill their Christian calling. Bushnell, however, was dubious of such interpretations. Rather than being saved through childbirth, she noted, many women in fact died in the process. And the suggestion that women could be saved from their sins by bearing children struck her as absurd. If such were the case, "then the childless widow, the old maid, and the barren wife" were "all on the broad road to perdition," while "the reckless mother who omitted the preliminary marriage ceremony" would find herself on the narrow way that leads to eternal life.[122] She had already discarded traditional interpretations of Genesis 3:16, thereby liberating women from the curse of compulsory, self-sacrificial motherhood, and here she rejected any idealization of motherhood as well; rather, she reduced motherhood to "the animal process of giving birth to children."[123]

For Bushnell, motherhood conveyed no mysterious or spiritual power upon women, and it certainly could not bring about women's salvation. Indeed, she reminded her readers, Christ himself rejected the significance of women's physical motherhood when he neglected his own mother in the Gospel of Matthew, declaring: "Whosoever shall do the will of my Father which is in heaven, the same is my mother" (Matt. 12:50).[124] Bushnell, then, had ample reason to reject traditional interpretations of 1 Timothy 2:15. Instead, she translated it to read: "woman shall be saved by *the* childbearing, by the birth of Christ." It was not women's physical motherhood, but rather Eve's spiritual motherhood that brought about women's redemption, social and spiritual.[125]

Bushnell pointed out, however, that Paul had made women's social redemption conditional on whether women continued "in faith and love and sanctification with sobriety." Woman's "social rescue" would come only when "the chain that binds her to the lusts of her own, and of man's flesh is broken, and she maintains the inviolability of free-will . . . towards every human being, including her husband."[126] But alas, Bushnell lamented, women had failed to do so. Within fifty years of Paul's writing, women "had largely yielded their faith,—that they were to be saved on precisely the same condition as men. They accepted the mischievous teaching that in addition to meeting the conditions laid down for men sinners, they must do penance for the sin of Eve (as though Christ's atonement had not been sufficient for Eve's transgression). Faith went; love and loyalty to Jesus Christ and His atonement waned; and finally they accepted a precisely opposite condition to the one laid down by Paul so impressively."[127]

But Bushnell held out hope that the long-awaited liberation of women was at hand. In the book of Jeremiah she found a rather obscure and "mysterious prophecy" relating to women, which she translated: "How long wilt thou keep turning away, O thou turning away daughter? For the Lord hath created [something] new in the earth, Female will lead male about" (Jer. 31:22). "In other words," Bushnell explained, "it seems God's design that the 'new woman' in Christ Jesus, shall no more 'turn away,' as did Eve, to her husband, but remaining loyal to God alone, and true to her destiny as the mother of that Seed,—both the literal, Jesus, and the mystical Christ, the Church,—shall lead man about,—out of the wilderness of the inefficiency of egotism into the glorious liberty of the children of God."[128] Bushnell was optimistic that *God's Word to Women* would help usher in the fulfillment of this prophecy and return women to their rightful place in the church of Christ.

7

Liberal Conservatives

GOD'S WORD TO *Women* was a remarkable achievement. Bushnell had fashioned a sophisticated and comprehensive critique of traditional Christian theology, one that undermined the very foundations of Victorian society and placed women's rights at the heart of the gospel. In depth and scope, the book went far beyond feminist theologies penned by earlier generations. Yet what was perhaps most notable about Bushnell's work was that she achieved her radical results while upholding the Scriptures as the inspired and authoritative word of God. The book confounded conventional categories; it was at once progressive and traditional, radical and conservative. Ultimately, however, *God's Word to Women* failed to accomplish the social and religious revolution that Bushnell had hoped to achieve. As it turned out, the book that transcended simple categorization proved ill-suited to an era marked by the increasing polarization of American Protestantism. With liberals and conservatives sorting themselves into opposing camps, the once-vibrant Protestant women's culture that had flourished in late-Victorian America began to break down, and with it the cultural space that had been vital to the development of a robust Christian feminism.

Bushnell published the first full edition of *God's Word to Women* in 1916, while residing in England, and the book garnered a number of favorable reviews. J. W. Thirtle, editor of *The Christian* (London), approvingly characterized Bushnell as "a sympathetic and trustworthy guide in all Biblical investigation," and prominent biblical scholar Alphonse Mingana praised her book as "the outcome of a solid erudition," a work that "cut a new path in the domain of textual criticism."[1] The Keswick-inspired Welsh evangelist Jessie Penn-Lewis was so impressed with Bushnell's book that she excerpted considerable portions of it in her 1919 *Magna Charta of Woman*. (Penn-Lewis believed there was an urgent need for the insights Bushnell offered, but feared that many women would lack the foundational knowledge to grasp Bushnell's extended treatise, and worried that the price of the book would inhibit its widespread circulation.) Like others who encountered *God's Word to Women*, Penn-Lewis agreed that the time had come for Christian women to explain themselves: "They profess, as Christians, obedience to the Word of God. They think that St. Paul forbade women to speak in public, and that he discountenanced women teachers of the Bible. Yet they teach and pray and preach. . . ." Women either needed to "equip themselves, as biblical scholars, to explain St. Paul . . . or else they should keep silence in the churches." According to Penn-Lewis, contemporary events had only exacerbated the urgency of the situation; with the Great War the emancipation of women had "burst upon the world," and it remained to be seen whether Christian women would share in this emancipation. What was at stake, then, was not merely "the authority and infallibility of the Word of God," but also "its Divine fitness to meet the needs of every generation." It was up to Christian women to demonstrate to the world that the Bible was not in fact "an antiquated Book, out of harmony with the present times."[2]

God's Word to Women did not have the same initial impact on the other side of the Atlantic, but in 1921 a reviewer in the *Moody Bible Institute Monthly* offered a hearty endorsement of the book. Concurring with Bushnell that "it is time a woman should interpret what the Bible says about women," the reviewer added that "no woman seems better qualified for this work than the author." The reviewer judged Bushnell's work "scholarly and erudite, but devout, and loyal to the Bible," and noted that Bushnell did not dodge any of the Bible's difficult "woman-problems." Like Penn-Lewis, the reviewer concluded that "by new translation, scholarly exegesis, bold interpretation, logical reasoning and common sense," Bushnell had not only come "to the defense and religious emancipation of women, but to the defense of the Bible."[3] Bushnell was pleased with what she deemed an "unstinting recommendation" of her teachings, and hoped that the approval of the Moody Bible Institute would enhance her American influence.[4]

In 1923 she published another edition of her book, generating a number of additional reviews in the United States and around the world. Helen Barrett Montgomery's assessment in *The Baptist* was typical, judging Bushnell "quite competent from her knowledge of Hebrew and

Greek," praising her exposition as "always reverent, often stimulating, sometimes startling," and recommending the "unique book" as worthy of "close study."[5] A reviewer in the *Watchman-Examiner* concurred, deeming Bushnell's "distinctly original and iconoclastic" project "the most extensive on womanhood that we have seen," and recommending the book as "a worthwhile study of a great question."[6]

It is noteworthy that despite the audacity of its claims, *God's Word to Women* received several enthusiastic endorsements from conservative Protestants. Even if they quibbled over particular interpretations, conservatives found common cause with Bushnell when it came to her respect for Scriptural authority. A reviewer in *The Australasian Biblical Recorder*, for example, praised Bushnell for her unfailing "loyalty to the Word," and for relying neither upon "feeble piety" nor upon "the weapons of rationalism." The reviewer approvingly noted that Bushnell, whom he considered "more learned in relative Biblical knowledge than any half-dozen professors," asked no one to accept her conclusions unless her interpretation proved to be "in agreement with the scope of the whole Revelation and Record." Though he refrained from offering an unqualified endorsement of Bushnell's efforts ("Whether all her inferences will be accepted at all points might be too much to expect in the fortunes of any writer on a profound subject"), he lauded the book as "a substantial contribution to one of the most important problems of the Biblical Revelation and of modern life."[7]

Other reviewers similarly expressed reservations about aspects of Bushnell's work but nonetheless applauded her efforts. A reviewer in *The Christian* judged the scope of Bushnell's "remarkable book" impressive, and her treatment of the subject "not only reverent but sane," yet cautioned, "that does not necessarily mean that we would follow Dr. Bushnell in all her claims and inferences." Even upon points of disagreement, however, the reviewer noted that one could not dispute the "soundly constructive purpose" that lay "behind her every endeavor."[8] In a similar manner, a reviewer in *The Glory of Israel* took issue with Bushnell's interpretations of Paul's writings, but nevertheless admired her "ingenuity," praised her for her commitment to "the authority and inviolability of the original text," and assured readers that whether or not they agreed with Bushnell, they could not fail to read her book "with interest and enjoyment."[9]

Perhaps the most critical review of *God's Word to Women* appeared in a 1924 issue of *The Sunday School Times*. On the one hand, the reviewer, W. H. Griffith Thomas, noted how refreshing it was to observe Bushnell's "attitude to the Bible as inspired, infallible, and inviolable. Nothing approaching Modernism in any degree is permitted." He thought it "impossible to speak too highly" of Bushnell's "ability and earnestness" and fully agreed that men had indeed "been guilty of giving wrong impressions of many important passages," and that it was therefore necessary for women to interpret what the Scriptures said about women. However, notwithstanding evidence of Bushnell's "great ability, real learning, and true loyalty to Scripture," he found her "convincing exegesis" marred by "special pleading" and an "overeagerness to prove her case"; too often, alongside her "illuminative and delightful suggestions," he encountered "interpretations which cannot stand the test of Hebrew and Greek scholarship," and he advised those unacquainted with the original languages to approach her work "with very great caution."[10]

On the whole, however, Bushnell was pleased with the book's sympathetic and often enthusiastic reception among theologians. Despite this favorable scholarly response, however, the book failed to achieve widespread influence among American Protestants in her own time. This was due in part to the very nature of the book. A jumbled and often dense theological treatise, it was a book that demanded careful study and did not lend itself to casual perusal. Having originated as a series of correspondence course lessons, the book was at times disjointed and repetitive, and would have benefited from a strong editorial hand. Lacking connections to prominent seminaries and publishing houses, Bushnell resorted to self-publishing the book, and so she lacked not only editorial oversight but also assistance in marketing her book to wider audiences. But there were also larger theological developments at play that inhibited the reception of her book. During the time in which she researched and revised *God's Word to Women,* deep divisions were taking hold within American churches—divisions that would significantly alter the landscape of twentieth-century Protestantism and dramatically diminish the potential audience for a radical, biblically based feminist theology.

When Bushnell first took up her theological investigations in the late 1870s, she had positioned herself as a critic of Christianity. Yet even as she spoke with a prophetic voice, she remained the product of mainstream religious and cultural currents. Not only was Protestantism the dominant faith in Victorian America, but establishment Protestantism drew heavily on the Methodist tradition in which Bushnell had been raised. By the late nineteenth century, even the holiness movement had so permeated American evangelicalism that Bushnell's faith was in many ways as representative as it was oppositional.[11]

Late-Victorian Protestantism was a forward-looking, socially oriented faith in which Christians worked together to reform society along broadly conceived notions of biblical truth. Within this context, Protestant women, deemed particularly suited to the work of reforming the world, enjoyed positions of relative power. By the 1920s, however, much had changed. As liberals and conservatives contended for the faith, the notion of a unified Christian audience could no longer be sustained. No longer could it be assumed that the Bible served as an undisputed arbiter of public belief, and for many Christians the link between Christianity and social reform had been severed. Together, these developments would profoundly affect the status of Christian women and would inhibit the reception of Bushnell's work.

The theological issues that drove a wedge between twentieth-century Protestants could be traced back to two forces that arrived on the American religious scene during the second half of the nineteenth century: Darwinism and higher criticism. By explaining human origins without the agency of the supernatural, the Darwinian theory of evolution called into question the historicity of the book of Genesis, and thereby threatened to undermine the authority of the Bible as a whole. In like manner, higher criticism rejected the supernatural origins of the Scriptures and instead subjected the Bible, and Christianity itself, to naturalistic investigation.

Christians responded in different ways to these challenges. Liberal Protestants sought to adapt their faith to modern thought, reasoning that by doing so they could fashion a faith that would stand the test of time. Refusing to choose between faith and reason, they embraced the latest scientific theories and sought God's purpose within them. In adopting an evolutionary view of knowledge, many modernists elevated modern scientific knowledge over traditional theological expertise.[12] Though the Bible might remain a useful source book for general moral ideals, it no longer served as the foundation for sophisticated and authoritative theologies.

Not all Protestants agreed, however. To conservatives, Darwinism and higher criticism undermined the very fundamentals of the faith: the authority of Scripture, the supernatural works of God, and the divinity of Christ.[13] To defend the faith from the evils of modernism, conservatives championed the literal and "inerrant" truth of the Bible, and insisted that scientific findings be interpreted in light of biblical truths. Liberals and conservatives parted ways when it came to social reform, as well. Whereas liberal Protestants touted "deeds, not creeds," and located social reform at the very heart of the gospel, many conservatives increasingly sought to distance themselves from liberal Protestants' "godless social service nonsense."[14] In a shift that historians have dubbed "the Great Reversal," many conservatives began to withdraw from the reform efforts that had long been hallmarks of nineteenth-century evangelicalism, preferring instead to emphasize personal morality and soul-saving revivalism.[15]

By the 1920s, then, members of the Protestant establishment were largely separating themselves into rival factions. Bushnell, however, did not fit comfortably in either camp. When it came to her understanding of the authority of Scripture, she remained firmly within the conservative fold.[16] Believing that the Bible contained within it the true source of women's liberation, she refused to accept "destructive" methods of higher criticism that threatened to diminish the power of the original text. Warning in no uncertain terms that modern rationalism would stifle a younger generation and wreak "treacherous havoc" in the pulpit, Bushnell situated Christian women firmly within the camp of conservative orthodoxy, and then used the threats of modernism to press her claim for female religious authority: "A very fire of hell is raging all about us, even though largely unrecognized, in modern rationalism," she contended. "We women have no alternative but to help to extinguish the fire or be scorched by it, and see our children perish in its flames. Shall we women, at such a time as this, sit still and remember our sex? Never! We will brush aside the opposition of those who can think only in terms of sex, and go up 'to the help of the Lord against the mighty.'"[17] Bushnell also deviated from liberalism when it came to the liberal faith in modern science, and in the perpetual progress of society. Although she looked forward to a new era of Christianity, she refused to see contemporary religious and social arrangements as the culmination of evolutionary advance, and she remained skeptical of modern science and its role in social reform, particularly a science dominated by male investigators.

Yet in other ways it is difficult to characterize Bushnell as a conservative. Highly critical of tradition, she found little worth conserving when it came to conventional understandings of gender, family, and society. She insisted on a radical reassessment of traditional theology in order to render the word of God relevant to modern America, and though she claimed to uphold the "inspired," "infallible," and "inviolable" nature of the biblical text, she employed a more flexible view of inspiration than did many conservatives, some of whom, by the 1920s, had abandoned even lower critical methods of interpretation. She believed that Christian truth must be distinguished from the cultural context in which it was communicated, and she turned to modern scholarship to illuminate the historical settings of Scriptural texts. Finally, Bushnell maintained a firm commitment to social reform. She studied theology in order to restructure society; she believed that true salvation would be facilitated by Christ's atonement, but realized through a redeemed social order.

Bushnell was not alone in finding herself caught between the emerging factions within American Protestantism. As the once-flourishing Protestant women's culture began to erode, women of Bushnell's generation, whose commitments to both biblical theology and social reform had long placed them securely within the religious mainstream, inhabited an increasingly precarious space where they would find their power diminished, and at times under siege. Madeline Southard, a friend and colleague of Bushnell, articulated well the challenges that such women faced. Writing in her personal journal in 1923, she struggled to place herself within the changing religious landscape, finally settling on the term "liberal conservative." But the stalwart reformer who had once accompanied Carrie Nation on her saloon-smashing crusade quickly added, "What would I have done [in] my college years had any one dared call me a conservative!"[18] As a Methodist preacher, women's rights advocate, and WCTU activist, Southard, like Bushnell, refused to separate social reform from evangelical theology, and she attributed her dual commitment to her position as a Christian woman. But she recognized that she was increasingly out of step with the prevailing directions of American Protestantism, and in fact blamed the diminishing space within Protestantism for those who united the conversionist and activist aspects of Christianity on the widespread exclusion of women from positions of church leadership.[19] Women who combined social reform with passionate Christianity had frequently been prevented from doing so within the church, she pointed out, and she suggested that had the church opened its ministry to women, it was "quite probable that these two aspects of the Gospel would not have become so estranged." But by stifling the work of women, the church had allowed "certain great social impulses born of the Christian spirit to crystallize in secular movements which are indifferent, sometimes hostile, to formulated Christianity." Southard suggested that the church was only beginning to awaken to its loss.[20]

The Masculinization of American Protestantism

Together with the growing estrangement of evangelical theology and social reform, additional factors within both liberal and conservative strands of Protestantism eroded the authority of women like Bushnell and Southard. By the early twentieth century, American Protestants of all persuasions found themselves in a world in which Victorian economic and social arrangements no longer prevailed. With women and men increasingly sharing the same social spaces at amusement parks, movie theaters, and even workplaces, the ideology of separate spheres had begun to break down. And as women began to abandon the private refuge of the home for the responsibilities and amusements of modern life, the construct of female moral superiority fell out of favor. Accordingly, depictions of women as naturally pure and especially religious lost their hold on popular imagination. In the wake of these changes, the long-standing overrepresentation of women in religious organizations suddenly became objectionable. This sentiment was powerfully conveyed by the thousands of men who joined forces in the Men and Religion Forward Movement of 1911 and 1912 in order to bring the purportedly three million "missing men" back into American churches. Though they failed to achieve this goal, they did succeed in masculinizing many of those churches, and in reclaiming religion as a masculine endeavor.[21]

Liberals and conservatives experienced this masculinization of American Protestantism in different ways. For conservatives, the decline in female religious authority meant that their staunch commitment to biblical inerrancy, dispensational theology, and antimodernism often resulted in masculinist, and on occasion blatantly misogynistic, rhetoric and practices.[22] Although fundamentalists embraced various and at times conflicting views of women, most continued to uphold the Victorian family ideal that relegated women to the home as wives and mothers. But even as they did so, they rejected notions of female purity and moral superiority that had long empowered women in those roles. Instead, many conservatives resurrected the symbol of Eve. Depicting women as weak—and vulnerable to doctrinal error—they assigned truth a masculine quality; indeed, fundamentalist men often characterized the theological perversions of liberal Protestantism as an "effeminate" squandering of the virility of true Christian doctrine.[23] To make matters worse, fundamentalists were losing their hold on Protestant denominations just as women were

appealing for greater rights within those denominations. Given their associations of right doctrine with masculine virility, it was not difficult for
fundamentalists to project a conspiracy between theological liberals and
modern women, and it was not long before women's rights and the evils
of modernism became firmly linked in the minds of many conservatives.[24]

Although liberal Protestants differed from their conservative counterparts on a host of issues, they, too, largely abandoned notions of female
moral superiority, and they, too, tended to espouse surprisingly conservative views when it came to women's societal roles. Though more likely
than fundamentalists to support women's suffrage and far less likely to
employ harsh antifeminist rhetoric, liberal Protestants nonetheless persisted in upholding the domestic ideal for women. Liberal Protestants'
embrace of female domesticity was due in part to their enthusiasm for
modern science. As Social Darwinists, many liberal Protestants considered the Victorian family not only the basis of a Christian social order,
but also the height of social evolutionary development, and thus essential
to the advance of civilization.[25] Indeed, many proponents of the Social
Gospel came to view the traditional family as "virtually synonymous" with
"the Kingdom of God."[26] Many liberal Protestants also welcomed eugenics
as a leading application of modern science,[27] and by assigning women vital
roles as mothers of the race, eugenics reinforced domesticity as central to
women's identity and vocation.

Institutional dynamics within liberal Protestantism further contributed to women's declining influence. By the late 1920s liberal and mod-
erate factions had largely wrested control of mainline denominations
from their conservative rivals, leaving many conservatives to retreat to
their own institutions and organizations. Within smaller conservative
sects, particularly those with decentralized power structures and those
influenced by holiness or Pentecostal teachings, it was not uncommon
for women to attain positions of power. Even as pronouncements on
women's inferiority and denunciations of the sins of modern women
abounded in fundamentalist literature, many conservative women persisted in their religious work, particularly in missions and religious education, but also in some cases in preaching and evangelism.[28] Their more
liberal sisters, however, confronted mainline Protestantism's centralized
power structures that often inhibited their advancement, and increasingly stripped them of what power they once enjoyed. Although mainline
Protestants included more "token" women on their national boards than
did their conservative counterparts, women ended up exerting little real

denominational power, and their active participation rarely extended to the local level.[29]

It is worth noting, however, that the story of Protestant women's diminished power is not one in which women themselves had no agency. With the rise of professionalization and a growing emphasis on scientific expertise, many Protestant women took advantage of educational opportunities and themselves came to adopt a gender-neutral, "objective" approach to social issues. Many women's organizations, too, began to downplay emotion and female solidarity for the sake of "efficiency" and professionalization.[30] In light of these developments, however, women could no longer lay special claim to reform work, and more traditionally minded women were less motivated to devote their time and money to organizations that prized efficiency and professionalism over women's special calling.[31]

Women were not oblivious to their declining religious power, and many initially expressed alarm at the changes taking place. In the 1920s, churchwomen issued frequent warnings to male religious leaders, arguing that if women were not allowed to participate actively and on an equal basis with men, they would simply look to secular avenues of advancement and turn their backs on religion altogether.[32] But such warnings went unheeded, and by the next generation the majority of women who remained within Protestant churches had come to accept their subordinate positions. A study conducted by the Federal Council of Churches in 1946 and 1947, for example, revealed that most churchwomen did not wish to take on greater responsibility for fear that men would "lose all interest" in church affairs were they to do so. The majority of women who achieved leadership positions in mainline denominations served small rural churches as deacons or trustees, and these women were frequently held to higher standards than their male counterparts. Churchwomen themselves agreed that a successful woman needed to be "not over-aggressive, nor yet afraid to speak up, cooperative, tactful, capable . . . free from petty jealousy, not eager for power and prestige"; a woman who failed to meet such stringent qualifications was "likely to be considered proof positive . . . that women cannot do the job."[33]

When Bushnell embarked upon her theological investigations at the end of the nineteenth century, she had imagined herself part of an uprising of Christian women on the cusp of reforming the world for Christ, and Christianity for women. Even as she neared completion of her book, she remained optimistic that she was witness to the dawn of a new era.

Suffrage seemed within reach, a new generation of university-educated women was entering the workforce and the ministry, and new possibilities seemed to abound. But with the polarization of American Protestantism, her intended audience was fast dissolving. Neither liberal nor conservative Protestants would prove particularly receptive to Bushnell's gospel for women—a radical gospel of female empowerment, based on a conservative hermeneutic, that sought to liberate women, socially and religiously, from the bonds of domesticity. Her impassioned denunciations of modernism surely did little to endear her to liberal Protestants, but even in the absence of such strident rhetoric it is doubtful that Bushnell's painstaking theological research would have counted for much among those who had abandoned traditional theological investigation. Feminist biblical interpretation could do little to disrupt enduring conservative gender commitments among those who no longer viewed the Scriptures as an authoritative guide to worldly matters. At the same time, Bushnell failed to influence conservative debates over women's rights to any considerable measure. Among those who shared Bushnell's commitment to the authority of the Scriptures, deepening hostility to female religious authority, together with a growing reluctance to accept even lower critical methods, undoubtedly inhibited the widespread acceptance of her ideas. The theological setting of the 1920s, then, was hardly conducive to a radical feminist re-examination of the Scriptures, particularly one penned by an evangelical woman committed to upholding the authority of the biblical text.

8

A Prophet Without Honor

EVEN AT THE height of her public work, Bushnell had envisioned herself an outsider of sorts. In her efforts to reform Victorian society and traditional Christianity, she seemed most comfortable when advancing a prophetic critique against the status quo. And yet, during the 1880s and 1890s, she was in many ways at the very center of things. As a prominent member of one of the world's largest and most influential women's organizations, Bushnell was known and admired by women across the globe. She was a crusading "New Woman" at a time when a new era for women seemed imminent, and she was a leading evangelical reformer at the height of American Protestantism's cultural influence. But in the span of roughly two decades, stretching from her resignation from the WCTU to the publication of God's Word to Women, Bushnell found herself relegated to the peripheries, not only out of step with transformations within American Protestantism, but also increasingly at odds with the mainstream women's movement.

Bushnell's marginalization coincided with the decline of the dynamic Protestant women's culture that had fostered and sustained her work. Even as transitions within American Christianity divested evangelical women of their considerable social influence, developments within the women's movement further limited their public authority. These changes were especially visible in the erosion of the social purity movement, one of the primary sites of cooperation between late nineteenth-century evangelicals and women's rights activists. As the Victorian era gave way to new social and economic realities, a growing number of feminists began to abandon a sexual ethic based on restraint in favor of one that championed sexual expression. In doing so, they parted ways with evangelical reformers who continued to recommend purity and restraint as the means to women's freedom and empowerment. In the wake of these changes, old-school purity reform gradually gave way to the more professionalized and scientific "social hygiene" movement, a process that frequently pitted evangelical reformers against scientists, and against a new generation of women's rights activists.

This growing estrangement between faith and feminism became particularly apparent by the 1920s and 1930s when it came to debates over contraception. Whereas proponents of women's rights increasingly came to understand birth control as a means to ensure women's freedom, women like Bushnell continued to advocate restraint, and feared that contraception would only increase women's vulnerability to male vice. Bushnell ardently opposed birth control until her death in 1946, and it was in this regard that she most clearly broke ranks with modern feminists. Decades later, tensions over sexuality and morality, freedom and restraint, continue to plague efforts to fashion a viable Christian feminism. In this way, the difficulties that Bushnell encountered in the closing decades of her career can illuminate some of the most entrenched challenges confronting Christian feminists today.

From Crusader to Crank

For years Bushnell had immersed herself in her theological research, but the outbreak of the First World War prompted her to leave Britain in 1917 to return to Oakland, California, and plunged her back into the world of purity activism. Bushnell would soon come to realize, however, that the purity movement in which she had long labored had declined dramatically in her absence, and that she herself had become increasingly marginalized within the broader American women's movement.

When President Wilson had announced the United States' entry into the war that spring, he had characterized it as a noble endeavor to protect democracy the world over. Bushnell, however, immediately feared for the democratic rights of American women, and watched warily as the country mobilized for war. Her fears soon materialized with the introduction of the "American Plan," a set of wartime measures reminiscent of the Contagious Diseases Acts that Bushnell and other purity activists had combated decades earlier. Aimed at preventing the spread of venereal disease in the military, the Plan not only called upon soldiers to report women suspected of disease, but also subjected accused women to compulsory physical examinations and forced incarceration without due process. In the context of wartime euphoria, most Americans lauded the measures as scientific and patriotic, but for Bushnell the stakes were clear: the Plan effectively endorsed prostitution, upheld the sexual double standard, and promoted the state-sanctioned subordination of women.[1] Rather than seeing the measures as the product of modern scientific progress, Bushnell contended that by treating women as men's chattel, the measures did nothing less than graft "modern hygiene onto medieval policies." To her mind, even national security could not warrant the injustice.[2]

Bushnell protested the new measures from the day they were first unveiled. But Elizabeth Andrew, her faithful friend and companion of twenty-six years, had fallen ill earlier that year and died, and so Bushnell was almost entirely alone in this effort.[3] Bushnell would later reflect that "the co-operation of her wonderful, well-balanced and highly cultured mind kept me from many a rash move,"[4] and in the coming months and years she would sorely miss her friend's wisdom and companionship. Reluctantly setting aside her biblical studies, Bushnell quickly produced a series of pamphlets to alert the public to the threat the Plan posed to public morality, and to the rights of women.[5] Employing classic social purity rhetoric, Bushnell railed against a double standard that targeted women in order to offer men a "false hope of healthier vice." Her previous experiences with military men, together with her suspicion of men in general, led her to resist the allure of patriotism and instead to question soldiers' trustworthiness in these circumstances. And she insisted that "detective methods to ferret out clandestine prostitution" would only lead to blackmail and to the entrapment of the innocent along with the guilty.[6]

She contested the measures on legal grounds as well, arguing that by allowing for the arrest of women on mere suspicion of "being a source of peril to fornicators" and denying them the right of *habeas corpus*, the measures "trampled underfoot" women's basic constitutional rights.[7] "Produce all male citizens walking about the streets of New York at night," she wrote. "Give them police court examinations to find out what their past has been. Publish the facts with their names attached in all the newspapers that everyone of their women acquaintances might read it, and hear the cry about individual liberty that will arise."[8] Rather than depriving women of their rights through compulsory examinations and arrest, Bushnell recommended instead the establishment of "wholly voluntary clinics and hospitals for venereal diseases."[9] Compulsion attached stigma to disease, she insisted, and would only discourage people from seeking treatment.

In response to her tireless protests, the federal government dispatched two representatives of the Interdepartmental Social Hygiene Board to Oakland to meet with her. Accustomed to confronting government officials in the interest of purity, Bushnell wasted no time in commencing the interview with an examination of the men's credentials. Upon learning that one representative was a lawyer, Bushnell demanded to know if he was familiar with "Judge Sheldon Amos' large law book on the Regulation of Vice," a favorite among purity activists. The man, however, "had never heard of it." She then asked "if he knew the valuable work by Benjamin Scott," the British anti-vice crusader. But no, "he had never heard of that, etc., etc." She found it "deplorable" that the United States government would "institute nation-wide methods, born of inexperience, to quell diseases spread by vice, and, professedly at least, to rehabilitate prostitutes," in "total ignorance" of the vast literature going back to the time of Napoleon chronicling the successes and failures of European attempts to implement such legislation.[10] Confident that her own investigations, together with Butler's work and that of other purity reformers, had decisively dispelled the purported benefits of regulationism, Bushnell was astonished that anyone could disregard their sound conclusions and commit again the errors of the past.

Not only were the government representatives unaware of the long history of antiregulationism, but they were also oblivious to Bushnell's pivotal role in the movement. Thus they did not realize the utterly incongruous nature of their request when they solicited Bushnell's support for American Plan. In exasperation, she contemptuously discharged the representatives at the end of their meeting, and decided instead to appeal to higher levels of command; she wrote a letter to the Secretary of the Navy to warn him that such egregious violations of women's constitutional rights would lead to social unrest, and "three times over" she sent personal letters or pamphlets on the subject to President Wilson, his cabinet, and every member of Congress.[11] Bushnell, however, had not been the only one to leave the meeting frustrated and dismissive. The two government representatives had been more than a little taken aback by Bushnell's scathing response to their seemingly innocuous request. One of the men described her reaction in a letter to the Surgeon General: "Her voice trembled, her hands shook, and she acted altogether like a fanatic, or insane person." Clearly amused by the older woman's antics, the government representatives quickly dismissed Bushnell as a "'crank' without many supporters."[12]

How had Bushnell gone from being a respected and internationally known reformer to a "crank without many supporters," in only two decades? For in their assertion that Bushnell lacked support, the government representatives were indeed correct. Bushnell was the "lone American woman" to oppose the American Plan at its inception.[13] Though she sought assistance from women's rights leaders like Anna Howard Shaw, Carrie Chapman Catt, and Lucy Stone Blackwell, only Blackwell took up the issue to any extent, and she informed Bushnell that she stood "almost alone, among suffragists," who had largely accepted the regulatory measures on scientific and patriotic grounds.[14] Surprised and dismayed that the appalling injustices that seemed obvious to her were lost on others, Bushnell could only conclude that, having never endured their own Contagious Diseases Acts, Americans lacked the capacity to recognize the dangers lurking within the wartime measures. She acknowledged as well her own lack of influence, which she attributed to having lived abroad for so many years; with her "record as an experienced purity worker" virtually unknown, she considered herself "a 'prophet,' without honour in my own country."[15]

In England, where the names Bushnell and Andrew were still "household words" among older purity reformers, and where "social hygiene" had remained truer to its social purity origins, Bushnell's protest aroused widespread attention and action. British reformers circulated more than 29,000 copies of one of Bushnell's pamphlets, and considered it instrumental in defeating similar regulatory measures in England.[16] But Bushnell continued to encounter *"very little* sympathy . . . on this side of the water,"[17] and though she pleaded with her British colleagues to intervene, they were reluctant to interfere in American affairs.[18] Members of the British Association for Moral & Social Hygiene did, however, agree to supply Bushnell with a letter of commendation and a small sum of money, which she immediately put toward the production and dissemination of additional pamphlets intended for governmental representatives, ministers, and anyone else who might assert influence on her behalf.[19] She also founded the Union to Combat the Sanitation of Vice, but by her own admission it never amounted to more than "a mere scarecrow" organization made up of a few of her friends and neighbors.[20] From time to time she managed to stir up a bit of controversy, but for the most part her appeals to authorities were "summarily dismissed." As far as she could see, her cause was "completely beaten."[21]

From Purity to Hygiene

Bushnell was stunned by her decisive defeat. She had been accustomed to facing formidable resistance in her purity work, but she had always been able to count on faithful allies within the women's movement, and within the Protestant fold, to help rally supporters to her cause. But by the dawn of the First World War, the American purity movement as she had known it had effectively ceased to exist, and the alliance between evangelical reformers and women's rights activists had begun to unravel. Even as Bushnell had been pursuing her biblical studies overseas, she had not been entirely unaware of the transformations taking place within the American purity movement, and it was to this history that she turned in her efforts to come to terms with her failure to overturn the American Plan.[22]

At the close of the nineteenth century, Bushnell and her fellow anti-regulationist purity reformers seemed to have won the day. They had succeeded in convincing most physicians of the inefficacy and impracticality of regulation, and of the need for men, as well as women, to exercise moral restraint.[23] For a time, the interests of religion, science, and public morality appeared closely aligned, and the "Christianized medicine" that Bushnell and others advocated seemed to have prevailed. Pleased with this new détente, many purity reformers abandoned their antagonism toward the scientific community and became increasingly receptive to the role that science could play in dictating proper attitudes toward sexuality and morality. In doing so, however, they unwittingly ceded their social power to the expertise of scientists, facilitating the eventual domination of scientific over religious frameworks for social morality.[24] This shift in power was evident in the growing popularity of the scientific social hygiene movement, which gradually displaced the earlier purity crusade.

The earliest signs of this transformation had become apparent after the appointment of O. Edward Janney to the presidency of the American Purity Alliance in 1900.[25] Though Janney advocated the "Christian medicine" that Bushnell championed, he also worked to professionalize the social purity movement, and it was under his tenure that the transformation from purity to hygiene began in earnest. (The name of the organization was first changed to the American Vigilance Association, and then, after a merger in 1914 with the American Federation for Sex Hygiene, to the American Social Hygiene Association.) Despite his emphasis on professionalization, Janney continued to respect the voices of the female reformers who had been instrumental in the movement's initial success.

But not all members were so inclined, and it was not long after the merger that Janney was ousted from the association and replaced by Charles William Eliot as president, and William F. Snow as secretary. Under this new leadership, it soon became clear just how far the social hygiene movement had drifted from its purity roots. As Secretary of the Association, Snow helped ensure the preeminence of medical professionals by relegating religious and women's groups to auxiliary roles within the emerging coalition. Although he continued to pay lip service to the role that religion played in supporting public health, it was clear that moral issues would "not be permitted to cloud the biological side of the movement," and that tensions between the two would be resolved by social hygienists.[26]

Perhaps most disturbing, as far as Bushnell was concerned, Snow began to express regulationist leanings as early as 1910.[27] Since both Snow and Eliot continued to employ the familiar vocabulary of purity, however, only astute observers noticed the extensive changes taking place within the movement.[28] Whereas in England "social hygiene" continued to respect social purity principles, maintaining a robust critique of the sexual double standard and concern for women's rights, in the United States it came to entail a very different set of values. Indeed, by abandoning a careful consideration of social factors and without strong connections to the women's movement, social hygiene would eventually become nothing more than "a euphemism for sexual regulation and the control of venereal diseases."[29]

Further forsaking their social purity roots, Eliot and Snow began to incorporate eugenics into the social hygiene movement.[30] Eugenic theory had emerged during the last two decades of the nineteenth century, in response to growing doubts about the inevitability of civilization's advance. Fearing that the very trappings of civilization had begun to render the civilized vulnerable, Victorians looked to modern science to avert civilization's decline; through selective reproduction, eugenics promised to ensure the vitality of Anglo-Saxon civilization.[31] Although Bushnell and other purity activists had explored the role of heredity in the perpetuation of social vice as early as the 1870s and 1880s, in Lamarckian fashion they had emphasized the significance of moral and environmental factors in shaping physical traits passed down from one generation to the next. Social hygienists and eugenicists, however, favored purely physical explanations, and in Bushnell's opinion they advanced their professional, scientific analysis at the expense of a thorough critique of the social and religious factors that perpetuated the abuse of women.

In particular, Bushnell took issue with social hygienists' tendency to label prostitutes "feeble-minded."[32] Historians have demonstrated how gendered distinctions very similar to Victorian constructions of virtue became inscribed in this new, "scientific" diagnosis; among men, feeble-mindedness was associated with criminal behavior or the failure to succeed economically, while among women it was "defined almost exclusively in sexual terms."[33] In 1915, for instance, a spokesperson for the American Social Hygiene Association estimated that at least half of the prostitutes taken into custody were mentally defective.[34] Bushnell, in contrast, rejected the "stupid assumption that prostitution proves feeble-mindedness," and asserted that any deficiencies likely resulted from their "abuse in sexual matters by men," rather than from any "inherited condition."[35]

Bushnell opposed eugenics both because she rejected the underlying discourse of civilization upon which it was based, and because she believed that eugenics would only exacerbate the subjugation of women. She understood that by effectively erasing the role that social or religious factors played in contributing to a culture of prostitution, eugenicists ended up placing the responsibility for contagious diseases squarely upon "defective" young women—women presumed to be genetically disposed toward prostitution. As far as eugenicists and social hygienists were concerned, then, it was in the public interest to control such women, without regard to their constitutional rights.

Bushnell did all she could to combat eugenics and social hygiene, but she found that her efforts mattered little in the face of the enormous influence the new scientific discourses wielded. In 1918, for instance, even as she was scraping together her meager resources to combat the American Plan (drawing funding from her few supporters, generally in amounts ranging from thirty-five cents to five dollars[36]), she learned that Snow had secured four million dollars in funding to inaugurate his social hygiene program throughout the nation.[37] That same year she also discovered that the Federal Council of Churches was incorporating social hygiene into its Sunday school curriculum.[38] She was left feeling as though she were "trying to turn Niagara around with a feather."[39]

Although the ascendancy of social hygiene can in some ways be seen as the triumph of "masculine" professionalization over the "feminine" approaches of female reformers—a view Bushnell certainly shared—it is important to note that this characterization can obscure the role that women themselves played in the process. Not only did many nineteenth-century purity reformers eventually come to endorse scientific approaches to morality, but as social hygiene gained prominence in the early decades of the twentieth century, it was often female social workers who edged out evangelical reformers.[40] Many women's rights activists, too, believed that modern science could help them in their cause, and it was not uncommon for early twentieth-century feminists to draw on the rhetoric of social hygiene and eugenics in their efforts to advance their aims. Proponents of women's rights, for example, argued that greater educational opportunities for women, public sex education, and access to birth control would strengthen women and their offspring.

Only over time did it become clear that this shift from purity to hygiene—from environmental to scientific explanations for social behavior—entailed unanticipated consequences for women. For example, despite the efforts of women's rights advocates to incorporate eugenics on behalf of their purposes, the heightened role that eugenic theory assigned to motherhood meant that "every eugenic argument was in the long run more effective in the hands of antifeminists than feminists."[41] The early twentieth-century "race suicide" scare exemplified this tendency, with white women once again relegated to the home in order to ensure that they fulfilled their domestic and reproductive duties in the interest of perpetuating the Anglo-Saxon race. Bushnell was among those who opposed the race suicide scare, openly questioning the motives of the "many foolish men," including President Theodore Roosevelt, who were "constantly talking of the nation's need of proliferous mothers," but she, and other women who shared her critique, encountered keen opposition.[42]

Further working against women's interests was the fact that social hygienists' neglect of environmental and social factors meant that public attention to the injustices perpetuated by the double standard, and concern for the rights of women—even those of dubious character—declined markedly. Even as purity activists had opposed prostitution, they had generally expressed sympathy for prostitutes and championed their rights in the face of government regulation. But among social hygienists, prostitutes came to be seen as "pariahs charged with spreading syphilis into the nation's bloodstream."[43] Divisions over the nature of prostitution had a marked effect on the women's movement. For decades, women's activists from a wide array of backgrounds had found common ground battling prostitution and the sexual double standard, but by the end of the Great War any consensus on these matters had vanished.[44] Indeed, by that time, consensus on any questions relating to sexuality and morality had become highly improbable, for the years in which Bushnell researched and wrote

God's Word to Women coincided with a period of profound social transformation that indelibly altered the American women's movement.[45]

Feminism, Sexuality, and the "New Morality"

In the early 1900s, a second generation of "New Women" had come of age; having benefited from access to higher education and greater participation in the workforce, this generation inhabited a world very different from Bushnell's. In 1912, eager to leave behind the vestiges of Victorianism, a number of "the newest of New Women" came together to launch a new movement, which they christened "Feminism."[46] Demanding a comprehensive social revolution, Feminists sought radical departures from convention, including cutting ties with Christianity. Though a certain degree of secularization had already occurred within the American women's movement in the aftermath of the *Woman's Bible* controversy, the majority of women active in the movement continued to draw upon the general teachings of the Christian faith. Many Feminists, however, freely condemned religion.[47]

Unfettered by the constraints of traditional Christian morality, Feminists parted ways with earlier generations of reformers by identifying sexual freedom as one of the central tenets of women's emancipation.[48] Nineteenth-century reformers like Bushnell had been closely attuned to the danger sexuality posed to women in the form of sullied reputations, contagious diseases, and unwanted and potentially perilous pregnancies. Within a Victorian social order that separated men and women into distinct spheres and spaces, reformers had developed an antagonistic worldview that not only emphasized men's difference, but also men's potential to harm women. Even those like Bushnell, who resisted Victorian constructions of virtue, persisted in seeing sexuality as latent with danger; indeed, temperance and purity workers focused almost exclusively on protecting women from men's moral shortcomings. Twentieth-century Feminists, too, identified sexuality as one of the key sources of women's oppression. But freed from the social and economic constraints of Victorian culture and unrestrained by Christianity, they proposed dramatically different remedies. They sought to undo the sexual double standard not by elevating male purity, but rather by abandoning all appeals to female purity. Instead they advocated women's freedom to fulfill their sexual desires without social, political, or religious restraint.[49] Drawing on the scientific expertise of sexologists and psychologists like Havelock

Ellis and Sigmund Freud, they touted the active pursuit of sexual pleasure as both normative and healthy. In doing so, they transformed the salvific self-control that Victorians had long extolled into something unhealthy, and even immoral.[50] In essence, they redefined morality.

This new sexual ethic found a receptive audience among early twentieth-century Americans. As a younger generation embraced new consumer pleasures and commercial leisure possibilities, the "feminine" morality of self-restraint had come to seem unduly restrictive. Both modern science and mass culture, then, conveyed powerful new "truths" when it came to sexuality and morality.[51] The newer model of sexual pleasure, however, did not fully supersede the former. Even as many women's rights activists joined Feminists and sexologists in recommending women's pursuit of pleasure, others continued to espouse the older ideals, underscoring women's vulnerability to men's passions and advocating restraint, rather than fulfillment. For members of an earlier generation of New Women, the emphasis on sexual freedom was not only foreign, but in many cases it contradicted their life's work. Having long labored to protect women from sexual danger (and to guard the women's movement against associations with "free love" and promiscuity), women of the older generation—many of whom were reaching their fifties and sixties by the 1920s—watched in dismay as a younger cohort embraced an opposing set of values.[52] By continuing to advocate sexual restraint, however, such women increasingly came to be treated as objects of ridicule and scorn; in the eyes of the younger generation, they seemed hopelessly old-fashioned, prudish, and "repressed."[53] Defining the advancement of women in contradictory ways, then, these conflicting frameworks coexisted uneasily within the early twentieth-century women's movement.

Clashing conceptions of sexuality came to a head in widespread disagreements over birth control in the 1920s and 1930s. On the one hand, women like Margaret Sanger and Emma Goldman considered contraception essential to women's advancement. They recognized that in removing the fear of unwanted pregnancies, contraception could bolster the identification of sexuality with health and pleasure. Additionally, contraception could serve eugenic ends by facilitating selective reproduction.[54] Other women, however, feared that birth control would do more harm than good. Although the majority of women's rights advocates would eventually embrace contraception as essential to women's emancipation, in the early decades of the twentieth century it was not yet clear whether birth control would enhance women's control over their own bodies, or men's control over women. Though nineteenth-century women's rights activists had enthusiastically promoted voluntary motherhood—women's right to control their reproduction through periodic abstinence—most feared that artificial means of contraception would sever too thoroughly the relationship between sexuality and reproduction, thereby discouraging men from taking responsibility for their sexual behavior. As historian Linda Gordon explains, the single most compelling reason for men to marry women seemed to be the fact that children resulted from sexual intercourse, and in the social and economic milieu of the nineteenth century, "women needed marriage more than men." Working within a framework where men's sexual freedom threatened the well-being of women, most women's rights proponents had believed it to be in women's best interest to increase, rather than diminish, the taboos against extramarital sex.[55]

A product of the nineteenth-century purity movement, Bushnell vigorously opposed the "Birth-Control delusion," which she insisted would "accomplish none of the good things it promises."[56] She feared that artificial means of contraception could be commandeered by the state to control women's bodies, and she expressed alarm at connections between birth control proponents and a small but growing movement for abortion.[57] Though she remained an ardent supporter of voluntary motherhood, she argued that "modern human devices" for contraception would "give full rein to irresponsible fleshly desire."[58] Believing that birth control advocates erred in thinking that "indulgence of the flesh is inevitable, and self-control unmanageable," Bushnell maintained that men ought to exercise self-control "unless the full responsibility of reproduction is faced and accepted by the wife." Rather than resorting to artificial means of contraception, which she thought reduced a wife to the "humiliating position of a mere 'vessel' to receive the excreta of the male," she recommended "a dignified, calm assertion of the natural rights of women" as the strongest protection that could be offered women.[59]

For Bushnell, birth control was at its heart a moral issue, and she noted that its proponents seemed to agree. Sanger herself had openly challenged "the revealed and dogmatic basis of morality," characterizing religious morality as "moral imbecility," and had boasted that birth control placed within women's hands "an instrument which becomes *ipso facto a power for the development of the New Morality.*"[60] Dubbing Sanger the "High Priestess of the cult" of New Morality,[61] Bushnell denounced this new morality as "anti-God, anti-Christian . . . anti-moral-marriage," and an attack upon women's chastity.[62] She attempted to combat birth control on scientific grounds as well, claiming that no effective measures of contraception existed apart from continence, and urging skepticism toward a medical profession eager to experiment on women's bodies. And she criticized proponents of the "new morality" for their "assumption of 'scientific' and 'philosophic' pretensions," accusing men like Bertrand Russell and Havelock Ellis of "swagger[ing] on the high stilts of scientific and philosophic wordiness" in order to deceive people into abandoning true morality.[63]

Deeming birth control an "imminent moral peril" to the nation, Bushnell worked "to the limit of [her] strength" to oppose the movement.[64] When a bill to repeal the Comstock Law and legalize contraceptive devices came before Congress in 1934, Bushnell, who was then approaching eighty years of age, sent personal letters of protest to all members of both Houses, helping to defeat the measure.[65] Ultimately, however, Bushnell was fighting a losing battle. Her calls for sexual restraint made sense in the Victorian cultural landscape but seemed out of touch with developments in modern America, and as more and more women came to see birth control as essential to women's emancipation, Bushnell became increasingly alienated from the modern women's movement.

By the 1930s, even her former purity allies in Britain had parted ways with her over birth control, objecting to her recalcitrant position and criticizing her for her "over-forced" or "feverishly self-assertive" tone. Alison Neilans, the secretary of the British Association for Moral and Social Hygiene and Bushnell's staunch ally in the battles over wartime regulationism, thought Bushnell "so obsessed by this new morality business and birth control that she simply cannot understand any argument which seems to put her in the wrong." Privately, Neilans dismissed Bushnell as an "absolutely obsessed fanatic," and she sought to discredit Bushnell among her British colleagues by noting Bushnell's close ties to "the fundamentalist movement which denies evolution, accepts every word of the bible [as] literally true, and is one of the most reactionary, so-called religious movements in the world today."[66] When the Association, of which Bushnell remained an honorary vice president, refused to denounce birth control, Bushnell resigned in protest; Neilans welcomed the decision.[67]

By the 1930s, then, Bushnell had become personally and professionally alienated from the movements in which she had once played a leading role. To a new generation of reformers, she appeared outmoded and reactionary, an example of the "prudish" Victorianism that had constrained women in the past. Bushnell, however, still perceived herself as an intrepid crusader for women's rights. Even as she had spent her career exposing the hypocrisies of the Victorian moral system, however, her critique remained rooted in the economic, social, and religious realities of that era; when she leveled a similar critique at the "new morality" of the modern era, she incurred both resistance and ridicule. Bushnell appeared to be on the wrong side of history.

Over time, however, historians have come to question whether this revolt against Victorianism constituted an unmitigated victory for modern feminism. Upon closer examination, the new arrangements often turned out to be less liberating than proponents had anticipated. As Christina Simmons explains, the myth of Victorian repression effectively "rehabilitated male sexuality and cast women as villains if they refused to respond to, nurture, or support it." And, Simmons adds, "by identifying women with Victorianism and men with a progressive and realistic understanding of sex, it confirmed men's sexual dominance as normative in modern marriage." The new sexual discourse amounted to a rejection of Victorian "repression," then, inasmuch as "repression" denoted the regulation of sexual activity. But in more precise terms, it was a calculated and largely successful "attack on *women's* control over *men's* sexuality." The "liberation" celebrated by sex radicals in fact entailed a new set of restrictions reflecting men's fear of female power.[68]

For instance, new rules of conduct that emphasized heterosexual intimacy ended up placing new restrictions on the kinds of relationships deemed acceptable for women. By the 1920s, the intimate friendships common among female reformers of Bushnell's generation had come to be viewed with suspicion, and relationships that had long contributed to female solidarity now seemed to threaten the normative heterosexual ideal. In an era in which one historian has situated "the invention of heterosexuality,"[69] women who did not comply with the new expectations of heterosexual intimacy could be labeled deviant and disruptive, or simply discounted as antiquated "cranks" or "prudes."[70] By advancing an ethic based on heterosexual pleasure, then, modern feminists unwittingly contributed to the growing suspicion of female intimacy that had long sustained the women's movement. And by discrediting old-school reformers, they helped to dismantle the protections against male sexual power that "prudish" reformers had worked for decades to construct.

As it turns out, Bushnell was not alone in expressing reservations about the changing sexual standards. Charlotte Perkins Gilman, too, had cautioned that the "New Morality" would end up reinforcing male supremacy and playing into the hands of "oversexed" males. Freud was popular, she claimed, because he gave "scientific" approval to man's "misuse of the female." Unlike many of her contemporaries, Gilman rejected the cultural hostility to all things Victorian, and contended that denouncing sexual excess did not amount to "Puritanism"; indeed, she believed that it would be in women's best interest to decrease the social emphasis on sex, since sexual equality, in the absence of pervasive cultural reform, would inevitably fail to liberate women.[71] Over time, many radicals themselves discovered that sexual freedom could not undo the systemic oppression of women that persisted in American society. There proved to be a "dark edge to sexual modernism": enduring inequalities that pervaded the very sexual relationships that were supposed to liberate women.[72] As Christine Stansell explains, "the structures of sexual modernism proved highly elastic in their ability to accommodate elements of the old sexual hierarchies"; even within seemingly egalitarian frameworks, male privilege endured.[73]

Historians have at times wondered at the shortsightedness of radicals who failed to discern "the infiltration of sexism into sex itself," who "somehow imagined that the assertion of female sexuality could erase deeply rooted male supremacy in the culture and in the economy."[74] But having embraced the new model of liberated womanhood, and having downplayed the differences between women and men, a new generation of feminists lacked the resources upon which to draw to formulate a coherent critique. The limitations of the new sexual framework were not readily apparent at the height of the revolution, however, and women like Bushnell who might have helped construct an alternative were quickly written off as reactionary vestiges of a time gone by.[75]

It is important to recall, however, that Bushnell remained as critical of Victorian morality as she was of the "new morality," and she considered both detrimental to the rights of women. And despite her marginalization within the movement, she continued to share a number of convictions with modern feminists. She, too, believed that women's social inequalities could not be sufficiently addressed in the political sphere alone, and she considered the sexual double standard, together with the traditional, patriarchal family, to be the chief obstacles to women's emancipation. And, like feminists, she believed that traditional Christianity had contributed significantly to the oppression of women.

In her attempt to chart an alternative course to both Victorian and modern arrangements, Bushnell was joined by a number of other Protestant women. In the 1920s, for example, several of Bushnell's fellow members of the Association of Women Preachers (the organization over which her friend Madeline Southard presided) pointedly refused to express alarm at the purported decline of American morality, even in the midst of the sexual emancipation of the "jazz age." Since they judged the Victorian moral system, with its double standard and systemic oppression of women, to be highly *immoral*, they considered modern departures fully comprehensible—even if not always ideal—for in the absence of an alternative, *truly* moral framework, they deemed the sexual license flaunted by young flappers a reasonable reaction to the injustices endemic to "traditional" morality.[76] Like Bushnell, these committed Christian women were sympathetic toward the anti-Christian sentiments that many feminists expressed, and they reasoned that radicals had good reason to claim that the church "had hindered more than helped the woman's cause."[77] They, too, shared Bushnell's vision that Christianity and morality must be transformed in order to bring proponents of women's rights back into the Christian fold, and in order to overcome an enduring cultural "feminitis."[78] But the voices of these women remained muted, both within American Protestantism and within the larger women's movement. As a result, little progress was made within American churches to envision a new sexual ethic, one both Christian and feminist, one based on biblical teachings yet committed to the emancipation and empowerment of women, and attuned to the realities of the modern world.

Conclusion

THE CHALLENGE OF CHRISTIAN FEMINISM

OVER THE COURSE of Bushnell's lifetime, changes within the American women's movement, together with developments within American Protestantism, dramatically altered the world in which Christian women found themselves. By the time of her death, the once-vibrant relationship between Christianity and feminism had diminished to the point that it did indeed seem difficult, if not impossible, to be both feminist and Christian. In her declining years, Bushnell was left to grapple with this disappointing reality.

In 1928, no longer at home in her own country, she returned to China, where she worked with evangelist Dora Yu at the Bible Study and Prayer House near Shanghai. While there, she continued to advocate social purity, hoping to counter the global reach of Snow's social hygiene program,[1] and also "to steady, a little, young women from taking their emancipation along perilous ways."[2] She remained in China until the Japanese invasion of Manchuria in 1931, which occasioned her return to Oakland.[3] Over the next decade she pursued her unrelenting crusade against birth control, alienating her former friends and supporters; by withdrawing from the British Association for Moral and Social Hygiene, she removed herself from the last community keeping alive the memory of her earlier crusades. Though she would never again command a national or international audience, Bushnell persisted in her waning years in authoring various Bible studies and social commentaries on sexuality and morality.[4] She continued to find solace in female companionship, and sought to share her home with women who functioned as secretaries, housekeepers, and confidants.[5] As late as 1943, her eyesight and hearing faltering, Bushnell was still attempting to recruit someone to carry on her purity work "in Mrs. Butler's uncompromising way." But even then, she did not consider her purity efforts to be her work of greatest significance; her "deeper interests" remained her biblical studies. As she reflected on her life's work in her last years, she lamented how the church, which at times had served as women's greatest resource, frequently "cabined, cribbed, confined, [and] bound down" women by promulgating traditional roles. And though she believed that she had made "some but slow progress in the emancipation of the church woman," she acknowledged that the work had "cost [her] heavily—it has been a hard field to labor in."[6] Despite the disappointments she had encountered, however, she remained certain that Christ was "the great emancipator of women," and that "if women were given their God-ordained place in the church, Christendom would expand in breadth and height of influence."[7]

Three years later, at the age of ninety, Bushnell fell ill. Even on her deathbed, however, she exhibited the pluck and devotion that had characterized so much of her life. Perhaps inspired by her "little pictured motto" of Phil. 4:13 ("I can do all things through Christ who strengthened me") that she kept with her to the end,[8] she gathered up her last remaining strength to witness to one of her neighbors, one final time.[9] On January 26, 1946, ten days shy of her ninety-first birthday, Bushnell died, an obscure and largely forgotten figure, a relic of a time gone by. The window of opportunity for women in church and society seemed to have closed. Few noted her passing, and the memory of her life and legacy quickly faded. In the words of her pastor, her work seemed like "a rock dropped to the bottom of the ocean. Kerplunk, it was gone, the end of it."[10]

Even with the rise of "second-wave" feminism in the 1960s and 1970s, Bushnell remained largely lost to history. Her devout religious faith, her unwavering commitment to a sexual ethic rooted in self-restraint, and her staunch opposition to birth control undoubtedly contributed to her exclusion from feminist histories of the women's movement.[11] It would be a mistake, however, to consider Bushnell's life's work a lost cause. As it turned out, a small number of devoted followers kept alive her memory in the decades after her death. Indeed, rather than a stone dropped in water, sunken into obscurity, her legacy might be better compared to ripples radiating across the water's surface, the influence of her life and work spreading slowly, sometimes almost imperceptibly, across time and space.

Even in the years before her death, copies of *God's Word to Women* continued to circulate around the globe; in the 1930s, the book was available at a number of "depots of supply" in England, Australia, New Zealand, India, China, Korea, and Germany, reflecting her earlier global travels.[12] Other writers, too, helped disseminate her teachings. In addition to Jessie Penn-Lewis's *Magna Charta of Women,* which was reprinted in 1929 and again in 1948, Lee Anna Starr's *Bible Status of Woman* drew heavily upon *God's Word to Women.*[13] First published in 1926, and again in 1955 by Alma White's Pillar of Fire Church, Starr's *Bible Status* provided a more readable account of several of Bushnell's key arguments. In 1940, as the Revised Version of the Bible was undergoing its own revision—once again at the hands of a committee composed entirely of men—Bushnell's friend Madeline Southard sent the head of the translation committee a copy of Starr's book, explaining that "a considerable number of church women" were "deeply concerned that the American Standard Bible . . . shall not perpetuate certain injustices to women."[14] A few months later, the chair of the committee informed Southard that they had found Starr's book to be "of real value," and assured her that they were doing their best "to guard against the sort of unfairness of which she writes."[15]

It would be outside the centers of power in American Protestantism, however, that *God's Word to Women* would exert the most influence. Passed along quietly from woman to woman, Bushnell's writings provided generations of Christian women with a biblical defense of female preaching and religious authority. Women like Georgia Harkness (a Methodist theologian and advocate for women's ecclesiastical rights), Theodora Gordon Hall (the daughter of Adoniram Judson Gordon, the Baptist founder of Gordon College and Gordon-Conwell Seminary), and Helena White Hubbard (an ordained Pentecostal minister and the mother of David Hubbard, the long-serving president of Fuller Theological Seminary) cherished their copies of *God's Word to Women.*[16] Not surprisingly, it was often among Pentecostals, heirs to the nineteenth-century holiness movement, that Bushnell's message found its most dedicated followers.

Only a few years after Bushnell's death, Ray Munson, a Pentecostal evangelist, came across Penn-Lewis's *Magna Charta* while holding a revival on an Indian reservation. Inspired by Penn-Lewis's excerpts of Bushnell's *God's Word to Women,* Munson set out to secure a copy of Bushnell's book. Despite being told it was "practically impossible to obtain," Munson persisted, and after several years he managed to locate a copy of the 1923 edition, which he then began to reproduce and distribute. He initially resorted to using a "miniature hand-copying machine" requiring nearly a week of labor per copy, and it wasn't until 1975 that he was able to reprint the book in greater quantities. Eight years later, Munson was joined in his efforts by two fellow Pentecostals, Cosette Jolliff and Bernice Menold, who, like Munson, had come across Bushnell's writings and wished to introduce her work to new audiences.[17]

As *God's Word to Women* became more widely available, its influence grew among a new generation of Christian feminists. A product of an earlier era, Bushnell's book enabled many evangelical women and men to envision a biblical feminism independent of the much-maligned "secular feminism" of their own time. Linked to the sexual revolution of the 1960s, this "second-wave" feminism paralleled in many ways the radical Feminism advanced by their early twentieth-century forebears. Embracing a sexual ethic based on liberation rather than restraint, many 1970s feminists championed birth control and abortion rights as essential to women's emancipation. And despite the involvement of many religious women in the early years of "second-wave" feminism, this resurgence of feminism was often stridently anti-Christian in tone.[18] This antagonism between Christianity and feminism was only heightened by the public re-emergence of conservative evangelicalism during the same period. As evangelicals began to mobilize politically in the 1970s and 1980s, issues of sexual morality frequently took center-stage. In opposition both to the sexual revolution and to modern feminism, evangelicals instead touted "traditional family values," advancing staunchly pronatalist positions that sacralized motherhood as women's God-given duty while opposing abortion and homosexuality as manifestations of sin and "crimes against reproduction."[19]

But Bushnell's theology provided an alternative to both "secular feminism" and "family-values" evangelicalism. By adhering to a conservative biblical hermeneutic while advancing feminist claims of female empowerment, Bushnell's book resonated with evangelicals searching for ways to reconcile their faith with contemporary gender arrangements. Even as Bushnell rejected a sexual ethic based on liberation, she nonetheless resisted the pronatalism and celebration of female domesticity that frequently characterized evangelical discussions of gender. As a new generation of Christian feminists discovered within Bushnell's writings a biblical foundation for women's rights, along with the basis for a powerful Christian critique of the abuse of women,[20] organizations like the Evangelical Women's Caucus and Christians for Biblical Equality helped recover Bushnell's memory and promote a new awareness of her work. In 1998, a group of Pentecostal women assisted in this effort by setting up a website that made available the entire text of *God's Word to Women*, along with several of Bushnell's other writings.[21]

When Bushnell first published *God's Word to Women*, the audience for a feminist theology based on a conservative hermeneutic was fast disappearing. But a century later, the audience for Bushnell's theology appears to be expanding, not only in light of the enduring presence of conservative evangelicalism in America, but also—and perhaps ultimately more significant—due to the remarkable growth of the Christian church in the developing world.[22] Through the efforts of Western missionaries, the global reach of the Internet, and the international presence of organizations such as Christians for Biblical Equality, Bushnell's teachings are once again finding a global audience.[23] Women and men in places as varied as Pakistan, Kenya, Ghana, Hungary, and Mexico are turning to Bushnell's writings in their efforts to discern God's will for women.[24]

Though it may at first seem incongruous that the nearly forgotten work of an American Victorian woman might find a receptive audience in the twenty-first-century global church, observers have in fact noted striking parallels connecting these seemingly disparate worlds. Like Victorians, many global Christians today are undertaking a profound re-examination of their cultural inheritance. And just as Victorian Christians looked to their faith to restructure society, present-day Christians in the global South are looking to the Bible as a guide to everyday matters ranging from gender and family structures to poverty and development.[25] Mirroring the efforts of Victorian reformers, many women in the "two-thirds world" are looking to the Scriptures for resources for female empowerment. Bushnell's efforts to redefine virtue for women and men, her insistence on the incompatibility of Christianity and patriarchy, and her defense of female preaching can be valuable tools in the hands of such women—women for whom a biblically based defense of women's rights may conform better to their own values and needs than do secular Western feminist ideologies. Given the theological creativity that cross-cultural engagement frequently sparks, it may well be that women in the global South, perhaps those finding inspiration in Bushnell's writings, will be among those to generate the most innovative and compelling feminist theologies to challenge and guide the Christian church in the next century.[26]

Bushnell has also received renewed attention in recent years from Christians working to combat human trafficking, in America and around the world. Organizations such as the Salvation Army and the International Justice Mission have found inspiration in Bushnell's life and work as they wage contemporary battles against the sexual oppression of women and children.[27] Reminiscent of the earlier social purity movement, contemporary anti-trafficking efforts have exhibited the rare potential to unite liberal feminists and evangelical Christians in common cause. It remains to be seen, however, whether contemporary activists will prove able to free themselves of the imperialistic assumptions that have so often accompanied Western women's endeavors to rescue and uplift "the oppressed heathen woman."[28] In their efforts to address the sexual oppression of women in the developing world, for example, evangelical organizations have tended to draw attention to backward cultural traditions, or to the actions of "evil" men, rather than to large-scale socio-economic issues—conditions in which Westerners themselves are often complicit.[29] It is also evident that, as in Bushnell's day, evangelicals' anti-trafficking efforts may have the potential to stifle a thoughtful critique of their own gender arrangements by focusing attention on the comparatively greater oppression of women globally. But it was Bushnell's willingness to turn a critical eye upon her own tradition that set her apart from her contemporaries, and that ultimately inspired her innovative feminist theology. Yet it remains unclear whether her example can provoke Western Christians today to reflect critically on the ways in which their own traditions might reinforce structures and ideologies that facilitate the oppression of women, both at home and abroad.

Given this renewed interest in Bushnell among twenty-first-century activists and Christians, it is appropriate to consider further the lessons that might be gleaned from her life and work. On the one hand, Bushnell exemplifies the potential for a robust Christian feminism. Her story demonstrates how conservative theological methods can foster progressive ends—a lesson worth considering in light of the remarkable resilience that conservative religious traditions have demonstrated in the modern world. Conversely, the exclusion of women like Bushnell from our histories can lend contemporary antagonisms between Christianity and feminism a sense of historical inevitability.

In the early stages of her career, Bushnell was buoyed by a close alliance with the larger women's movement. When that alliance broke down, the impact she could achieve within her own tradition, and beyond, was significantly diminished. Those working for the liberation of women within religious traditions have frequently labored—out of choice or necessity—in isolation from the larger feminist movement, but as Bushnell's story demonstrates, there may be much to be gained by opening up meaningful conversations between "secular" feminists and women in conservative religious traditions. Confronting entrenched patriarchies is a complicated endeavor, and one marked by contradictions and compromises. By giving ear to the voices of those on the margins, including women within conservative traditions, feminists may find ways to draw upon a longer and more varied tradition of feminism, one that might more effectively facilitate the development of a diversity of feminisms suited to the needs of the contemporary world.

Inasmuch as Bushnell's story discloses the productive possibilities of a faith-based feminism, however, her life and legacy also reveal the central problem confronting Christian feminists today: the challenge of constructing a thoroughly biblical, feminist sexual ethic. Even as the majority of American evangelicals have come to embrace more progressive gender roles, evangelicals remain sharply divided from feminists, and indeed from the majority of their fellow Americans, when it comes to sex.[30] Indeed, in opposition to the perceived promiscuity of contemporary society, which they attribute to the influences of modern feminism and its sexual ethic of liberation, many evangelicals have attempted to resurrect the nineteenth-century idealization of female purity. Through an elaborate "purity culture" consisting of scripted purity pledges, father-daughter balls, purity rings, and the rhetoric of warriors and princesses, evangelicals have worked to reinstitute an ethic of feminine restraint.[31]

On the surface, Bushnell's work might seem to support this emphasis on purity. Bushnell, too, emphasized purity and restraint, and found much to criticize in a feminist ethic of liberation. However, whereas contemporary evangelical purity culture focuses chiefly on the purity of young women—effectively re-establishing a sexual double standard reminiscent of Victorian morality—Bushnell ardently opposed such unequal measures. Remaining vigilant to the harm that such ideals could inflict upon women, Bushnell preferred instead to emphasize the need for men to exhibit purity and restraint. And whereas evangelical purity culture reinforces patriarchal relationships by assigning husbands and fathers prominent roles in guarding the purity of their wives and daughters, Bushnell denounced patriarchy, female domesticity, and any notion of women's inferiority or subordination. Most significant, Bushnell situated her ethic of restraint within a theology of women's social and religious emancipation. She opposed sexual liberation, birth control, and abortion not because she feared the emancipatory powers of female sexuality, but because she was convinced that the new sexual ethic would ultimately disempower women and play into the hands of sinful men. Bushnell's theology, then, presents a compelling challenge to contemporary evangelical purity culture, one that might offer useful guidance to twenty-first-century Christian feminists.

While Bushnell's writings can offer insight into contemporary issues, however, they do not offer a clear blueprint for Christian feminists seeking to construct a viable sexual ethic. As the trajectory of her own career makes clear, a sexual ethic formulated in the social and economic milieu of Victorian America may well be ill-suited to the realities of the modern world. Bushnell's social vision remained rooted in a Victorian worldview that highlighted women's vulnerability and advanced an antagonistic view of the relationship between women and men. While these perspectives made sense in the context of Victorian culture, they do not accurately reflect contemporary arrangements. The task for Christian feminists today, then, is to develop a sexual ethic based upon the Christian gospel—one of grace and liberation, for women and men—suited to the realities of the modern world.

It is unlikely, and perhaps even undesirable, that Christian feminists and their secular counterparts will see eye to eye on all questions relating to sexuality and morality, but the time may be right for religious and secular feminists to initiate dialogue around the issues that most divide them. As feminists continue to come to terms with the failure of feminism to liberate sex itself from the bonds of patriarchy, evangelicals, too, have begun to confront the limitations of their own value systems, particularly in light of a younger generation's unwillingness to practice the purity that their elders continue to preach. This may well be a propitious moment, for feminists and Christians alike, to reassess notions of sexuality, liberation, purity, and empowerment.[32] Recent studies, for example, have revealed the alarming inability of young women, evangelical and non-religious alike, to identify and resist sexual assault. It seems that both the evangelical purity culture and the sexualized "hook-up" culture on college campuses have left women ill-equipped to exercise agency over their own sexual experiences and identities.[33]

Among Christians and feminists, then, there remains a pressing need to develop a sexual ethic that both protects and empowers women, one linked to a vision for women's social, economic, and religious emancipation. This is true not only in America, but globally as well, where issues of sexuality and morality remain closely linked with women's rights, public health, and international development. Bushnell's global encounters triggered her innovative and critical theology; in an era of global Christianity, the voices of women from the two-thirds world promise to reshape existing frameworks and extend the conversation in ways yet to be seen.

In her own lifetime and today, Bushnell defies simple categorization. By placing women's rights at the very heart of the gospel, she was both liberal and conservative, orthodox and radical, feminist and Christian. Though her inability to fit securely within any movement limited her influence in her own day, it is precisely this transcendence of ideological, theological, and even geographic boundaries that enables her to provide fresh insights into critical issues today. Bushnell had long looked forward to a new era for women, to a time when the "new woman" in Christ would no more turn away from God and submit to man, as had Eve, but rather would remain "loyal to God alone"—to a time when women would lead men "out of the wilderness of the inefficiency of egotism into the glorious liberty of the children of God."[34] It remains the task of Christian feminists today to discover what shape that freedom might take for twenty-first-century women and men, the world over.

Works Cited

PRIMARY SOURCES

Manuscript Collections

Anne Henrietta Martin Papers, ca. 1892–1951; Bancroft Library, University of California, Berkeley.

Ethel Sturges Dummer Papers, ca. 1866–1954; Schlesinger Library, Radcliffe Institute, Harvard University, Cambridge, MA.

Josephine Butler Letters Collection, The Women's Library collections at LSE, London, England.

Luther Allan Weigle Papers, Sterling Memorial Library, Yale University, New Haven, CT.

M. Madeline (Mabel Madeline) Southard Papers, ca. 1878–1998; Schlesinger Library, Radcliffe Institute, Harvard University, Cambridge, MA.

Records of the Association for Moral & Social Hygiene, The Women's Library collections at LSE, London, England.

Records of the Northern Wisconsin "Slave" Investigation, 1882–1889, State Historical Society of Wisconsin, University of Wisconsin, Oshkosh.

Papers of Henry Joseph Wilson, The Women's Library collections at LSE, London, England.

Papers of Mrs. F. White, The Women's Library collections at LSE, London, England.

Papers of the Standard Bible Committee, Yale Divinity School, New Haven, CT.

Selected Newspapers, Magazines, and Journals

Heathen Woman's Friend
The Light
Medical Woman's Journal
Storm-Bell
The Union Signal

Works Cited

Watchman-Examiner
Woman Citizen
The Woman's Pulpit
W.C.T.U. State Work

Contemporary Printed Material

Andrew, Elizabeth W., and Katharine C. Bushnell. *A Fatal Mistake: To the W.C.T.U.* 1897.

Andrew, Elizabeth W., and Katharine C. Bushnell. *Heathen Slaves and Christian Rulers*. 1907. Project Gutenberg, 2004. http://www.gutenberg.org/catalog/world/readfile?fk_files=1999559.

Andrew, Elizabeth W., and Katharine C. Bushnell. *Reply of Dr. Katharine Bushnell and Mrs. Elizabeth Andrew to Certain Statements in a Published Letter Addressed by Lady Henry Somerset to a Correspondent on the Regulation of Vice in India*. London: Ladies' National Association, 1897.

Andrew, Elizabeth W., and Katharine C. Bushnell. *The Queen's Daughters in India*. London: Morgan and Scott, 1899. http://books.google.com/books?id=JJ9j8KKdNLQC.

Baker, Franc. *Historical Sketches of the Northwestern Branch of the Women's Foreign Missionary Society of the Methodist Episcopal Church*. Chicago: Jameson & Morse Co., 1887.

Beebe, Henry S. *The History of Peru*. Peru, IL: J. F. Linton, 1858. Digitized by the University of Illinois at Urbana-Champaign and available online at http://hdl.handle.net/10111/UIUCOCA:historyofperu00beeb.

Bushnell, Katharine C. *101 Questions Answered. A Woman's Catechism*. 1910.

Bushnell, Katharine C. *The Badge of Guilt and Shame*. Oakland, CA, n.d.

Bushnell, Katharine C. *Bible Interleaves: A Series of Notes*. 1920.

Bushnell, Katharine C. *A Clean Life*. 1896. Reprint, Chicago: Revell, 1901.

Bushnell, Katharine C. *Covet to Prophesy*. Oakland, CA, n.d.

Bushnell, Katharine C. *Dr. Katharine C. Bushnell: A Brief Sketch of Her Life Work*. Hertford: Rose & Sons, 1932.

Bushnell, Katharine C. *God's Word to Women: One Hundred Bible Studies on Woman's Place in the Divine Economy*. Oakland, CA: Katharine C. Bushnell, 1923. Reprint, Peoria, IL: Cosette McCleave Jolliff and Bernice Martin Menold, n.d.

Bushnell, Katharine C. *Mother's Catechism on Adam and Eve*. Oakland, CA, 1924.

Bushnell, Katharine C. *Mother's Catechism on the Seventh of First Corinthians*. Oakland, CA, 1938.

Bushnell, Katharine C. *The Reverend Doctor and His Doctor Daughter*. Oakland, CA, 1924.

Bushnell, Katharine C. *The Supreme Virtue*. Oakland, CA, 1924.

Bushnell, Katharine C. *The Vashti-Esther Bible Story*. Piedmont, CA, 1945.

Bushnell, Katharine C. "What's Going On? A Report of Investigations by Katharine C. Bushnell Regarding Certain Social and Legal Abuses in California That Have Been in Part Aggravated and in Part Created by the Federal Social Hygiene Programme." Oakland, CA, n.d.

Bushnell, Katharine C. *The Woman Condemned*. New York: Funk & Wagnalls, 1886.

Butler, Josephine. *The Constitution Violated*. Edinburgh: Edmonston & Douglas, 1871.

Butler, Josephine. "The Present Aspect of the Abolitionist Cause in Relation to British India." Reprinted in *Josephine Butler and The Prostitution Campaigns: Diseases of the Body Politic*, edited by Jane Jordan and Ingrid Sharp. London: Routledge, 2003.

Catalogue of the Officers and Students of the Northwestern Female College and Male and Female Preporatory. Chicago: R. L. & C. L. Wilson & Col., 1856.

Cavert, Inez M. *Women in American Church Life: A Study Prepared under the Guidance of a Counseling Committee of Women Representing National Interdenominational Agencies*. New York: Friendship Press, published for the Federal Council of the Churches of Christ in America, 1949.

Drysdale, Euphemia. "Woman and the Ministry." *Homiletic Review* 33, no. 5 (May 1922): 347–353.

Fitzpatrick, Kathleen. *Lady Henry Somerset*. Boston: Little, Brown, and Company, 1923.

Foster, John O. *Life and Labors of Mrs. Maggie Newton Van Cott*. Cincinnati, OH: Hitchcock and Walden, 1872.

Gifford, Carolyn De Swarte, ed. *Writing Out My Heart: Selections from the Journal of Frances E. Willard, 1855–96*. Urbana: University of Illinois Press, 1995.

Gordon, Anna A. *The Beautiful Life of Frances E. Willard*. Chicago: Women's Temperance Publishing Association, 1898.

Gracey, Annie Ryder. *Medical Work of the Woman's Foreign Missionary Society, Methodist Episcopal Church*. Dansville, NY: A. O. Bunnell, 1881.

Grimké, Sarah. *Letters on the Equality of the Sexes, and the Condition of Woman: Addressed to Mary S. Parker*. Boston: I. Knapp, 1838.

History of La Salle County, Illinois. Chicago: Inter-State Pub. Co., 1886. http://books.google.com/books?id=IYE_AAAAYAAJ.

Minutes of the National Woman's Christian Temperance Union at the Eleventh Annual Meeting in St. Louis, Missouri, 1884. Chicago: Woman's Temperance Publication Association, 1884.

Minutes of the Second Biennial Convention of the World's Woman's Christian Temperance Union. Chicago: Woman's Temperance Publishing Association, 1893.

Minutes of the Third Biennial Convention and Executive Committee Meetings of the World's Woman's Christian Temperance Union. London: The White Ribbon Company, 1895.

"Miss Kate Bushnell." In *A Woman of the Century*, edited by Frances E. Willard and Mary A. Livermore. Buffalo, NY: Charles Wells Moulton, 1893.

Penn-Lewis, Jessie. *The Magna Charta of Woman According to the Scriptures: Being Light Upon the Subject Gathered from Dr. Katherine Bushnell's Text Book, "God's Word to Women."* Bournemouth, England: The Overcomer Book Room, 1919.

Reeling, Viola Couch. *Evanston: Its Land and Its People.* Evanston, IL: Daughters of the American Revolution, Evanston Chapter, 1928.

Sanger, Margaret. "The Civilizing Force of Birth Control." 1929. In *Sex in Civilization,* edited by V. F. Calverton and Samuel Daniel Schmalhausen, 525–537. New York: The Macaulay Co., 1939.

Stanton, Elizabeth Cady. *Woman's Bible.* 1895–1898. Reprint, New York: Arno Press, 1972.

Stead, William T. *The Americanization of the World, or the Trend of the Twentieth Century.* New York: Horace Markley, 1902. https://openlibrary.org/books/OL13514186M/The_Americanization_of_the_world.

Twelfth Annual Announcement and Catalogue of the Woman's Medical College of Chicago. Chicago: Brown Pettibone & Kelley, 1881.

Willard, Frances. *A Classic Town: The Story of Evanston.* Chicago: Woman's Temperance Publishing Association, 1891. http://books.google.com/books?id=_tUNAQAAMAAJ.

Willard, Frances. *Glimpses of Fifty Years: The Autobiography of an American Woman.* Chicago: H. J. Smith & Co., published by the Woman's Temperance Publication Association, 1889. http://books.google.com/books?isbn=1152924893.

Willard, Frances. *Woman in the Pulpit.* Boston: D. Lothrop, 1888.

Wilson, Elizabeth. *A Scriptural View of Woman's Rights and Duties, in All the Important Relations of Life.* Philadelphia: Wm. S. Young, 1849.

Women's Medical School: Northwestern University (Woman's Medical College of Chicago) Class Histories 1870–1890. Chicago: H. G. Butler, 1896.

SECONDARY SOURCES

Banks, Adelle M. "Evangelicals Say It's Time for Frank Talk about Sex." Religion News Service. Accessed January 9, 2013. http://archives.religionnews.com/culture/gender-and-sexuality/Evangelicals-say-its-time-for-frank-talk-about-sex.

Barkan, Elazar, and Ronald Bush. "Introduction." In *Prehistories of the Future: The Primitivist Project and the Culture of Modernism,* edited by Barkan and Bush. Stanford, CA: Stanford University Press, 1995.

Beatty, William. "Katharine Bushnell, M.D.—Evangelist and Investigator." *Union Signal.* July, August, & September, 1997.

Beaver, R. Pierce. *All Loves Excelling: American Protestant Women in World Mission.* Grand Rapids, MI: Eerdmans, 1968.

Bederman, Gail. *Manliness and Civilization: A Cultural History of Gender and Race in the United States, 1880–1917.* Chicago: University of Chicago Press, 1995.

Bederman, Gail. "'The Women Have Had Charge of the Church Work Long Enough': The Men and Religion Forward Movement of 1911–1912 and the Masculinization of Middle-Class Protestantism." *American Quarterly* 41, no. 3 (September 1989): 432–465.

Bendroth, Margaret Lamberts. *Fundamentalism and Gender: 1875 to the Present.* New Haven, CT: Yale University Press, 1996.

Bendroth, Margaret Lamberts. "Religion, Feminism, and the American Family: 1865–1920." In *Religion, Feminism, and the Family,* edited by Anne E. Carr and Mary Stewart Van Leeuwen, 183–196. Louisville, KY: Westminster John Knox Press, 1996.

Berg, Barbara J. *The Remembered Gate: Origins of American Feminism: The Woman and the City, 1800–1860.* New York: Oxford University Press, 1978.

Bernstein, Elizabeth. "Militarized Humanitarianism Meets Carceral Feminism: The Politics of Sex, Rights, and Freedom in Contemporary Antitrafficking Campaigns." *Signs* 36 (Autumn 2010): 45–71.

Bloch, Ruth. "Republican Virtue: The Gendered Meanings of Virtue in Revolutionary America." Chap. 7 in *Gender and Morality in Anglo-American Culture, 1650–1800.* Berkeley: University of California Press, 2003.

Bordin, Ruth. *Frances Willard: A Biography.* Chapel Hill: University of North Carolina Press, 1986.

Bordin, Ruth. *Woman and Temperance: The Quest for Power and Liberty, 1873–1900.* Philadelphia: Temple University Press, 1981.

Bosch, David J. *Transforming Mission: Paradigm Shifts in Theology of Mission.* Maryknoll, NY: Orbis Books, 1991.

Boyd, Lois A., and R. Douglas Brackenridge. *Presbyterian Women in America: Two Centuries of a Quest for Status.* Westport, CT: Greenwood Press, 1983.

Boylan, Anne. "Women in Groups: An Analysis of Women's Benevolent Organizations in New York and Boston, 1797–1840." *Journal of American History* 71 (December 1984): 497–523.

Braude, Ann. "A Religious Feminist—Who Can Find Her? Historiographical Challenges from the National Organization for Women." *Journal of Religion* 84, no. 4 (October 2004): 555–572.

Braude, Ann. "Women's History is American Religious History." In *Retelling U.S. Religious History,* edited by Thomas A. Tweed, 87–107. Berkeley: University of California Press, 1997.

Brekus, Catherine A. *Strangers and Pilgrims: Female Preaching in America, 1740–1845.* Chapel Hill: University of North Carolina Press, 1998.

Brereton, Virginia Lieson. "United and Slighted: Women as Subordinated Insiders." In *Between the Times: The Travail of the Protestant Establishment in America, 1900–1960,* edited by William R. Hutchison, 143–167. Cambridge: Cambridge University Press, 1989.

Brumberg, Joan Jacobs. "The Ethnological Mirror: American Evangelical Women and Their Heathen Sisters, 1870–1910." In *Women and the Structure of Society,* edited by Barbara J. Harris and JoAnn McNamara, 108–208. Durham, NC: Duke University Press, 1984.

Bullard, Roger A. "Feminine and Feminist Touches in the Centenary New Testament." *Bible Translator* 38 (January 1987): 118–122.

Bunkle, Phillida. "The Origins of the Women's Movement in New Zealand: The Woman's Christian Temperance Union 1885–1895." In *Women in New Zealand Society*, edited by Phillida Bunkle and Beryl Hughes, 52–76. Auckland, New Zealand: George Allen & Unwin, 1980.

Burton, Antoinette. *Burdens of History: British Feminists, Indian Women, and Imperial Culture, 1865–1915*. Chapel Hill: University of North Carolina Press, 1994.

Calvert-Koyzis, Nancy, and Heather Weir, eds. *Breaking Boundaries: Female Biblical Interpreters Who Challenged the Status Quo*. New York: T & T Clark, 2010.

Case, Jay Riley. *An Unpredictable Gospel: American Evangelicals and World Christianity, 1912–1920*. New York: Oxford University Press, 2012.

Clark, Elizabeth Battelle. "The Politics of God and the Woman's Vote: Religion in the American Suffrage Movement, 1848–1895." PhD dissertation, Princeton University, 1989.

Cott, Nancy F. *The Bonds of Womanhood: "Woman's Sphere" in New England, 1780–1835*. New Haven, CT: Yale University Press, 1977.

Cott, Nancy F. *The Grounding of Modern Feminism*. New Haven, CT: Yale University Press, 1987.

Cox, Jeffrey. *Imperial Fault Lines: Christianity and Colonial Power in India, 1818–1940*. Stanford, CA: Stanford University Press, 2002.

Dannenbaum, Jed. *Temperance Reform in Cincinnati from the Washington Revival to the WCTU*. Urbana: University of Illinois Press, 1984.

Dayton, Donald W. *Discovering an Evangelical Heritage*. New York: Harper & Row, 1976.

De Berg, Betty. *Ungodly Women: Gender and the First Wave of American Fundamentalism*. Minneapolis: Fortress Press, 1990.

De Groot, Christiana, and Marion Ann Taylor, eds. *Recovering Nineteenth-Century Women Interpreters of the Bible*. Atlanta, GA: Society of Biblical Literature, 2007.

Demers, Patricia. *Women as Interpreters of the Bible*. Mahwah, NJ: Paulist Press, 1992.

D'Emilio, John, and Estelle B. Freedman. *Intimate Matters: A History of Sexuality in America*. 3rd ed. Chicago: University of Chicago Press, 2012.

Dieter, Melvin E. *The Holiness Revival of the Nineteenth Century*. Metuchen, NJ: Scarecrow Press, 1980.

Donovan, Brian. *White Slave Crusades: Race, Gender, and Anti-Vice Activism, 1887–1917*. Urbana: University of Illinois Press, 2006.

Douglas, Ann. *The Feminization of American Culture*. New York: Knopf, 1977.

Dowd, Sharyn. "Helen Barrett Montgomery's *Centenary Translation* of the New Testament: Characteristics and Influences." *Perspectives in Religious Studies* 19 (Summer 1992): 133–150.

Du Mez, Kristin Kobes. "Reorienting American Religious History: The Case of Katharine Bushnell." In *American Evangelicalism: George Marsden and the State of American Religious History*, edited Darren Dochuk, Thomas S. Kidd, and Kurt W. Peterson, 180–198. Notre Dame: University of Notre Dame Press, 2014.

Earhart, Mary. *Frances Willard: From Prayers to Politics.* Chicago: University of Chicago Press, 1944.

Epstein, Barbara Leslie. "Family, Sexual Morality, and Popular Movements in Turn-of-the-Century America." In *Powers of Desire: The Politics of Sexuality*, edited by Ann Snitow, Christine Stansell, and Sharon Thompson, 117–130. New York: The Monthly Review Press, 1983.

Epstein, Barbara Leslie. *The Politics of Domesticity: Women, Evangelism, and Temperance in Nineteenth-Century America.* Middletown, CT: Wesleyan University Press, 1981.

Fishburn, Janet Forsythe. *The Fatherhood of God and the Victorian Family: The Social Gospel in America.* Philadelphia: Fortress Press, 1981.

Fitzgerald, Maureen. "Losing Their Religion: Women, the State, and the Ascension of Secular Discourse, 1890–1930." In *Women and Twentieth-Century Protestantism*, edited by Margaret Lamberts Bendroth and Virginia Lieson Brereton, 280–303. Urbana: University of Illinois Press, 2002.

Flammang, Lucretia A. " 'And Your Sons and Daughters Will Prophesy': The Voice and Vision of Josephine Butler." In *Women's Theology in Nineteenth-Century Britain: Transfiguring the Faith of Their Fathers*, edited by Julie Melnyk, 151–164. New York: Garland, 1998.

Freitas, Donna. *Sex and the Soul: Juggling Sexuality, Spirituality, Romance, and Religion on America's College Campuses.* New York: Oxford University Press, 2008.

Gifford, Carolyn De Swarte. " 'The Woman's Cause Is Man's'? Frances Willard and the Social Gospel." In *Gender and the Social Gospel*, edited by Wendy J. Deichmann Edwards and Carolyn De Swarte Gifford, 21–34. Urbana: University of Illinois Press, 2003.

Ginzberg, Lori D. *Women and the Work of Benevolence: Morality, Politics, and Class in the Nineteenth-Century United States.* New Haven, CT: Yale University Press, 1990.

Gordon, Linda. *The Moral Property of Women: A History of Birth Control Politics in America.* 3rd ed. Urbana: University of Illinois Press, 2002.

Gordon, Linda. "What's New in Women's History." In *Feminist Studies/Critical Studies*, edited by Theresa de Lauretis, 20–30. Bloomington: Indiana University Press, 1986.

Greenlee, J. Harold. *Introduction to New Testament Textual Criticism.* Peabody, MA: Hendrickson, 2005.

Gripe, Elizabeth Howell. "Women, Restructuring and Unrest in the 1920s." *Journal of Presbyterian History* 52 (Summer 1974): 188–199.

Hall, Catherine. *Civilising Subjects: Colony and Metropole in the English Imagination, 1830–1867.* Chicago: University of Chicago Press, 2002.

Hamilton, Michael S. "Women, Public Ministry, and American Fundamentalism, 1920–1950." *Religion and American Culture* 3, no. 2 (Summer 1993): 171–196.

Hardesty, Nancy A. *Women Called to Witness: Evangelical Feminism in the Nineteenth Century.* Nashville, TN: Abindon Press, 1984

Hardesty, Nancy, Lucille Sider Dayton, and Donald W. Dayton. "Women in the Holiness Movement: Feminism in the Evangelical Tradition." In *Women of Spirit: Female Leadership in the Jewish and Christian Traditions,* edited by Rosemary Radford Ruether and Eleanor McLaughlin, 225–254. New York: Simon & Schuster, 1979.

Hardwick, Dana. *Oh Thou Woman That Bringest Good Tidings: The Life and Work of Katharine C. Bushnell.* Kearney, NE: Morris Publishing, published for Christians for Biblical Equality, 1995.

Hassey, Janette. *No Time for Silence: Evangelical Women in Public Ministry Around the Turn of the Century.* Grand Rapids, MI: Academie Books, 1986.

Hatch, Nathan O. "The Puzzle of American Methodism." In *Methodism and the Shaping of American Culture,* edited by Nathan O. Hatch and John H. Wigger, 23–40. Nashville, TN: Kingswood Books, 2001.

Haugen, Gary. *Good News about Injustice: A Witness of Courage in a Hurting World.* Rev. ed. Downers Grove, IL: InterVarsity Press, 2009.

Hearn, Virginia. "New Publishers of Katherine Bushnell." *Update: Newsletter of the Evangelical Women's Caucus* 11, no. 4 (Winter 1987–1988): 7–8.

Hewitt, Nancy A. *Women's Activism and Social Change: Rochester, New York, 1822–1872.* Ithaca: Cornell University Press, 1984.

Hill, Patricia. *The World Their Household.* Ann Arbor: University of Michigan Press, 1985.

Hobson, Barbara Meil. *Uneasy Virtue: The Politics of Prostitution and the American Reform Tradition.* New York: Basic Books, 1987.

Hoppin, Ruth. "The Legacy of Katherine Bushnell." *Priscilla Papers* 9, no. 1 (Winter 1995): 8–10.

Hutchison, William R. *The Modernist Impulse in American Protestantism.* Durham, NC: Duke University Press, 1992.

Hunter, Jane H. *The Gospel of Gentility: American Women Missionaries in Turn-of-the-Century China.* New Haven, CT: Yale University Press, 1984.

Hunter, Jane H. "Women's Mission in Historical Perspective: American Identity and Christian Internationalism." In *Competing Kingdoms: Women, Mission, Nation, and the American Protestant Empire, 1812–1960,* edited by Barbara Reeves-Ellington, Kathryn Kish Sklar, and Connie A. Shemo, 19–42. Durham, NC: Duke University Press, 2010.

Hlavka, Heather R. "Normalizing Sexual Violence: Young Women Account for Harassment and Abuse." *Gender & Society* 28 (February 2014): 337–358.

Isenberg, Nancy. *Sex and Citizenship in Antebellum America.* Chapel Hill: University of North Carolina Press, 1998.

Jayawardena, Kumari. *The White Woman's Other Burden: Western Women and South Asia during British Colonial Rule*. New York: Routledge, 1995.

Jenkins, Philip. *The New Faces of Christianity*. New York: Oxford University Press, 2006.

Joiner, Thekla Ellen. *Sin in the City: Chicago and Revivalism, 1880–1920*. Columbia: University of Missouri Press, 2007.

Jordan, Jane, and Ingrid Sharp, eds. *Josephine Butler and the Prostitution Campaigns: Diseases of the Body Politic*. London: Routledge, 2003.

Kaplan, Amy. "Manifest Domesticity." *American Literature* 70, no. 3 (September 1998): 581–606.

Katz, Jonathan Ned. *The Invention of Heterosexuality*. New York: Dutton, 1995.

Keller, Rosemary Skinner, and Hildah F. Thomas. "The Status of Women in Institutional Church Life." Section IV in *Women in New Worlds: Historical Perspectives on the Wesleyan Tradition*. Nashville, TN: Abingdon Press, 1981.

Kerber, Linda K. *Women of the Republic: Intellect and Ideology in Revolutionary America*. Published for the Omohundro Institute of Early American History and Culture. Chapel Hill: University of North Carolina Press, 1980.

Kern, Kathi. *Mrs. Stanton's Bible*. Ithaca, NY: Cornell University Press, 2002.

Kraditor, Aileen S. *The Ideas of the Woman Suffrage Movement*. 1965. Reprint, New York: W. W. Norton & Company, 1981.

Kroeger, Catherine Clark. "The Legacy of Katherine Bushnell: A Hermeneutic for Women of Faith." *Priscilla Papers* 9, no. 4 (Fall 1995): 1–5.

Kunzel, Regina G. *Fallen Women, Problem Girls: Unmarried Mothers and the Professionalization of Social Work, 1890–1945*. New Haven, CT: Yale University Press, 1993.

Larsen, Timothy. *A People of One Book: The Bible and the Victorians*. New York: Oxford University Press, 2011.

Lerner, Gerda. "One Thousand Years of Feminist Biblical Criticism." Chap. 7 in *The Creation of Feminist Consciousness from the Middle Ages to Eighteen-Seventy*. New York: Oxford University Press, 1993.

Levine, Philippa. *Prostitution, Race, and Politics: Policing Venereal Disease in the British Empire*. New York: Routledge, 2003.

Levine, Philippa. "Sexuality and Empire." In *At Home with Empire: Metropolitan Culture and the Imperial World*, edited by Catherine Hall and Sonya O. Rose, 122–142. Cambridge: Cambridge University Press, 2006.

Loades, Ann. "Elizabeth Cady Stanton's *The Woman's Bible*." In *The Oxford Handbook of the Reception History of the Bible*, edited by Michael Lieb, Emma Mason, and Jonathan Roberts, 307–322. New York: Oxford University Press, 2011.

Long, Kathryn T. "Consecrated Respectability: Phoebe Palmer and the Refinement of American Methodism." In *Methodism and the Shaping of American Culture*, edited by Nathan O. Hatch and John H. Wigger, 281–308. Nashville, TN: Kingswood Books, 2001.

MacKell, Jan. *Red Light Women of the Rocky Mountains.* Albuquerque: University of New Mexico Press, 2009.

Marsden, George M. *Fundamentalism and American Culture.* New York: Oxford University Press, 1980.

Mathers, Helen. "The Evangelical Spirituality of a Victorian Feminist: Josephine Butler, 1828–1906." *Journal of Ecclesiastical History* 52, no. 3 (April 2001): 282–312.

McAlister, Melani. "The Politics of Persecution." *Middle East Report*, no. 249 (Winter 2008): 18–27.

McLoughlin, William A. *Billy Sunday Was His Real Name.* Chicago: University of Chicago Press, 1955.

Meyerowitz, Joanne. "Sexual Geography and Gender Economy: The Furnished Room Districts of Chicago, 1890–1930." *Gender & History* 2, no. 3 (Autumn 1990): 274–297.

Moberg, David O. *The Great Reversal: Evangelism versus Social Concern.* Philadelphia: Lippincott, 1972.

Moreton, Bethany. "Why Is There So Much Sex in Christian Conservatism and Why Do So Few Historians Care Anything about It?" *Journal of Southern History* 75, no. 3 (August 2009): 717–738.

Newsom, Carol A., Sharon H. Ringe, and Jacqueline E. Lapsley, eds. *The Women's Bible Commentary.* 3rd ed. Louisville, KY: Westminster John Knox, 2012.

Noll, Mark A. *The New Shape of World Christianity.* Downers Grove, IL: IVP Academic, 2009.

Nolland, Lisa Severine. *A Victorian Feminist Christian: Josephine Butler, the Prostitutes and God.* Waynesboro, GA: Paternoster, 2004.

Pascoe, Peggy. *Relations of Rescue: The Search for Female Moral Authority in the American West, 1874–1939.* New York: Oxford University Press, 1990.

Pellauer, Mary D. *Toward a Tradition of Feminist Theology: The Religious Social Thought of Elizabeth Cady Stanton, Susan B. Anthony, and Anna Howard Shaw.* Brooklyn, NY: Carlson Publishing, 1991.

Pivar, David J. *Purity and Hygiene: Women, Prostitution, and the "American Plan," 1900–1930.* Westport, CT: Greenwood Press, 2002.

Pivar, David J. *Purity Crusade: Sexual Morality and Social Control, 1868–1900.* Westport, CT: Greenwood Press, 1973.

Putnam, Robert D., and David E. Campbell. *American Grace: How Religion Divides and Unites Us.* New York: Simon & Shuster, 2010.

Pruitt, Lisa Joy. *A Looking-Glass for Ladies: American Protestant Women and the Orient in the Nineteenth Century.* Macon, GA: Mercer University Press, 2005.

Renda, Mary A. "Conclusion: Doing Everything: Religion, Race, and Empire in the U.S. Protestant Women's Missionary Enterprise, 1812–1960." In *Competing Kingdoms: Women, Mission, Nation, and the American Protestant Empire, 1812–1960,* edited by Barbara Reeves-Ellington, Kathryn Kish Sklar, and Connie A. Shemo, 367–390. Durham, NC: Duke University Press, 2010.

Robert, Dana L. *American Women in Mission: A Social History of Their Thought and Practice*. Macon, GA: Mercer University Press, 1996.

Robert, Dana L. *Christian Mission: How Christianity Became a World Religion*. Chichester, UK: Wiley-Blackwell, 2009.

Robert, Dana L. "The 'Christian Home' as a Cornerstone of Anglo-American Missionary Thought and Practice." In *Converting Colonialism: Visions and Realities in Mission History, 1706–1914*, edited by Dana L. Robert, 134–165. Grand Rapids, MI: Eerdmans, 2008.

Robert, Dana L. "The Influence of American Missionary Women on the World Back Home." *Religion and American Culture* 12, no. 1 (Winter 2002): 59–89.

Robert, Dana L. "World Christianity as a Women's Movement." *International Bulletin of Missionary Research* 30, no. 4 (2006): 180–188.

Rosen, Christine. *Preaching Eugenics: Religious Leaders and the American Eugenics Movement*. New York: Oxford University Press, 2004.

Rosen, Ruth. *The Lost Sisterhood: Prostitution in America, 1900–1918*. Baltimore, MD: The Johns Hopkins University Press, 1982.

Rosenberg, Emily. *Spreading the American Dream: American Economic and Cultural Expansion, 1890–1945*. New York: Hill and Wang, 1982.

Ryan, Mary P. *Cradle of the Middle Class: The Family in Oneida County, New York, 1780–1865*. Cambridge: Cambridge University Press, 1981.

Rydell, Robert W. *All the World's a Fair: Visions of Empire at American International Expositions, 1876–1916*. University of Chicago Press, 1987.

Saiving Goldstein, Valerie. "The Human Situation: A Feminine View." *The Journal of Religion* 40, no. 2 (April 1960): 100–112.

Sanneh, Lamin O. *Encountering the West: Christianity and the Global Cultural Process: The African Dimension*. Maryknoll, NY: Orbis Books, 1993.

Scanzoni, Letha Dawson, and Susan Setta. "Women in Evangelical, Holiness, and Pentecostal Traditions." In *Women and Religion in America*, Volume 3: *1900–1968*, edited by Rosemary Radford Ruether and Rosemary Skinner Keller, 223–265. San Francisco: Harper & Row, 1986.

Schmidt, Jean Miller. *Souls or the Social Order: The Two-Party System in American Protestantism*. Brooklyn: Carlson Publishing, 1991.

Schneider, A. Gregory. *The Way of the Cross Leads Home: The Domestication of American Methodism*. Bloomington: Indiana University Press, 1993.

Secrest, Clark. *Hell's Belles: Prostitution, Vice, and Crime in Early Denver*. Revised edition. Boulder: University Press of Colorado, 2002.

Selvidge, Marla. *Notorious Voices: Feminist Biblical Interpretations, 1500–1920*. New York: Continuum, 1996.

Shemo, Connie Anne. *The Chinese Medical Ministries of Kang Cheng and Shi Meiyu, 1872–1937*. Bethlehem, PA: Lehigh University Press, 2011.

Simmons, Christina. "Modern Sexuality and the Myth of Victorian Repression." In *Passion and Power: Sexuality in History*, edited by Kathy Peiss and Christina Simmons, 157–177. Philadelphia: Temple University Press, 1989.

Sklar, Kathryn Kish. *Catharine Beecher: A Study in American Domesticity*. New Haven, CT: Yale University Press, 1973.

Smith Rosenberg, Carroll. "The Female World of Love and Ritual: Relations Between Women in Nineteenth-Century America." *Signs* 1, no. 1 (Autumn 1975): 1–29.

Smith-Rosenberg, Carroll. "The New Woman as Androgyne: Social Order and Gender Crisis, 1870–1936." In *Disorderly Conduct: Visions of Gender in Victorian America*, 245–296. New York: A. A. Knopf, 1985.

Stanley, Brian. *The Bible and the Flag: Protestant Missions and British Imperialism in the Nineteenth and Twentieth Centuries*. Leicester, UK: Apollos, 1990.

Stanley, Susie C. "Wesleyan/Holiness Churches: Innocent Bystanders in the Fundamentalist/Modernist Controversy." In *Re-Forming the Center: American Protestantism, 1900 to the Present*, edited by Douglas Jacobsen and William Vance Trollinger, Jr., 172–193. Grand Rapids, MI: Eerdmans, 1998.

Stansell, Christine. *American Moderns: Bohemian New York and the Creation of a New Century*. New York: Metropolitan Books, 2000.

Stansell, Christine. *City of Women: Sex and Class in New York, 1789–1860*. New York: Alfred A. Knopf, 1986.

Stocking, George W. *Victorian Anthropology*. New York: Free Press, 1987.

Stoler, Ann Laura. *Race and the Education of Desire: Foucault's History of Sexuality and the Colonial Order of Things*. Durham, NC: Duke University Press, 1995.

Synan, Vinson. *The Holiness-Pentecostal Movement in the United States*. Grand Rapids, MI: Eerdmans, 1971.

Taves, Ann. *The Household of Faith: Roman Catholic Devotions in Mid-Nineteenth-Century America*. Notre Dame, IN: University of Notre Dame Press, 1986.

Taylor, Marion Ann, and Agnes Choi, eds. *Handbook of Women Biblical Interpreters: A Historical and Bibliographical Guide*. Grand Rapids, MI: Baker Academic, 2012.

Taylor, Marion Ann, and Heather E. Weir, eds. *Let Her Speak for Herself: Nineteenth-Century Women Writing on the Women of Genesis*. Waco, TX: Baylor University Press, 2006.

Theusen, Peter J. *In Discordance with the Scriptures: American Protestant Battles over Translating the Bible*. New York: Oxford University Press, 1999.

Thorne, Susan. "Missionary-Imperial Feminism." In *Gendered Missions: Women and Men in Missionary Discourse and Practice*, edited by Mary Taylor Huber and Nancy C. Lutkehaus, 39–65. Ann Arbor: University of Michigan Press, 1999.

Thorne, Susan. "Religion and Empire at Home." In *At Home with Empire: Metropolitan Culture and the Imperial World*, edited by Catherine Hall and Sonya O. Rose, 143–165. Cambridge: Cambridge University Press, 2006.

Tyrrell, Ian. *Woman's World/Woman's Empire: The Woman's Christian Temperance Union in International Perspective, 1880–1930*. Chapel Hill: University of North Carolina Press, 1991.

Tyrrell, Ian. "Women, Missions, and Empire: New Approaches to American Cultural Expansion." In *Competing Kingdoms: Women, Mission, Nation, and the American Protestant Empire, 1812–1960*, edited by Barbara Reeves-Ellington, Kathryn Kish Sklar, and Connie A. Shemo, 43–68. Durham, NC: Duke University Press, 2010.

Uglow, Jenny. "Josephine Butler: From Sympathy to Theory." In *Feminist Theorists: Three Centuries of Key Women Thinkers*, edited by Dale Spender, 146–164. New York: Pantheon Books, 1983.

Wacker, Grant. "The Holy Spirit and the Spirit of the Age in American Protestantism, 1880–1910." *Journal of American History* 72 (June 1985): 45–62.

Walkowitz, Judith R. *City of Dreadful Delight: Narratives of Sexual Danger in Late-Victorian London*. Chicago: University of Chicago Press, 1992.

Walkowitz, Judith R. "Male Vice and Female Virtue: Feminism and the Politics of Prostitution in Nineteenth-Century Britain." In *Powers of Desire: The Politics of Sexuality*, edited by Ann Snitow, Christine Stansell, and Sharon Thompson, 419–438. New York: The Monthly Review Press, 1983.

Walkowitz, Judith R. *Prostitution and Victorian Society: Women, Class and the State*. Cambridge: Cambridge University Press, 1980.

Walls, Andrew F. "Christian Scholarship in Africa in the Twenty-first Century." *Journal of African Christian Thought* 4, no. 2 (December 2001): 44–52.

Walls, Andrew F. *The Cross-Cultural Process in Christian History*. Maryknoll, NY: Orbis Books, 2002.

Walls, Andrew F. *The Missionary Movement in Christian History: Studies in the Transmission of Faith*. Maryknoll, NY: Orbis Books, 1996.

Welch, Claude. *Protestant Thought in the Nineteenth Century*. Vol. 2. New Haven, CT: Yale University Press, 1985.

Welter, Barbara. "The Cult of True Womanhood: 1820–1860." *American Quarterly* 18, no. 2 (Summer, 1966): 151–174.

Welter, Barbara. "The Feminization of American Religion." Ch. 6 in *Dimity Convictions: The American Woman in the Nineteenth Century*. Athens: Ohio University Press, 1976.

Wigger, John H. *Taking Heaven by Storm: Methodism and the Rise of Popular Christianity in America*. New York: Oxford University Press, 1998.

Williamson, Harold Francis, and Payson Sibley Wild. *Northwestern University: A History, 1850–1975*. Evanston, IL: Northwestern University Press, 1976.

Notes

1. In my efforts to situate Katharine Bushnell in terms of the history of feminism and "Christian feminism," I follow the lead of Nancy Cott when it comes to employing the term "feminism," attempting "to root the term in history without unnecessarily limiting its current applications" (Nancy F. Cott, *The Grounding of Modern Feminism* [New Haven, CT: Yale University Press, 1987], 4). I have thus taken the liberty, particularly in introductory and concluding comments, of utilizing an expansive understanding of the term "feminism" that transcends a particular time and place, one that draws on Cott's own definition of feminism as consisting of "three core components": the "opposition to sex hierarchy," the conviction "that women's condition is socially constructed," and a sense of gender consciousness as a precondition for social action (Cott, 4–5). Linda Gordon, too, offers a useful definition of feminism not restricted to particular historical circumstances: "Feminism is a critique of male supremacy, formed and offered in the light of a will to change it, which in turn assumes a conviction that it is changeable" (Linda Gordon, "What's New in Women's History," in *Feminist Studies/Critical Studies*, Theresa de Lauretis, ed. [Bloomington: Indiana University Press, 1986], 29). At the same time, the historical development of modern Feminism (originally capitalized by those who coined the term) in the early twentieth century and its divergences from the nineteenth-century "woman's movement" provide a crucial backdrop to Bushnell's life and work, a story that is recounted in Chapter 8. Within the historical narrative, then, I have taken pains when appropriate to distinguish "Feminism" as a specific historical movement from the more expansive and timeless definition of "feminism" otherwise employed.

2. Bushnell developed her ideas through her "Women's Correspondence Bible Class," which she issued and compiled in the years leading up to the publication of *God's Word to Women*. For further details on this publication history, see Chapter 4.

3. Bushnell, *God's Word to Women* (hereafter referred to as *GWTW*), 5.

4. The 1972 reprinting of Elizabeth Cady Stanton's *Woman's Bible* (1895–1898; repr., New York: Arno Press, 1972) exemplified this renewed interest. Later works include Mary D. Pellauer, *Toward a Tradition of Feminist Theology: The Religious Social Thought of Elizabeth Cady Stanton, Susan B. Anthony, and Anna Howard Shaw* (Brooklyn, NY: Carlson Publishing, 1991); Patricia Demers, *Women as Interpreters of the Bible* (Mahwah, NJ: Paulist Press, 1992); Gerda Lerner, "One Thousand Years of Feminist Biblical Criticism," in *The Creation of Feminist Consciousness from the Middle Ages to Eighteen-Seventy* (New York: Oxford University Press, 1993), 138–166; and Marla Selvidge, *Notorious Voices: Feminist Biblical Interpretation, 1500–1920* (New York: Continuum, 1996).

5. See Nancy A. Hardesty, *Women Called to Witness: Evangelical Feminism in the Nineteenth Century* (Nashville, TN: Abindon Press, 1984), and Janette Hassey, *No Time for Silence: Evangelical Women in Public Ministry Around the Turn of the Century* (Grand Rapids, MI: Academie Books, 1986).

6. See, for example, Ann Loades, "Elizabeth Cady Stanton's *The Woman's Bible*," in *The Oxford Handbook of The Reception History of the Bible*, ed. Michael Lieb, Emma Mason, and Jonathan Roberts (New York: Oxford University Press, 2011), 307–322.

7. Recent works in the history of women's biblical interpretation include Christiana de Groot and Marion Ann Taylor, eds., *Recovering Nineteenth-Century Women Interpreters of the Bible* (Atlanta, GA: Society of Biblical Literature, 2007); Nancy Calvert-Koyzis and Heather Weir, eds., *Breaking Boundaries: Female Biblical Interpreters Who Challenged the Status Quo* (New York: T & T Clark, 2010); Marion Ann Taylor and Agnes Choi, eds., *Handbook of Women Biblical Interpreters: A Historical and Biographical Guide* (Grand Rapids, MI: Baker Academic, 2012); Carol A. Newsom, Sharon H. Ringe, and Jacqueline E. Lapsley, eds., *The Women's Bible Commentary*, 3rd ed. (Louisville, KY: Westminster John Knox, 2012); and the ongoing international, multi-volume project *The Bible and Women: An Encyclopaedia of Exegesis and Cultural History*. www.bibleandwomen.org.

8. Andrew F. Walls, "The Gospel as Prisoner and Liberator of Culture," in *The Missionary Movement in Christian History: Studies in the Transmission of Faith* (Maryknoll, NY: Orbis Books, 1996), 10.

9. Bushnell to Butler, August 30, 1899, The Josephine Butler Letters Collection, The Women's Library collections at LSE, 3JBL/43/28.

10. Bushnell to Butler, August 30, 1899, The Josephine Butler Letters Collection, The Women's Library collections at LSE, 3JBL/43/28.

11. Bushnell to Butler, August 30, 1899, The Josephine Butler Letters Collection, The Women's Library collections at LSE, 3JBL/43/28.

12. Elizabeth Cady Stanton, *Woman's Bible* (1895–1898; repr., New York: Arno Press, 1972), 11–12; Kathi Kern, *Mrs. Stanton's Bible* (Ithaca, NY: Cornell University Press, 2002), 1.

13. Kern, *Mrs. Stanton's Bible*, 5.

14. Aileen S. Kraditor, *The Ideas of the Woman Suffrage Movement* (1965; repr., New York: W. W. Norton & Company, 1981), 93–95. It is not clear if Bushnell was familiar with Stanton's *Woman's Bible*. She was abroad during the time of its publication, and thus it is possible that she did not come across the book. Although Stanton's book inflamed conservative opposition, it is striking (but perhaps not surprising) how little influence it had in evangelical women's circles in the years after its publication.

15. Margaret Lamberts Bendroth points out in "Religion, Feminism, and the American Family," in Anne E. Carr and Mary Stewart Van Leeuwen, eds., *Religion, Feminism, and the Family* (Louisville, KY: Westminster John Knox Press, 1996), that already by the 1920s "it seemed no longer necessary, or perhaps truly possible, to be both a Christian and a feminist" (192).

CHAPTER 1

1. Bushnell was born Caroline Sophia, and later changed her name to Katharine. See Dana Hardwick, *Oh Thou Woman That Bringest Good Tidings: The Life and Work of Katharine C. Bushnell* (Kearney, NE: Morris Publishing, published for Christians for Biblical Equality, 1995), 13. As Hardwick notes, some secondary sources list her date of birth as 1856, but census data and family records confirm 1855 as her year of birth.

2. Henry S. Beebe, *The History of Peru* (Peru, IL: J. F. Linton, 1858), digitized by the University of Illinois at Urbana-Champaign, available at http://hdl.handle.net/10111/UIUCOCA:historyofperuoobeeb, 66–67.

3. Viola Couch Reeling, *Evanston: Its Land and Its People* (Evanston: Daughters of the American Revolution, Evanston Chapter, 1928), 434; and William Beatty, "Katharine Bushnell, M.D.—Evangelist and Investigator," *Union Signal*, July, August, & September, 1997, 13.

4. *Union Signal*, November 20, 1890, 4. The Bushnells were also distant relatives of the renowned theologian Horace Bushnell, though Katharine Bushnell does not seem to have had any contact with him.

5. John H. Wigger, *Taking Heaven by Storm: Methodism and the Rise of Popular Christianity in America* (New York: Oxford University Press, 1998), 174–75; Nathan O. Hatch, "The Puzzle of American Methodism," in *Methodism and the Shaping of American Culture*, ed. Hatch and John H. Wigger (Nashville: Kingswood Books, 2001), 27.

6. Beebe, *History of Peru,* 9–10.

7. *History of La Salle County, Illinois* (Chicago: Inter-state Pub. Co., 1886), 862, http://books.google.com/books?id=IYE_AAAAYAAJ.

8. Beebe, *History of Peru,* 71–74.

9. Franc Baker, *Historical Sketches of the Northwestern Branch of the Women's Foreign Missionary Society of the Methodist Episcopal Church* (Chicago: Jameson & Morse, 1887), 33.

10. Wigger, *Taking Heaven,* 192–193, 174–175.

11. Harold Francis Williamson and Payson Sibley Wild, *Northwestern University: A History, 1850–1975* (Evanston, IL: Northwestern University Press, 1976), 35.

12. *Union Signal,* November 20, 1890, 4.

13. Frances Willard, *A Classic Town: The Story of Evanston* (Chicago: Woman's Temperance Publishing Association, 1891), 58, http://books.google.com/books?id=_tUNAQAAMAAJ.

14. Willard, *Classic Town,* 365.

15. Willard, *Classic Town,* 366.

16. Willard, *Classic Town,* 365.

17. Hatch, "Puzzle," 28, 37; see also Catherine A. Brekus, *Strangers and Pilgrims: Female Preaching in America, 1740–1845* (Chapel Hill: University of North Carolina Press, 1998); and Dana L. Robert, *American Women in Mission: A Social History of Their Thought and Practice* (Macon, GA: Mercer University Press, 1996), 139.

18. See, for example, Barbara Welter, "The Cult of True Womanhood: 1820–1860," *American Quarterly* 18, no. 2 (Summer 1966): 151–174; and Kathryn Kish Sklar, *Catharine Beecher: A Study in American Domesticity* (New Haven, CT: Yale University Press, 1973).

19. A. Gregory Schneider, *The Way of the Cross Leads Home: The Domestication of American Methodism* (Bloomington: Indiana University Press, 1993), xxi. In *The Politics of Domesticity: Women, Evangelism, and Temperance in Nineteenth-Century America* (Middletown, CT: Wesleyan University Press, 1981), Barbara Leslie Epstein contrasts the Victorian elevation of motherhood with the way in which Puritans considered motherhood "only one of a woman's tasks" (76).

20. Methodists helped shape the ideology of domesticity, but they were hardly its exclusive practitioners. See Barbara Welter, "The Feminization of American Religion," in Welter, *Dimity Convictions: The American Woman in the Nineteenth Century* (Athens: Ohio University Press, 1976); Ann Douglas, *The Feminization of American Culture* (New York: Knopf, 1977); and Ann Taves, *The Household of Faith: Roman Catholic Devotions in Mid-Nineteenth-Century America* (Notre Dame, IN: University of Notre Dame Press, 1986).

21. Jay Riley Case, *An Unpredictable Gospel: American Evangelicals and World Christianity, 1812–1920* (New York: Oxford University Press, 2012), 144–145. See also Melvin E. Dieter, *The Holiness Revival of the Nineteenth Century* (Metuchen,

NJ: Scarecrow Press, 1980); and Vinson Synan, *The Holiness-Pentecostal Movement in the United States* (Grand Rapids, MI: Eerdmans, 1971).

22. Kathryn T. Long, "Consecrated Respectability: Phoebe Palmer and the Refinement of American Methodism," in *Methodism and the Shaping of American Culture*, 284; see also Nancy Hardesty, Lucille Sider Dayton and Donald W. Dayton, "Women in the Holiness Movement: Feminism in the Evangelical Tradition," in *Women of Spirit: Female Leadership in the Jewish and Christian Traditions*, ed. Rosemary Radford Ruether and Eleanor McLaughlin (New York: Simon & Schuster, 1979), 225–254.

23. For further discussion of the ways in which the ideology of female domesticity and "woman's sphere" could empower middle-class women, see Nancy F. Cott, *The Bonds of Womanhood: "Woman's Sphere" in New England, 1780–1835* (New Haven, CT: Yale University Press, 1977); Epstein, *Politics of Domesticity*; and Sklar, *Catharine Beecher*. On the relationship between domesticity, female reform, and the formation of the middle class in nineteenth-century America, see Mary P. Ryan, *Cradle of the Middle Class: The Family in Oneida County, New York, 1790–1865* (Cambridge: Cambridge University Press, 1981); Nancy A. Hewitt, *Women's Activism and Social Change: Rochester, New York, 1822–1872* (Ithaca, NY: Cornell University Press, 1984); and Christine Stansell, *City of Women: Sex and Class in New York, 1789–1860* (New York: Alfred A. Knopf, 1986).

24. *Catalogue of the Officers and Students of the Northwestern Female College and Male and Female Preparatory* (Chicago: R. L. & C. L. Wilson, 1856), 4–8. In addition, the school enrolled thirty-two male students.

25. Willard, *Classic Town*, 57.

26. Willard, *Classic Town*, 58–59.

27. Willard, *Classic Town*, 58.

28. Willard, *Classic Town*, 83–84.

29. Willard, *Classic Town*, 83–84.

30. Frances Willard, *Glimpses of Fifty Years: The Autobiography of an American Woman* (Chicago, H. J. Smith, published by the Woman's Temperance Publication Association, 1889), 188, http://books.google.com/books?isbn=1152924893.

31. Patricia Hill, *The World Their Household* (Ann Arbor: University of Michigan Press, 1985), 39.

32. R. Pierce Beaver, *All Loves Excelling: American Protestant Women in World Mission* (Grand Rapids, MI: Eerdmans, 1968), 19–67.

33. *Heathen Woman's Friend* 1 (May 1869), 1.

34. Hill, *World Their Household*, 5.

35. Robert, *American Women in Mission*, 130–137.

36. Hill, *World Their Household*, 5; *Heathen Woman's Friend* 1 (May 1869), 1.

37. As Lori D. Ginzberg argues, "the significance of the Civil War for Northern women lay more in heightening trends that had been apparent in the 1850s than in opening wholly new horizons" (*Women and the Work of Benevolence: Morality, Politics, and Class in the Nineteenth-Century United States* [New Haven, CT: Yale University Press, 1990], 136).

38. Hill, *World Their Household*, 38.

39. *Heathen Woman's Friend* 1 (May 1869), 2.

40. Though Congregationalist women organized their own society a few months earlier, Methodist women were the first to achieve a denomination-wide movement, and the WFMS quickly outpaced other societies both in terms of absolute numbers and in percentages of church members recruited. By 1895 WFMS membership stood at over 150,000; by 1910, 267,000; and by 1920 more than half a million (Hill, *World Their Household*, 46–49).

41. Baker, *Historical Sketches*, 7–8.

42. Baker, *Historical Sketches*, 8; Hill, *World Their Household*, 48. Eventually the WFMS included eleven branches across the nation.

43. Baker, *Historical Sketches*, 16–17.

44. Baker, *Historical Sketches*, 14.

45. Willard dates Van Cott's visit to the "first year of the new college (1871–72)" (*Glimpses*, 219).

46. John O. Foster, *Life and Labors of Mrs. Maggie Newton Van Cott* (Cincinnati, OH: Hitchcock and Walden, 1872), 70.

47. Willard, *Glimpses*, 220.

48. *Union Signal*, November 20, 1890, 4.

49. Willard, *Glimpses*, 576–589.

50. *Union Signal*, November 20, 1890, 4.

51. Willard, *Classic Town*, 63; see also *Glimpses*, 188 ff.

52. Mary Earhart, *Frances Willard: From Prayers to Politics* (Chicago: University of Chicago Press, 1944), 115.

53. Anna A. Gordon, *The Beautiful Life of Frances E. Willard* (Chicago: Woman's Temperance Publishing Association, 1898), 63.

54. Gordon, *Beautiful Life*, 63.

55. Earhart, *Prayers to Politics*, 116–118.

56. Willard, *Glimpses*, 229–230. In later years, when asked if speaking before large audiences made her nervous, Willard replied without hesitation: "You never taught the Freshman class in Northwestern University or you would not expect one who has done that to be frightened at anything"; in contrast to her former students, an audience was "like a well-bred person, quiet, attentive, sympathetic, and, best of all, not in a position to answer back!"

57. Gordon, *Beautiful Life*, 62.

58. Gordon, *Beautiful Life*, 65.

59. *Union Signal*, November 20, 1890, 4.

60. *Union Signal*, November 20, 1890, 4.

61. On Bushnell's medical training, see Annie Ryder Gracey, *Medical Work of the Woman's Foreign Missionary Society, Methodist Episcopal Church* (Dansville, NY: A. O. Bunnell, 1881), 182; *Twelfth Annual Announcement and Catalogue of the Woman's Medical College of Chicago* (Chicago: Brown Pettibone & Kelley,

1881, 11, 18; Bushnell, *Dr. Katharine C. Bushnell: A Brief Sketch of Her Life Work* (Hertford: Rose & Sons, 1932), 3; Baker, *Historical Sketches*, 100.

62. "Katharine C. Bushnell, M.D.," *Medical Woman's Journal* (November 1944): 29.

63. Willard, *Classic Town*, 60.

64. Baker, *Historical Sketches*, 142.

65. Carolyn De Swarte Gifford, ed. *Writing Out My Heart: Selections from the Journal of Frances E. Willard, 1855–96* (Urbana: University of Illinois Press, 1995), 200. The revival had a formative influence on Frances Willard.

66. Willard, *Classic Town*, 202.

67. Baker, *Historical Sketches*, 142. Another member of Hamline's generation who played a prominent role in Evanston's women's circle was Mary H. Brown, a member of the WFMS and advocate of temperance and reform work. Born in 1798 in upstate New York, Brown's childhood had been filled with old-school Methodist love-feasts and camp meetings. As a young woman she had studied Hebrew so that she could translate the Scriptures from their original language, and she served for a time as an itinerant minister alongside her husband, Arza Brown. In Evanston she was revered by the community's women for her knowledge of Christian history and doctrine, and for the way in which she combined faith and learning, and unapologetically placed Christ above custom (146).

68. Willard, *Classic Town*, 203.

69. Bushnell, *Brief Sketch*, 3–4. Here Bushnell was quoting Romans 8:28.

CHAPTER 2

1. Antoinette Burton, *Burdens of History: British Feminists, Indian Women, and Imperial Culture, 1865–1915* (Chapel Hill: University of North Carolina Press, 1994), 43. With regard to the British women's movement, Burton notes that "Christianity, and, more specifically, the Christian commitments of British women, contributed not just to emancipation ideology but to justifications for women's emancipationist activity as well." She adds that "feminist argument in the pre-WWI period never completely lost touch with its religious roots. . . . And yet feminists' call for moral improvement, for all that it depended on Christian validation, was in many respects a secular project, with the moral elevation of British social and political life as its objective."

2. Several historians have illuminated both the radical and conservative possibilities inherent in nineteenth-century women's activism and moral reform work. See, for example, Cott's *Bonds of Womanhood*; Barbara J. Berg, *The Remembered Gate: Origins of American Feminism: The Woman and the City, 1800–1860* (New York: Oxford University Press, 1978); Ginzberg's *Women and the Work of Benevolence*; and Anne Boylan, "Women in Groups: An Analysis of Women's Benevolent Organizations in New York and Boston, 1797–1840," *Journal of American History* 71 (December 1984): 497–523. While historians have primarily concerned

themselves with ways in which religious commitments either enhanced or constrained feminism, many have treated Christianity in static terms, and have thus failed to investigate ways in which Christian women active in the women's movement also sought to reshape Christianity itself.

3. Whereas "Jiujiang" is the modern *pinyin* romanization currently in use in the People's Republic of China, I utilize the earlier Wade-Giles Romanization of "Kiukiang," which was the system Bushnell and her fellow missionaries employed.

4. Connie Anne Shemo, *The Chinese Medical Ministries of Kang Cheng and Shi Meiyu, 1872–1937* (Bethlehem, PA: Lehigh University Press, 2011), 22.

5. Gracey, *Medical Work*, 176. This purpose was not lost on the local inhabitants, among whom a rumor spread that the medical missionaries had "a mirror which we hold before their hearts, which causes them to forget their homes and friends and to neglect their daily worship before their idols" (180).

6. Gracey, *Medical Work*, 176.

7. Jane Hunter, *Gospel of Gentility: American Women Missionaries in Turn-of-the-Century China* (New Haven, CT: Yale University Press, 1984), 15. For more on female medical missions, see Lisa Joy Pruitt, *A Looking-Glass for Ladies: American Protestant Women and the Orient in the Nineteenth Century* (Macon, GA: Mercer University Press, 2005), 114–143.

8. Shemo, *Chinese Medical Ministries*, 23; Robert, *American Women in Mission*, 162.

9. On the significance of domesticity in Christian missions, see Dana L. Robert, "The 'Christian Home' as a Cornerstone of Anglo-American Missionary Thought and Practice," in Dana L. Robert, ed., *Converting Colonialism: Visions and Realities in Mission History, 1706–1914* (Grand Rapids, MI: Eerdmans, 2008), 134–165.

10. Robert, *American Women in Mission*, 175.

11. Robert, *American Women in Mission*, 162.

12. Robert, *American Women in Mission*, 136.

13. Dana L. Robert, *Christian Mission: How Christianity Became a World Religion* (Chichester, UK: Wiley-Blackwell, 2009), 93.

14. Burton, *Burdens*, 17.

15. Amy Kaplan, "Manifest Domesticity," *American Literature* 70, no. 3 (September 1998): 586.

16. Kaplan, "Manifest Domesticity," 597.

17. Susan Thorne, "Missionary-Imperial Feminism," in *Gendered Missions: Women and Men in Missionary Discourse and Practice*, ed. Mary Taylor Huber and Nancy C. Lutkehaus (Ann Arbor: University of Michigan Press, 1999), 45, 60.

18. Burton, *Burdens*, 21, 96. Western women also exhibited a tendency to speak for their non-Western "sisters," a tendency Bushnell certainly shared.

19. Shemo, *Chinese Medical Ministries*, 4. On the opportunities imperialism provided British women, see Catherine Hall, *Civilising Subjects: Colony and*

Metropole in the English Imagination, 1830–1867 (Chicago: University of Chicago Press, 2002).

20. Shemo, *Chinese Medical Ministries*, 5, 33.

21. See, for example, Burton's opening chapter in *Burdens*, "The Politics of Recovery: Historicizing Imperial Feminism, 1865–1915," 1–32.

22. Thorne, "Missionary-Imperial Feminism," 45.

23. *Leeds Mercury*, October 3, 1883, 7, cited in Thorne, "Missionary-Imperial Feminism," 45.

24. Amy Kaplan, "Manifest Domesticity," 582.

25. Burton, *Burdens*, 11, 42–43.

26. Robert, *Christian Mission*, 128. Robert notes that by the early twentieth century American women missionaries came to outnumber male missionaries by roughly two to one.

27. Joan Jacobs Brumberg, "The Ethnological Mirror: American Evangelical Women and Their Heathen Sisters, 1870–1910," in *Women and the Structure of Society*, ed. Barbara J. Harris and JoAnn K. McNamara (Durham, NC: Duke University Press, 1984), 115.

28. Brumberg, "Ethnological Mirror," 109.

29. Brumberg, "Ethnological Mirror," 115; see also Thorne, "Missionary-Imperial Feminism," 45.

30. Shemo, *Chinese Medical Ministries*, 8.

31. Shemo, *Chinese Medical Ministries*, 6.

32. Jane H. Hunter, "Women's Mission in Historical Perspective: American Identity and Christian Internationalism," in *Competing Kingdoms: Women, Mission, Nation, and the American Protestant Empire, 1812–1960*, ed. Barbara Reeves-Ellington, Kathryn Kish Sklar, and Connie A. Shemo (Durham, NC: Duke University Press, 2010), 22. As Hunter notes, "This fluidity in the past is suggestive for those who might see gendered activism as a source of hope in a divided present."

33. Walls, "Gospel as Prisoner and Liberator," 7.

34. Walls, "Gospel as Prisoner and Liberator," 8.

35. Walls, "Gospel as Prisoner and Liberator," 9. As Walls explains, the indigenizing principle "associates Christians with the *particulars* of their culture and group," whereas the pilgrim principle, "by associating them with things and people outside the culture and group, is in some respects a *universalizing* factor."

36. Andrew F. Walls, "From Christendom to World Christianity: Missions and the Demographic Transformation of the Church," in *The Cross-Cultural Process in Christian History* (Maryknoll, NY: Orbis Books, 2002), 49.

37. Andrew F. Walls, "The Ephesian Moment: At a Crossroads in Christian History," in *Cross-Cultural Process*, 78.

38. Andrew F. Walls, "Christianity in the Non-Western World: A Study in the Serial Nature of Christian Expansion," in *Cross-Cultural Process*, 43.

39. Walls, "Christianity in the Non-Western World," 44.

40. Walls, "Christianity in the Non-Western World," 42–43. For additional interpretations of Christianity, imperialism, and the missionary experience, see Brian Stanley, *The Bible and the Flag: Protestant Missions and British Imperialism in the Nineteenth and Twentieth Centuries* (Leicester, UK: Apollos, 1990); Lamin O. Sanneh, *Encountering the West: Christianity and the Global Cultural Process: The African Dimension* (Maryknoll, NY: Orbis Books, 1993); and Jeffrey Cox, *Imperial Fault Lines: Christianity and Colonial Power in India, 1818–1940* (Stanford, CA: Stanford University Press, 2002).

41. Case, *Unpredictable Gospel,* 8–9.

42. Case, *Unpredictable Gospel,* 6.

43. *Baptist Missionary Magazine,* November 1895, 543–544, quoted in Case, *Unpredictable Gospel,* 6.

44. Robert, *American Women in Mission,* 149, 147.

45. For more on the relationship between the women's missionary movement and women's rights, see Dana L. Robert, "The Influence of American Missionary Women on the World Back Home," *Religion and American Culture* 12, no. 1 (Winter 2002): 59–89.

46. Baker, *Historical Sketches,* 100.

47. Shemo, *Chinese Medical Ministries,* 5.

48. WFMS minutes, 1880–1881, 40–41, cited in Shemo, *Chinese Medical Ministries,* 33.

49. WFMS minutes, 1880–1881, 40–41; 1882, 29–31, cited in Shemo, *Chinese Medical Ministries,* 34.

50. Gracey, *Medical Work,* 183; Baker, *Historical Sketches,* 100.

51. Bushnell, *Brief Sketch,* 4–5; Gracey, *Medical Work,* 182–183; Baker, *Historical Sketches,* 100.

52. Bushnell, *Brief Sketch,* 5. The accident resulted in a painful spinal curvature; Bushnell claimed she "never knew a well day for years afterwards" and in her biographical sketch attributed the end of her missionary service (two years later) to this event.

53. Bushnell, "Letter from China," February 25, 1881, published in *The Chicago Medical Journal and Examiner* (1881), 520.

54. Bushnell, *Brief Sketch,* 4.

55. Gracey, *Medical Work,* 187.

56. Bushnell, *Brief Sketch,* 4.

57. Baker, *Historical Sketches,* 100.

58. Gracey, *Medical Work,* 187.

59. Bushnell, "Letter from China," 520.

60. Baker, *Historical Sketches,* 155–157.

61. For more on Shi Meiyu see Shemo, *Chinese Medical Ministries.* As Shemo notes, the medical training of indigenous women such as Shi Meiyu further

complicates simplistic interpretations of missions, and medical missions in particular, as unidirectional expressions of cultural imperialism (33).

62. As Dana Robert notes, missionary women who returned due to ill health, or who left the mission field for any reason other than martyrdom, were considered "failures" and were quickly forgotten by their community of supporters (*American Women in Mission*, 49).

63. Bushnell, "Letter from China," 520. Bushnell nevertheless considered Chinese practices worth studying, and began her own investigation of traditional medicine as soon as she had gained proficiency in the language, with the help of three Chinese friends who practiced medicine. See also *The Medical and Surgical Reporter: A Weekly Journal* (July–December, 1885), Vol. LIII, 454.

64. Gracey, *Medical Work*, 184–185.

65. Catherine Clark Kroeger, "The Legacy of Katherine Bushnell: A Hermeneutic for Women of Faith," *Priscilla Papers* 9, no. 4 (Fall 1995): 2.

66. Bushnell, *Brief Sketch*, 20.

67. Bushnell, *Brief Sketch*, 20.

68. Bushnell, *Brief Sketch*, 5.

69. Ruth Bordin, *Frances Willard: A Biography* (Chapel Hill: University of North Carolina Press, 1986), 67; Barbara Epstein, *Politics of Domesticity*, 91–100. Epstein points out that the Woman's Crusade did have earlier precedents.

70. As Barbara Epstein explains, for a brief time in the late 1840s and early 1850s, temperance and women's rights intersected. Elizabeth Cady Stanton and other feminists published *The Lily*, a newspaper addressing temperance concerns, in which they explicitly connected feminism and temperance. But when temperance men excluded women from the national Sons of Temperance in 1852, female activists shifted their efforts from temperance to women's rights (*Politics of Domesticity*, 93).

71. Jed Dannenbaum, *Temperance Reform in Cincinnati from the Washingtonian Revival to the WCTU* (Urbana: University of Illinois Press, 1984), 181–182.

72. Willard, *Glimpses*, 340–341.

73. Carolyn De Swarte Gifford, "'The Woman's Cause Is Man's'? Frances Willard and the Social Gospel," in *Gender and the Social Gospel*, ed. Wendy J. Deichmann Edwards and Carolyn De Swarte Gifford (Urbana: University of Illinois Press, 2003), 26.

74. Bordin, *Willard*, 69.

75. Ian Tyrrell, *Woman's World/Woman's Empire: The Woman's Christian Temperance Union in International Perspective, 1880–1930* (Chapel Hill: University of North Carolina Press, 1991), 23. Tyrrell adds that holiness teachings "gave women on both sides of the Atlantic a shared set of assumptions concerning Christian service and sacrifice." In *American Women in Mission*, Dana Robert notes that "piety, especially that of the holiness movement," was "the gasoline that ran the engine of social reform" (144).

76. Phillida Bunkle, "The Origins of the Women's Movement in New Zealand: The Woman's Christian Temperance Union 1885–1895," in *Women in New Zealand Society*, ed. Phillida Bunkle and Beryl Hughes (Auckland, New Zealand: George Allen & Unwin, 1980), 67–69.

77. Alcohol interfered far less with earlier modes of work, which was often undertaken at home and at a more flexible pace. Drinking habits, too, had changed by the nineteenth century. Whereas earlier drinking had taken place in the home or in community taverns, by the nineteenth century "drinking moved from the home to the tavern and increasingly became a men's occupation." See Epstein, *Politics of Domesticity*, 108.

78. Bunkle, "Origins," 67.

79. As Lori D. Ginzberg makes clear, this antagonistic attitude toward men motivated female moral reform work in earlier decades of the nineteenth century as well (*Women and the Work of Benevolence*, 20).

80. As her friends later recalled, "Miss Willard did not come to woman suffrage through temperance, but was a suffragist first, last, and all the time" (*Woman's Journal* [March 5, 1892], quoted in Earhart, *Prayers to Politics*, 150).

81. Hunter, "Women's Mission in Historical Perspective," 25.

82. On the relationship between temperance and feminism, see Ruth Bordin, *Woman and Temperance: The Quest for Power and Liberty, 1873–1900* (Philadelphia: Temple University Press, 1981). Bordin goes so far as to claim that "temperance became the medium through which nineteenth-century women expressed their deeper, sometimes unconscious, feminist concerns" (162).

83. Earhart, *Prayers to Politics*, 193.

84. Earhart, *Prayers to Politics*, 198.

85. Earhart, *Prayers to Politics*, 206–207.

86. Clark Secrest, *Hell's Belles: Prostitution, Vice, and Crime in Early Denver*, rev. ed. (Boulder: University Press of Colorado, 2002), 133.

87. Peggy Pascoe, *Relations of Rescue: The Search for Female Moral Authority in the American West, 1874–1939* (New York: Oxford University Press, 1990), 12.

88. Pascoe, *Relations of Rescue*, 12.

89. Pascoe, *Relations of Rescue*, 13.

90. Pascoe, *Relations of Rescue*, 20.

91. Pascoe, *Relations of Rescue*, 13.

92. Pascoe, *Relations of Rescue*, 6.

93. Pascoe, *Relations of Rescue*, 36–37.

94. Pascoe, *Relations of Rescue*, xvi.

95. Beatty, "Katharine C. Bushnell, M.D," 14.

96. *Union Signal*, March 4, 1886.

97. Secrest, *Hell's Belles*, 155; 181–182.

98. Jan MacKell, *Red Light Women of the Rocky Mountains* (Albuquerque: University of New Mexico Press, 2009), 116.

99. *Union Signal,* December 4, 1884, 9; *Women's Medical School: Northwestern University (Woman's Medical College of Chicago) Class Histories 1870–1890* (Chicago: H. G. Butler, 1896), 137; *Minutes of the National Woman's Christian Temperance Union at the Eleventh Annual Meeting in St. Louis, Missouri, 1884* (Chicago: Woman's Temperance Publication Association, 1884), xliv.

100. Even after Bushnell left Denver for Chicago, the work of the Colorado Union continued. According to Pascoe, members "sponsored a kitchen garden (to train domestics), a woman's exchange (to allow homemakers to sell handicrafts on consignment), a day and night nursery, and a home for 'friendless' women," as well as a "fledgling Denver Florence Crittenton Home for the rehabilitation of prostitutes" and the more popular Colorado Cottage Home for unmarried mothers (Pascoe, *Relations of Rescue,* 17). As Pascoe notes, 1880s Denver was a situation "ripe with opportunities for seduction and abandonment" (18).

101. David J. Pivar, *Purity Crusade: Sexual Morality and Social Control, 1868–1900* (Westport, CT: Greenwood Press, 1973), 25; see also Barbara Meil Hobson, *Uneasy Virtue: The Politics of Prostitution and the American Reform Tradition* (New York: Basic Books, 1987).

102. Tyrrell, *Woman's World,* 191–192; Judith R. Walkowitz, "Male Vice and Female Virtue: Feminism and the Politics of Prostitution in Nineteenth-Century Britain," in *Powers of Desire: the Politics of Sexuality,* ed. Ann Snitow, Christine Stansell, and Sharon Thompson (New York: The Monthly Review Press, 1983), 419. As Walkowitz explains, "few historical moments better demonstrate how sexual politics makes strange bedfellows."

103. Walkowitz, "Male Vice," 429.

104. Barbara Epstein, "Family, Sexual Morality, and Popular Movements in Turn-of-the-Century America," in *Powers of Desire,* 118.

105. Bunkle, "Origins," 74.

106. Philippa Levine, "Sexuality and Empire," in *At Home with Empire: Metropolitan Culture and the Imperial World,* ed. Catherine Hall and Sonya O. Rose (Cambridge: Cambridge University Press, 2006), 122. See also Epstein, "Family, Sexual Morality, and Popular Movements." Epstein argues that the rise of prostitution in nineteenth-century America "was directly linked to middle-class family arrangements," and that "men's visits to prostitutes were almost taken for granted" (121).

107. Bunkle, "Origins," 71–74. Springing up in newly industrialized urban areas, prostitution represented sexuality outside the bounds of the family, and thus threatened the social order. Prostitution not only separated sex from reproduction, but also "from love and intimacy." At the same time, as John D'Emilio and Estelle B. Freedman make clear, "the prostitute evoked fears of disease at a time of recurrent and inexplicable cholera epidemics and a growing incidence of syphilis. Thus women had legitimate concerns about threats to the health and stability of their families." John D'Emilio and Estelle B. Freedman,

Intimate Matters: A History of Sexuality in America, 3rd ed. (Chicago: University of Chicago Press, 2012), 141.

108. Barbara Epstein locates the roots of this antagonism as far back as the divergent social and religious experiences of women and men in the religious revivals of the late eighteenth and early nineteenth centuries (*Politics of Domesticity,* 62–65); Elizabeth Battelle Clark also identifies this gender antagonism within the early years of the American women's rights movement ("The Politics of God and the Woman's Vote: Religion in the American Suffrage Movement, 1848–1895" [PhD diss., Princeton University, 1989], 43).

109. Ruth Bloch, "Republican Virtue: The Gendered Meanings of Virtue in Revolutionary America," in *Gender and Morality in Anglo-American Culture, 1650–1800* (Berkeley: University of California Press, 2003), 140.

110. Bloch, "Republican Virtue," 139, 146.

111. See Linda K. Kerber, *Women of the Republic: Intellect and Ideology in Revolutionary America* (Chapel Hill: University of North Carolina Press, published for the Omohundro Institute of Early American History and Culture, 1980).

112. Bloch, "Republican Virtue," 137.

113. Linda Gordon, *The Moral Property of Women: A History of Birth Control Politics in America*, 3rd ed. (Urbana: University of Illinois Press, 2002), 114.

114. Tyrrell, *Woman's World,* 192; see also Epstein, *Politics of Domesticity.*

115. For a nuanced discussion of the uses of female moral authority, see Peggy Pascoe, *Relations of Rescue.*

116. Ann Braude, "Women's History Is American Religious History," in *Retelling U.S. Religious History,* ed. Thomas A. Tweed (Berkeley: University of California Press, 1997), 100.

117. Ruth Rosen, *The Lost Sisterhood: Prostitution in America, 1900–1918* (Baltimore, MD: The Johns Hopkins University Press, 1982), 6.

118. Hobson, *Uneasy Virtue,* 110–113.

119. Clergy and reformers had worked to rescue and reform prostitutes and combat the state regulation of prostitution since the 1820s. Their grassroots efforts, however, remained controversial, and many Protestants feared that public discussion of sexuality would only draw more people into a world of vice. And efforts often focused on the rehabilitation of prostitutes themselves, rather than on underlying social issues. On the longer history of purity reform, see Pivar, *Purity Crusade,* chapters 1–3.

120. A number of women's rights activists, including Elizabeth Cady Stanton, Susan B. Anthony, Ellen Battelle Dietrick, Lucy Stone, and Henry Blackwell, took up social purity in the closing decades of the nineteenth century.

121. Walkowitz, "Male Vice," 422.

122. Judith R. Walkowitz, *Prostitution and Victorian Society: Women, Class, and the State* (Cambridge: Cambridge University Press, 1980), 255. See also Bushnell's article on Butler in *Union Signal,* December 26, 1889, 10.

123. Lucretia A. Flammang, "'And Your Sons and Daughters Will Prophesy': The Voice and Vision of Josephine Butler," in *Women's Theology in Nineteenth-Century Britain: Transfiguring the Faith of Their Fathers*, ed. Julie Melnyk (New York: Garland, 1998), 151; see also Lisa Severine Nolland, *A Victorian Feminist Christian: Josephine Butler, the Prostitutes and God* (Waynesboro, GA: Paternoster, 2004). For a concise explication of Butler's evangelical faith, see Timothy Larsen, "Evangelical Anglicans: Josephine Butler and the Word of God," in *A People of One Book: The Bible and the Victorians* (New York: Oxford University Press, 2011), 219–246.

124. See Josephine Butler, *The Constitution Violated* (Edinburgh: Edmonston & Douglas, 1871), and Jenny Uglow, "Josephine Butler: From Sympathy to Theory," in *Feminist Theorists: Three Centuries of Key Women Thinkers*, ed. Dale Spender (New York: Pantheon Books, 1983). Uglow, however, tends to dismiss or regret the religious motivations behind Butler's activism. For a helpful balance to this perspective that highlights the "radical feminist theology" that Butler worked to develop, see Helen Mathers, "The Evangelical Spirituality of a Victorian Feminist: Josephine Butler, 1828–1906," *Journal of Ecclesiastical History* 52, no. 3 (April 2001): 282. In the 1870s American purity reformers successfully challenged the government regulation of prostitution as well, most notably in St. Louis, Missouri, and in Chicago (Pivar, *Purity Crusade*, 52–59).

125. Pivar, *Purity Crusade*, 132. On the social construction of these tales of seduction and abduction, see Judith R. Walkowitz, *City of Dreadful Delight: Narratives of Sexual Danger in Late-Victorian London* (Chicago: University of Chicago Press, 1992), 135.

126. Pivar, *Purity Crusade*, 85.

127. Bordin, *Willard*, 132; Willard, *Glimpses*, 418. On age-of-consent laws, see Pivar, *Purity Crusade*, 141–143.

128. Willard, *Glimpses*, 421.

129. Willard, *Glimpses*, 420.

130. Willard, *Glimpses*, 421.

131. As Pivar recounts (*Purity Crusade*, 116–117), Willard invited Aaron and Anna Powell of the New York Committee for the Suppression of Legalized Vice to head the WCTU's new department, but they declined. She later succeeded in appointing James H. and Ella Kellogg as national superintendents.

132. Bushnell, *Brief Sketch*, 5.

133. Baker, *Historical Sketches*, 158.

134. "Sayings and Doings of Women," *Good Housekeeping*, Vol. 10 (November 9, 1889–April 26, 1890), 67. See also Hardwick, *Oh Thou Woman*, 20–21, and *Union Signal*, April 22, 1886. On Chicago reformers' discomfort with urban vice, see Thekla Ellen Joiner, *Sin in the City: Chicago and Revivalism, 1880–1920* (Columbia: University of Missouri Press, 2007).

135. Pascoe, *Relations of Rescue*, 34.

136. *Union Signal*, May 5, 1887, 12.

137. "Miss Kate Bushnell," in *A Woman of the Century*, ed. Frances E. Willard and Mary A. Livermore (Buffalo: Charles Wells Moulton, 1893), 141.

138. *Union Signal*, February 21, 1889, 12.

139. Kate C. Bushnell, *The Woman Condemned* (New York: Funk & Wagnalls, 1886).

140. Bushnell, *Woman Condemned*, 9.

141. Bushnell, *Woman Condemned*, 4–5.

142. Bushnell, *Woman Condemned*, 7–9.

143. Bushnell, *Woman Condemned*, 10–11.

144. Bushnell, *Woman Condemned*, 13–14.

145. Bushnell, *Woman Condemned*, 17.

146. *Union Signal*, September 16, 1886, 9; see also *Union Signal*, May 5, 1887, 12.

147. *Union Signal*, May 5, 1887, 12.

148. *Union Signal*, August 26, 1886, 2.

149. *Union Signal*, March 15, 1888, 12.

150. Pivar, *Purity Crusade*, 136–137; *Union Signal*, March 24, 1887, 7, and September 8, 1887, 12.

151. "Where Satan Rules" was reprinted in the Wisconsin *W.C.T.U. State Work* (November 1888), 1–2.

152. *W.C.T.U. State Work*, 1–2.

153. *W.C.T.U. State Work*, 1–2.

154. *W.C.T.U. State Work*, 1–2.

155. *W.C.T.U. State Work*, 5.

156. *W.C.T.U. State Work*, 3–4. The "previous chaste character" clause could be found in the law titled "An act for the prevention of crime, and to prevent the abducting of unmarried women," No. 46, S., Chapter 214, *Laws of Wisconsin*; photocopy received from The State of Wisconsin Legislative Reference Bureau. The law was published April 28, 1887.

157. *W.C.T.U. State Work*, 3, 6.

158. *W.C.T.U. State Work*, 2–4. For an insightful cultural analysis of the "white slave" crusades, and of Bushnell's role in the movement, see Brian Donovan, *White Slave Crusades: Race, Gender, and Anti-Vice Activism, 1887–1917* (Urbana: University of Illinois Press, 2006).

159. *W.C.T.U. State Work*, 2–4.

160. *W.C.T.U. State Work*, 7. These women were reflecting common Victorian attitudes; as William Lecky explained in his *History of European Morals* (Vol. II [New York, 1870], 283), the prostitute, as "the supreme type of vice," was ultimately "the most efficient guardian of virtue" for the way in which she addressed the imbalance in a Victorian moral system that considered women naturally passionless and men at the mercy of persistent sexual needs.

161. *W.C.T.U. State Work*, 7. Bushnell judged that in some Northern Wisconsin towns, "a Social Purity member is as much a subject of hatred, even on the part of many professing Christianity, as is an abolitionist in the South."

162. *Union Signal*, November 8, 1888, 4.

163. *Union Signal*, March 7, 1889, 5.

164. *Union Signal*, April 11, 1889, 5.

165. *Union Signal*, April 11, 1889, 5; C. C. McCabe to Governor Hoard, February 2 and April 17, 1889, Records of the Northern Wisconsin "Slave" Investigation, 1882–1889, State Historical Society of Wisconsin, University of Wisconsin, Oshkosh, Box 6, Folder 1.

166. Pivar, *Purity Crusade*, 137.

167. Letter from C. C. McCabe to Governor Hoard, April 17, 1889, Records of the Northern Wisconsin "Slave" Investigation, 1882–1889, State Historical Society of Wisconsin, University of Wisconsin, Oshkosh, Box 6, Folder 1; *Union Signal*, February 14, 1889.

168. Bushnell, *Brief Sketch*, 7; *Union Signal*, January 31, 1889, 1.

169. As Dana Hardwick notes (*Oh Thou Woman*, 31–32), there is some confusion as to the precise nature of this legislation. Bushnell may be referring to the removal of the "previous chaste character" clause of the Wisconsin Senate Bill 46, Chapter 214, or to the adoption of prison sentences rather than fines for those operating houses of prostitution. Bushnell described the legislation as "drafted after my own heart's desire, but not by myself," and noted that it had "sent several men to long terms of imprisonment for trading in girls in the State of Wisconsin" (*Brief Sketch*, 7).

170. Bushnell, *Brief Sketch*, 8. In the spring of 1889 the *Union Signal* found it necessary to remind local unions that Bushnell "positively cannot speak but once a day" (*Union Signal*, April 11, 1889, 1).

171. Pivar, *Purity Crusade*, 10, 138–139.

CHAPTER 3

1. Bushnell, *Brief Sketch*, 8.

2. *Union Signal*, February 21, 1889, 1.

3. Bushnell, *Brief Sketch*, 8.

4. Notice of Bushnell's acceptance can be found in the *Union Signal*, December 25, 1890, 16.

5. Tyrrell, *Woman's World*, 20, 83.

6. Tyrrell, *Woman's World*, 36–37. Between 1888 and 1925 the WCTU commissioned 35 women as round-the-world missionaries; during that period Tyrrell estimates that "approximately 12.5 percent of all *Union Signal* copy was given over to reporting international events, places, and personnel."

7. Tyrrell, *Woman's World*, 4.

8. William T. Stead, *The Americanization of the World, or the Trend of the Twentieth Century* (New York: Horace Markley, 1902), 272, https://openlibrary.org/books/OL13514186M/The_Americanization_of_the_world; Tyrrell, 5.

9. Ian Tyrrell, "Women, Missions, and Empire: New Approaches to American Cultural Expansion," in *Competing Kingdoms*, 43. On American cultural expansion during this time, see Emily Rosenberg, *Spreading the American Dream: American Economic and Cultural Expansion, 1890–1945* (New York: Hill and Wang, 1982).

10. Tyrrell, *Woman's World*, 83.

11. Tyrrell, *Woman's World*, 96. As Tyrrell notes, "their universal mission made WCTU appointees suspicious of Western imperial adventures and critical of any temporizing toward moral corruption in imperial systems" (97–98).

12. Bushnell, *Brief Sketch*, 6.

13. Josephine E. Butler, "The Present Aspect of the Abolitionist Cause in Relation to British India," in *Josephine Butler and The Prostitution Campaigns: Diseases of the Body Politic*, ed. Jane Jordan and Ingrid Sharp (London: Routledge, 2003), 182.

14. Bushnell, *Brief Sketch*, 8–9.

15. Butler, "Present Aspect," 184.

16. Philippa Levine, *Prostitution, Race, and Politics: Policing Venereal Disease in the British Empire* (New York: Routledge, 2003), 95.

17. Elizabeth W. Andrew and Katharine C. Bushnell, *The Queen's Daughters in India* (London: Morgan and Scott, 1899), 17–18, http://books.google.com/books?id=JJ9j8KKdNLQC.

18. Bushnell, *Brief Sketch*, 11.

19. Butler, "Present Aspect," 184. In recounting Andrew's story, Butler added: "I would go further than this. I would reply, 'Just as I would to any other woman.' For we are all sinners" (201).

20. Bushnell, *Brief Sketch*, 9–11.

21. Butler to Mrs. Tanner and Miss Priestman, March 9, 1891, Josephine Butler Letters Collection, The Women's Library collections at LSE, 3JBL/30/13.

22. Andrew and Bushnell, *Queen's Daughters*, 24.

23. Bushnell, *Brief Sketch*, 11.

24. Andrew and Bushnell, *Queen's Daughters*, 24.

25. Bushnell, *Brief Sketch*, 12.

26. Bushnell, *Brief Sketch*, 14–15. Their account in *Queen's Daughters* provides a slightly more sympathetic account of this man (25).

27. Andrew and Bushnell, *Queen's Daughters*, 29.

28. Andrew and Bushnell, *Queen's Daughters*, 45, 48.

29. Andrew and Bushnell, *Queen's Daughters*, 37.

30. Andrew and Bushnell, *Queen's Daughters*, 32, 47.

31. Andrew and Bushnell, *Queen's Daughters*, 33.

32. Andrew and Bushnell, *Queen's Daughters*, 101–102.

33. Andrew and Bushnell, *Queen's Daughters*, 55–58. They also countered regulationists' insistence that cantonment women came from a "prostitute class." In their investigations they encountered "Hindus of all castes, from high-caste Brahmins down . . . [and] Mohammedans, Arabs, Egyptians, Afghans, Kashmiris, Jewesses." The closest thing they could find to a caste of *chakla* women were the daughters of Englishmen and prostitutes, who were themselves placed in *chaklas* (52).

34. Andrew and Bushnell, *Queen's Daughters*, 56–58. Bushnell's and Andrew's "Journal and Report" can be found in the Records of the Association for Moral & Social Hygiene, The Women's Library collections at LSE, 3AMS/C/03/03.

35. Andrew and Bushnell, *Queen's Daughters*, 56–57.

36. Andrew and Bushnell, *Queen's Daughters*, 20.

37. Andrew and Bushnell, *Queen's Daughters*, 76–77.

38. Andrew and Bushnell, *Queen's Daughters*, 20, 49.

39. Andrew and Bushnell, *Queen's Daughters*, 34, 73. On the regulation of sexuality in an imperial context, see Ann Laura Stoler, *Race and the Education of Desire: Foucault's* History of Sexuality *and the Colonial Order of Things* (Durham, NC: Duke University Press, 1995).

40. Andrew and Bushnell, *Queen's Daughters*, 41. Bushnell and Andrew continued: "Men and women, Governments and Armies, cannot, combined, reduce the estimate which He puts upon one immortal soul; but in a near judgement-day, these will have to drink the full measure appointed for such a crime as thwarting a woman in her God-given right to lead a decent moral life. When a Government begins to drag down the moral character of its subjects, it has begun to dig out its own foundations" (41–42).

41. Levine, *Prostitution, Race, and Politics*, 105; "Indian Journal," 1892, Papers of Henry Joseph Wilson, The Women's Library collections at LSE, 3HJW/F/05.

42. Bushnell, *Brief Sketch*, 13. For accounts of their Australia visit, see *Union Signal*, December 8, 1892, 5, 10.

43. "Is Vice Regulated by the State in India? Interview with General Lord Roberts," *Christian Commonwealth* 11 (May 1893): 519, cited in *Josephine Butler and the Prostitution Campaigns*, ed. Jane Jordan and Ingrid Sharp (London: Routledge, 2003), 209–213.

44. Andrew and Bushnell, *Queen's Daughters*, 88–89; see also Levine, *Prostitution, Race, and Politics*, 107. As Levine notes, five years earlier British viceroy Lord Dufferin had characterized repealers as "the raging sisterhood who are troubling our mental purity by their obscene correspondence" (99).

45. Andrew and Bushnell, *Queen's Daughters*, 91.

46. Andrew and Bushnell, *Queen's Daughters*, 91–96.

47. Letter from Josephine E. Butler to Stanley Butler, August 24, 1893, in *Josephine Butler and the Prostitution Campaigns*, ed. Jordan & Sharp, 381–382; Andrew and Bushnell, *Queen's Daughters*, 92–93.

48. Letter from Josephine E. Butler to Stanley Butler, August 24, 1893.

49. Robert W. Rydell, *All the World's a Fair: Visions of Empire at American International Expositions, 1876–1916* (Chicago: University of Chicago Press, 1987), 4–5, 39, 55.

50. Gail Bederman, *Manliness and Civilization: A Cultural History of Gender and Race in the United States, 1880–1917* (Chicago: University of Chicago Press, 1995), 35–41. These lessons were not lost on contemporary observers. Ida B. Wells and Frederick Douglass, for example, argued for the inclusion of African Americans' achievements in the hall of the White City, but the fair's organizers denied their request.

51. Bederman, *Manliness and Civilization*, 25–26.

52. Andrew and Bushnell, *Queen's Daughters*, preface to first edition; see also Tyrrell, *Woman's World*, 97–98. Tyrrell cautions, however, that "none of this chastisement of Christian and 'civilized' peoples changed the impact of the cultural messages of superiority imbedded in the WCTU's version of the Christian commitment" (103). Antoinette Burton, too, notes how challenging "the 'so-called civilization' of Britain was a popular tack in Victorian emancipationist literature" (*Burdens*, 90), even as British feminists continued to advance an imperial feminism. Far more than fellow critics of "so-called civilization," however, Bushnell turned her critique back on Western Christianity as the source of this hypocrisy.

53. *Union Signal*, November 2, 1893, 2–3; see also *Minutes of the Second Biennial Convention of the World's Woman's Christian Temperance Union* (Chicago: Woman's Temperance Publishing Association, 1893), 190–193.

54. *Union Signal*, November 2, 1893, 5.

55. *Union Signal*, November 2, 1893, 5.

56. *Union Signal*, November 2, 1893, 5.

57. *Union Signal*, November 2, 1893, 5.

58. Tyrrell, *Woman's World*, 7.

59. Hunter, "Women's Mission in Historical Perspective," 31.

60. Burton, *Burdens*, 3.

61. *Union Signal*, August 9, 1894, 3. Writing from Shanghai as she and Andrew continued on their world tour, Bushnell was trying to provide a practical solution to a problem she and other round-the-world missionaries faced, as they often found themselves swamped by letters "from women in every part of the world on all possible questions, submitting every sort of case to our judgment and making all manner of requests." And although she cautioned against any method that "seemed like a proposal to patronize and give charity to these distant unions," she nevertheless urged that a "home" union "take under its special charge for help and counsel" unions in India, China, Japan, Australia, or "wherever it may be." For more on Bushnell's "Reciprocity Plan," see *Minutes of the Third Biennial Convention and Executive Committee Meetings of the World's Woman's Christian Temperance Union* (London: The White Ribbon Company, 1895), 255.

62. *Union Signal*, January 17, 1895, 4.

63. For a nuanced and often sympathetic assessment of missionary women's rhetoric of "sisterhood," see Kumari Jayawardena, *The White Woman's Other Burden: Western Women and South Asia during British Colonial Rule* (New York: Routledge, 1995), 21–32.

64. Tyrrell, *Woman's World*, 213. Tyrrell cites Elizabeth Wheeler Andrew to Frances Willard, April 1, 1893, roll 19, WCTU Series, Ohio Historical Society, Columbus, Ohio; and Elizabeth W. Andrew to Henry Wilson, July 3, 1900, Josephine Butler Papers, The Women's Library collections at LSE.

65. *Union Signal*, March 21, 1895, 12.

66. Bushnell was not alone among evangelicals in her opposition to racist and imperialist thinking. As Case demonstrates in his *Unpredictable Gospel*, those influenced by holiness teachings and those in close contact with non-Western believers were most likely to formulate this prophetic critique (138, 245).

67. *Union Signal*, February 22, 1894, 11. While in China, Bushnell was also able to visit her old mission station in Kiukiang, which was an emotional homecoming after two decades (*Union Signal*, August 23, 1894, 4).

68. *Union Signal*, June 7, 1894, 1.

69. Bushnell, *Brief Sketch*, 19.

70. Hardwick, 51; *US*, August 16, 1894, 4.

71. Elizabeth Andrew and Katharine Bushnell, *Heathen Slaves and Christian Rulers* (1907; Project Gutenberg, 2004), http://www.gutenberg.org/catalog/world/readfile?fk_files=1999559, 74.

72. Andrew and Bushnell, *Heathen Slaves*. They did note that the buying and selling of children was restricted in important ways (11, 54–55).

73. Andrew and Bushnell, *Heathen Slaves*, 18.

74. Andrew and Bushnell, *Heathen Slaves*, 15.

75. Andrew and Bushnell, *Heathen Slaves*, 13.

76. Andrew and Bushnell, *Heathen Slaves*, 27.

77. Andrew and Bushnell, *Heathen Slaves*, 36.

78. Andrew and Bushnell, *Heathen Slaves*, 28.

79. Andrew and Bushnell, *Heathen Slaves*, 28.

80. Andrew and Bushnell, *Heathen Slaves*, 27. And, Bushnell and Andrew added, "One does not propose a license as a remedy for an evil, except as led to that view by secret sympathy with the evil" (61).

81. Andrew and Bushnell, *Heathen Slaves*, 12.

82. Bushnell, *Brief Sketch*, 19.

83. *Union Signal*, April 18, 1895, 4.

84. Bushnell, *Brief Sketch*, 18–19.

85. Andrew and Bushnell, *Heathen Slaves*, 4; on women's mission work in San Francisco, see Pascoe, *Relations of Rescue*.

86. Andrew and Bushnell, *Heathen Slaves*, 94–95.

87. Andrew and Bushnell, *Heathen Slaves*, 114.

88. Andrew and Bushnell, *Heathen Slaves*, 107.
89. Andrew and Bushnell, *Heathen Slaves*, 107.
90. Andrew and Bushnell, *Heathen Slaves*, 111.

CHAPTER 4

1. Butler to Mary Priestman, July 26, 1895, Josephine Butler Letters Collection, The Women's Library collections at LSE, 3JBL/34/39 26; Bushnell, *Brief Sketch*, 17–18.
2. Butler to Miss Forsaith, May 3, 1895, Josephine Butler Letters Collection, The Women's Library collections at LSE, 3JBL/34/22.
3. Butler to Priestman, July 26, 1895, Josephine Butler Letters Collection, The Women's Library collections at LSE, 3JBL/34/39. Perhaps a lingering resentment shaped Bushnell's actions later that fall, when she removed herself from the Executive Committee of the World's WCTU to protest the fact that Andrew had not also been nominated to the Committee. Reflecting on this decision, Butler suggested that the "noble characters" of her "dear American friends," were "marred by a certain self assertion, and a little jealousy," and she recommended to a coworker that these "little infirmities of the American workers" should be kept in mind in order to avoid offending them, "while we rejoice in their good work" (Butler to Priestman, October 2, 1895, Josephine Butler Letters Collection, The Women's Library collections at LSE, 3JBL/34/50).
4. Andrew and Bushnell, *Queen's Daughters*, 23.
5. Butler to Priestman, August 10, 1895, Josephine Butler Letters Collection, The Women's Library collections at LSE, 3JBL/34/45.
6. Kathleen Fitzpatrick, *Lady Henry Somerset* (Boston: Little, Brown, and Company, 1923), 197–199; see also Hardwick, *Oh Thou Woman*, 62.
7. Butler to Forsaith, May 22, 1897, Josephine Butler Letters Collection, The Women's Library collections at LSE, 3JBL/37/32. Sixty-one thousand women signed a petition to bring Butler out of retirement given the circumstances. Lady Henry's cause was not helped by the fact that doubts lingered as to her commitment to the absolute evils of alcohol.
8. See the *Times*, November 23, 1897; *The Shield*, January 1898; Andrew and Bushnell, *A Fatal Mistake: To the W.C.T.U.* (n.p., 1897); *Reply of Dr. Katharine Bushnell and Mrs. Elizabeth Andrew to Certain Statements in a Published Letter Addressed by Lady Henry Somerset to a Correspondent on the Regulation of Vice in India* (London: Ladies' National Association, 1897); and Levine, *Prostitution, Race, and Politics*, 118.
9. *Union Signal*, November 18, 1897, 4.
10. Andrew to Forsaith, March 10, 1898, Josephine Butler Letters Collection, The Women's Library collections at LSE, 3JBL/40/16.
11. "May God pity you," Bushnell wrote vituperatively to Willard, adding: "I do" (Fitzpatrick, *Lady Henry*, 201; Hardwick, *Oh Thou Woman*, 66–67).

12. Andrew to Forsaith, February 18, 1898, Josephine Butler Letters Collection, The Women's Library collections at LSE, 3JBL/39/31.

13. Andrew to Forsaith, February 19, 1898, Josephine Butler Letters Collection, The Women's Library collections at LSE, 3JBL/39/32.

14. Bushnell to Forsaith, February 21, 1898, Josephine Butler Letters Collection, The Women's Library collections at LSE, 3JBL/39/34; and February 22, 1898, Josephine Butler Letters Collection, The Women's Library collections at LSE, 3JBL/39/35.

15. *Union Signal*, August 4, 1898, 5–6.

16. Butler to Mrs. Spence Watson, March 15, 1898, Josephine Butler Letters Collection, The Women's Library collections at LSE, 3JBL/40/21. Butler noted she had been "bothered out of [her] life" by those who had been unable to put to rest "this unlucky Lady H. Somerset affair."

17. Bushnell to Forsaith, June 16, 1898, Josephine Butler Letters Collection, The Women's Library collections at LSE, 3JBL/41/21. The book had been published in America in 1896 by the Woman's Temperance Publishing Association. Bushnell did not blame the Somerset affair for her difficulties with the book. Rather, she pointed instead to the perennial unpopularity of her message, noting that "even the best of men generally 'fight shy' of anything that would carry the purity reform into a question of obeying the Golden Rule in the marriage relation."

18. Bushnell's and Andrew's support came entirely from "receipts from meetings" and donations. In the years encompassing their India campaign, they gave over one thousand addresses and raised over $4,000; the following two years, with attention to their investigations diminishing, they gave under 200 addresses and raised less than $1,000. See *Minutes of the Third Biennial Convention*, 184–185.

19. Bushnell to Henry Wilson, December 26, 1898, Josephine Butler Letters Collection, The Women's Library collections at LSE, 3JBL/41/60.

20. Bushnell to Butler, August 30, 1899, Josephine Butler Letters Collection, The Women's Library collections at LSE, 3JBL/43/28; Butler, "Dead Hands on the Threshold," *Storm-Bell*, July 1899, 202–206.

21. Bushnell to Butler, August 30, 1899, and Bushnell to Forsaith, June 16, 1898, Josephine Butler Letters Collection, The Women's Library collections at LSE, 3JBL/41/21. *A Clean Life* was republished in 1901 by Revell, Chicago.

22. Bushnell to Butler, August 30, 1899, Josephine Butler Letters Collection, The Women's Library collections at LSE, 3JBL/43/28.

23. Bushnell to Butler, August 30, 1899, Josephine Butler Letters Collection, The Women's Library collections at LSE, 3JBL/43/28.

24. Bushnell to Butler, August 30, 1899, Josephine Butler Letters Collection, The Women's Library collections at LSE, 3JBL/43/28.

25. Bushnell to Butler, August 30, 1899, Josephine Butler Letters Collection, The Women's Library collections at LSE, 3JBL/43/28.

26. Bushnell, *Brief Sketch*, 22–23. Bushnell noted that she "had reached [her] own conclusion about the matter, and it was fully corroborated in the course of time by Josephine Butler."

27. Bushnell, *Brief Sketch*, 23.

28. Martin Kähler, *Schriften zur Christologie und Mission* (1908, Munich: Chr. Kaiser Verlag, 1971), quoted and translated in David J. Bosch, *Transforming Mission: Paradigm Shifts in Theology of Mission* (Maryknoll, NY: Orbis Books, 1991), 16.

29. Walls, "Gospel as Prisoner and Liberator," 10.

30. Walls, "Ephesian Moment," 79.

31. Susan Thorne writes, for example, of "what Victorian Christians referred to as the 'reflux benefit' or influence of foreign missions on British audiences *at home*, and of the role missions played in bringing the Empire *home*" (Susan Thorne, "Religion and Empire at Home," in *At Home with Empire*, 146).

32. Bushnell, *Brief Sketch*, 20. Bushnell attributed her ability to concentrate in such circumstances to the "powers of detachment from surroundings" she developed by growing up "in a home crowded with nine children and little privacy."

33. Bushnell, *Brief Sketch*, 21–22.

34. In *Women and the Work of Benevolence*, Ginzberg writes of a declining faith in the ability of moral reform to accomplish social change on the part of reformers in the decades following the Civil War, and of a growing reliance on legislative solutions in order to ensure social morality (206). Bushnell, however, remained skeptical of the role the state could play in legislating social reform, and focused instead on reinvigorating moral regeneration by reforming the theological foundations of society.

35. Sarah Grimké, *Letters on the Equality of the Sexes, and the Condition of Woman: Addressed to Mary S. Parker* (Boston: I. Knapp, 1838); Angelina E. Grimké, *Appeal to Christian Women of the South* (New York: American Anti-Slavery Society, 1836); Elizabeth Wilson, *A Scriptural View of Woman's Rights and Duties, in all the Important Relations of Life* (Philadelphia: Wm. S. Young, 1849). In *Sex and Citizenship in Antebellum America* (Chapel Hill: University of North Carolina Press, 1998), Nancy Isenberg cites two published letters written by Stanton and Elizabeth Wilson McClintock, "Woman's Rights," National Reformer, September 21, 1848, and "To the Editors," Seneca County Courier, n.d., Elizabeth Cady Stanton Papers, Manuscript Division, Library of Congress, Washington, DC.

36. Timothy Larsen, *A People of One Book*, 1. Although Larsen writes on Victorian Britain, the Bible's cultural currency was pronounced in nineteenth-century America as well.

37. As Nancy Isenberg states, "religion had a distinctive influence on the women's rights movement, not only as a set of ideas about morality and sacred truths, but as a crucial medium for debating such pivotal concerns as public opinion." According to Isenberg, "churches represented the religious lens through which congregations viewed political issues; the clergy used the pulpit for decidedly political purposes; and male and female church members and ministers used a

formidable religious press to instruct, discipline, and create opinions for their religious reading public" (*Sex and Citizenship*, 77).

38. Clark, "Politics of God," 60, 39.

39. Clark, "Politics of God," 46, 230.

40. Clark, "Politics of God," 55.

41. Clark, "Politics of God," 274.

42. Bushnell to Martin, September 7, 1943, Anne Henrietta Martin Papers, ca. 1892–1951, Bancroft Library, University of California, Berkeley. Rhetoric of Christ as the emancipator of women was common among Christian women of Bushnell's generation.

43. Pascoe, *Relations of Rescue*, 44–45.

44. Pascoe, *Relations of Rescue*, 44. Throughout the 1880s, for example, Methodist women fought for ordination, and for their right to serve as delegates to the Methodist Church's General Conference.

45. Frances Willard, *Woman in the Pulpit* (Boston: D. Lothrop, 1888), 55.

46. Willard, *Woman in the Pulpit*, 57.

47. Willard, *Woman in the Pulpit*, 23.

48. Willard, *Woman in the Pulpit*, 45.

49. *Union Signal*, October 17, 1889, 10. The courses were taught by Alfred A. Wright, a former Methodist Episcopal pastor and Dean of the Chautauqua School of Theology.

50. *Union Signal*, December 27, 1888, 3; *Union Signal*, March 28, 1889, 7.

51. *Union Signal*, May 29, 1890, 9.

52. *Union Signal*, August 1, 1889, 12. The courses continued through the end of 1892 (*Union Signal*, November 17, 1892, 12).

53. Although Willard keeps the majority of her female sources anonymous in *Woman in the Pulpit*, she mentions a conversation with "a returned missionary from China" on the gendered translation of Phil. 4:3 as revelatory of the potential bias on the part of biblical translators and interpreters, and is here clearly alluding to Bushnell (31).

54. *Union Signal*, September 12, 1889, 7.

55. *Union Signal*, June 7, 1894, 3–4; see also *Union Signal*, June 14, 1894, 2–3, and June 21, 1894, 3.

56. *Union Signal*, January 3, 1895, 3–4; January 10, 1895, 4; January 17, 1895, 3–4. Willard, too, briefly addressed 1 Cor. 11 in *Woman in the Pulpit*, 25.

57. *Union Signal*, June 14, 1894, 2.

58. *Union Signal*, June 14, 1894, 2. Willard also notes the gendered translation of "deaconess" as "servant" in *Woman in the Pulpit*, 32. I am indebted to Nevada DeLapp for his assistance in providing Greek and Hebrew terms, in this chapter and in subsequent ones.

59. *Union Signal*, June 5, 1890, 4.

60. *Union Signal*, June 5, 1890, 4.

61. Bushnell to Mrs. White, March 21, 1911, Papers of Mrs. F. White, The Women's Library collections at LSE, 7FWH/C/1.

62. Bushnell to Mrs. White, March 21, 1911, Papers of Mrs. F. White, The Women's Library collections at LSE, 7FWH/C/1.

63. Katharine Bushnell, *101 Questions Answered: A Woman's Catechism* (n.p., 1910); "Literature List," in Anne Henrietta Martin Papers, ca. 1892–1951; Bancroft Library, University of California, Berkeley. Around this time she also wrote two additional booklets, *The Badge of Guilt and Shame* and *Covet to Prophesy*, both on Paul's writings on women.

64. Copies of the 1911 and 1913 editions of Bushnell's "Women's Correspondence Bible Class" are housed in the British Library collections (BL 3129.h.13 and BL L.17.f.4, respectively).

65. The 1916 edition of "The Women's Correspondence Bible Class: God's Word to Women" is also available at the British Library (BL 3125.df.29). While similarities exist between this edition and the 1911 and 1913 manuscripts, Bushnell made significant and substantive changes to her earlier drafts. Although Bushnell continued to edit the lessons between 1916 and 1923, the content of the two editions overlaps to a significant extent. For these reasons, together with the fact that Bushnell first used the title *God's Word to Women* in connection with her 1916 edition, I have identified 1916 as the initial publication date of *God's Word to Women*.

66. Peter J. Theusen, *In Discordance with the Scriptures: American Protestant Battles over Translating the Bible* (New York: Oxford University Press, 1999), 44–45, 49–50. Only one member of the Revised Version committee, William Robertson Smith, espoused higher critical methods.

67. Theusen, *In Discordance with the Scriptures*, 51–56.

68. Theusen, *In Discordance with the Scriptures*, 61, 116.

69. Theusen, *In Discordance with the Scriptures*, 96, 111–12.

70. Bushnell, *God's Word to Women* (hereafter *GWTW*), 144. Bushnell added that "the highest good of the other half" was "just as vitally concerned, if even more remotely and less visibly."

71. Bushnell, *GWTW*, 375. On the reorientation of nineteenth-century theology, see Claude Welch, *Protestant Thought in the Nineteenth Century*, vol. 2 (New Haven, CT: Yale University Press, 1985), 68.

72. Bushnell, *GWTW*, 172.

73. Bushnell, *GWTW*, 154.

74. Bushnell, *GWTW*, 20.

75. Bushnell, *GWTW*, 5. Here Bushnell quoted the German New Testament scholar Adolf Diessmann.

76. Bushnell, *GWTW*, 5–9.

77. Bushnell, *GWTW*, 374.

78. Bushnell acknowledged that a few women had in fact translated a part of the Bible, or the whole, but their work had been "allowed to perish" (*GWTW*, 377).

79. Bushnell, *GWTW*, 152, 391.

80. Bushnell, *GWTW*, 372.

81. Bushnell, *GWTW*, 616.
82. Bushnell, *GWTW*, 375.
83. Bushnell, *GWTW*, 616, 619.
84. Bushnell, *GWTW*, 447.
85. Bushnell, *GWTW*, 372,
86. Bushnell, *GWTW*, 622.
87. Bushnell, *GWTW*, 375.
88. Bushnell, *GWTW*, 13.
89. Bushnell, *GWTW*, 371.
90. Bushnell, *GWTW*, 375. Here Bushnell quoted Robert Herbert Story, an "eminent Scotch divine," cited in F. W. Farrar's *History of Interpretation* (London: Macmillan and Co., 1886), 29.
91. Bushnell, *GWTW*, 375.
92. Bushnell cited 2 Tim. 3:16 on the inspired nature of the Bible, Isaiah 40:8 on its infallibility, and John 10:35 on its inviolability (*GWTW*, 2), but she made clear that she was referring only to the original text, not to "any mere version" (*GWTW*, 5).
93. Bushnell, *GWTW*, 11.
94. Kraditor, *Ideas of the Woman Suffrage Movement*, 76; see also Margaret Lamberts Bendroth, *Fundamentalism and Gender: 1875 to the Present* (New Haven, CT: Yale University Press, 1996), 37.
95. Bushnell, *GWTW*, 2.
96. Bushnell, *GWTW*, 1.

CHAPTER 5

1. In *Sex and Citizenship*, Nancy Isenberg explains how a number of women's rights activists engaged the Christian creation story: "As a complex metaphor, the creation story details several overlapping allusions to explain marital and religious relationships. From the seventeenth through the nineteenth centuries, ministers and politicians used the creation story as their major proof text for defining the polity of the family" (10).
2. Bushnell, *GWTW*, 22.
3. Bushnell, *GWTW*, 98.
4. Bushnell, *GWTW*, 98.
5. Bushnell, *GWTW*, 98.
6. Bushnell, *GWTW*, 165.
7. Bushnell, *GWTW*, 88.
8. Bushnell, *GWTW*, 88. Bushnell was quoting from Tertullian's *De Culta Feminarum*.
9. Cotton Mather's granddaughter Hannah Mather Crocker based her treatise on women's rights on the first three chapters of Genesis (*Observations on the Real Rights of Women, with Their Appropriate Duties, Agreeable to Scripture,*

Reason and Common Sense [Boston, 1818]; twenty years later, Sarah Grimké anticipated some of Bushnell's insights in her *Letters on the Equality of the Sexes, and the Condition of Woman* (1838); and in 1849, Elizabeth Wilson began her *Scriptural View of Woman's Rights and Duties* with the book of Genesis. Other, less orthodox, revisions also appeared, particularly among Owenite socialist women in Britain in the 1830s and 1840s. For more on women's interpretations of Genesis, see Marion Ann Taylor and Heather E. Weir, eds., *Let Her Speak for Herself: Nineteenth-Century Women Writing on the Women of Genesis* (Waco, TX: Baylor University Press, 2006).

10. Stanton, *Woman's Bible*, 24, 26–27.
11. Bushnell, *GWTW*, 87. The book was known as *Ecclesiasticus*, or *The Wisdom of Ben Sira*.
12. Bushnell, *GWTW*, 85–86.
13. Bushnell, *GWTW*, 112.
14. Bushnell, *GWTW*, 23–24. Bushnell traced this idea "at least as far back" as the time of Christ, to the writings of Philo, and defended it in light of modern Darwinian research that revealed how some creatures, "at a very early embryonic period," possessed rudimentary reproductive glands of both sexes. (Though Bushnell did not accept Darwinian evolution in its entirety, she insisted that Darwinism would not have gained widespread acceptance were it not based upon "well-founded facts," and she believed that "the Scriptures in no way contradict scientific facts such as these, discovered only thousands of years afterwards by human research").
15. Bushnell, *GWTW*, 31. Bushnell cited Gen. 1:31 and 2:18.
16. Bushnell, *GWTW*, 31.
17. Bushnell, *GWTW*, 32.
18. Bushnell, *GWTW*, 33. Bushnell explained that by separating Eve out of Adam, "God intended the development of the social virtues, as an aid for Adam" (35).
19. Bushnell, *GWTW*, 34–35. The three exceptions could be found in Isa. 20:5; Eze. 12:14; and Dan. 11:34. The numbers of occurrences of terms that Bushnell provides do not always align precisely with counts provided by modern scholars.
20. Bushnell, *GWTW*, 39.
21. Bushnell, *GWTW*, 40.
22. Bushnell, *GWTW*, 39.
23. Bushnell, *GWTW*, 346. In *Woman in the Pulpit*, Frances Willard briefly addresses the issue of creation order as well (37).
24. Bushnell, *GWTW*, 346, 350. Here Bushnell cited W. M. Ramsay in *The Expositor*, 1909.
25. Bushnell, *GWTW*, 349.
26. Bushnell, *GWTW*, 348.
27. Bushnell, *GWTW*, 351.
28. Bushnell, *GWTW*, 352. Bushnell cited Acts 20:29; 2 Pet. 3:15–16; and 2 Cor. 4:2–3 as evidence of his opposition to the "Judaizers"; see also Gal. 2:14.

29. Bushnell, *GWTW*, 347.

30. Bushnell, *GWTW*, 351.

31. Here Bushnell cited Franz Delitzsch and Monroe Gibson, who defined the "seed of woman" as those who are spiritually her children, those who are "on the side of good, the side of God and righteousness" in the drama of redemption (Bushnell, *GWTW*, 83).

32. Bushnell explained that Eve was so inspired by God's promise that her seed would "crush the serpent's head," that she wrongly anticipated the birth of her first child, Cain, as the fulfillment of that promise, naming him "the Coming One" (Gen. 4:1), and demonstrating her belief in God's promise (Gen. 3:15).

33. Bushnell, *GWTW*, 77–79, 81.

34. Bushnell, *GWTW*, 345.

35. Bushnell, *GWTW*, 363.

36. Bushnell, *GWTW*, 113.

37. Bushnell, *GWTW*, 102.

38. On Eve's deception, see 1 Tim. 2:14 and 2 Cor. 11:3; on Adam's culpability, see 1 Tim. 2:14; 1 Cor. 15:22; Rom. 5:12–19 (Bushnell, *GWTW*, 91–92).

39. Bushnell, *GWTW*, 68; here Bushnell cited Gen. 3:12–13.

40. Bushnell, *GWTW*, 69. Although modern biblical interpreters often point out that the serpent of Genesis 3 is not in fact identified as Satan in the text, Bushnell advanced the view common in her day that the serpent and Satan were one and the same. Drawing on the German scholar John Peter Lange, Bushnell added that perhaps because Adam had been charged with watching and protecting the garden from an "existing power of evil," he had declined to mention Satan, who had somehow been let inside (36).

41. Bushnell, *GWTW*, 71.

42. Bushnell, *GWTW*, 104.

43. Bushnell, *GWTW*, 99. Here Bushnell noted that "despite the popular cry regarding the 'universal Fatherhood of God, and the universal brotherhood of man,' which is in part true, we who accept the Scriptures as authority must not forget that Satan, as well as God, has his children—moral and spiritual delinquents—among men" (73).

44. Bushnell, *GWTW*, 99.

45. Bushnell, *GWTW*, 100–101.

46. Bushnell, *GWTW*, 114.

47. Bushnell, *GWTW*, 117.

48. Bushnell, *GWTW*, 121. Bushnell pointed to Ruth 4:13 and Hosea 9:11 for the proper spelling of "conception," which she transliterated as "HRJWN" (הריון).

49. Bushnell, *GWTW*, 121.

50. Bushnell, *GWTW*, 139.

51. Bushnell, *GWTW*, 107–108. Here Bushnell quoted William E. Addis and the British Methodist scholar Adam Clarke. Bushnell added that Calvin had written that here woman was "cast into servitude"; it was as if God said: "Thou

shalt desire nothing but what thy husband wishes." As Bushnell put it, "Calvin would have us believe God first ordained marriage, but afterwards substituted 'servitude.'"

52. Bushnell, *GWTW*, 142–143.

53. Bushnell, *GWTW*, 108. Bushnell quoted Karl August Knobel, Johann Karl Keil and Franz Delitzsch, and August Dillman.

54. Bushnell, *GWTW*, 108. Bushnell added that if this sensuality were indeed "the state of woman's mind in general, it would not be necessary to starve women out of industrial lines, and put a check upon their mental development, lest they be disinclined to marry if capable of self support," yet precisely these methods had been used to "maintain the 'domestic' desires of women."

55. Bushnell, *GWTW*, 109.

56. Bushnell, *GWTW*, 125–144.

57. Bushnell, *GWTW*, 124.

58. According to Bushnell, the Greek Septuagint, the Syriac Peshitta, the Samaritan Pentateuch, and the Old Latin, Sahidic, Bohairic, and Ethiopic texts all rendered the word as a form of "turning," while the Babylon Targum, a text penned much later than those listed above and described by Bushnell as "purely rabbinical teaching," translated *teshuqa* as "lust" in Gen. 3:16, but as "turning" in Gen. 4:7 (Bushnell, *GWTW*, 138–144).

59. Bushnell, *GWTW*, 127.

60. Bushnell, *GWTW*, 167.

61. Bushnell, *GWTW*, 127.

62. Bushnell, *GWTW*, 418.

63. Bushnell, *GWTW*, 127.

64. Bushnell, *GWTW*, 124.

65. Bushnell, *GWTW*, 96.

66. Bushnell, *GWTW*, 97.

67. Bushnell, *GWTW*, 96.

68. Bushnell, *GWTW*, 122. Though Eve repented, there was no evidence Adam did. Bushnell surmised that "before Cain could have been born (Gen. 4:1) either Adam must have repented and become again the child of God, or Eve must have turned from God and followed Adam out of Eden. The fact that Cain was a murderer certainly argues that Eve followed Adam."

69. In redefining sin in this way, Bushnell anticipated Valerie Saiving's critical observation nearly half a century later that would help spawn a new era of feminist theology (Valerie Saiving Goldstein, "The Human Situation: A Feminine View," *The Journal of Religion* 40, no. 2 [April 1960]: 100–112). Saiving's gendered analysis of sin influenced other feminist theologians such as Mary Daly and Judith Plaskow. See, for example, Plaskow's *Sex, Sin and Grace: Women's Experience and the Theologies of Reinhold Niebuhr and Paul Tillich* (Washington, DC: University Press of America, 1980).

70. Bushnell, *GWTW*, 390. Here Bushnell quoted Arthur Penryn Stanley, Dean of Westminster.

71. Bushnell, *GWTW*, 391. Bushnell wavered on whether she believed this to be a deliberate act or simply a reflection of man's sinful state. Elsewhere she allowed that the mistranslation of Genesis 3:16 might be attributed to "men of old," who, coming across a phrase "beyond their comprehension" that "seemed to have to do with woman's relation to her husband," unconsciously "consulted their own ideas of what a wife *should be*, in her relation to her husband, and inserted those ideas into their interpretation." Other men then accepted this interpretation without challenge, "because it conformed to their unsanctified wishes," and so it was handed on "from generation to generation, until it became weighty through 'tradition'" (Bushnell, *GWTW*, 112).

72. Bushnell to Ethel Dummer, May 20, 1921, Ethel Sturges Dummer Papers, ca. 1866–1954, Schlesinger Library, Radcliffe Institute, Cambridge, MA.

73. Bushnell, *GWTW*, 623; *Union Signal*, June 14, 1894, 2.

74. Bushnell, *GWTW*, 624.

75. Bushnell, *GWTW*, 633.

76. Bushnell, *GWTW*, 625. Bushnell noted that the Septuagint renders Ruth 3:11: "'*Thou art a woman of power*' (dunamis)."

77. Bushnell, *GWTW*, 626.

78. Bushnell, *GWTW*, 628.

79. Bushnell, *GWTW*, 629.

80. Bushnell, *GWTW*, 629.

81. Bushnell, *GWTW*, 630.

82. Bushnell, *GWTW*, 631.

83. Bushnell, *GWTW*, 630.

84. Bushnell, *GWTW*, 632.

85. Bushnell, *GWTW*, 633. Bushnell added that in this case the Septuagint translates the passage "a *masculine* woman," and noted that when Syriacist Alphonse Mingana reviewed her work he added that "another point in your favour is that the Syriac text has actually a 'strong, powerful, virile woman'" (630).

86. Bushnell, *GWTW*, 639.

87. Bushnell, *GWTW*, 639.

88. Bushnell, *GWTW*, 640. The word in question was *sophrosune*.

89. Bushnell, *GWTW*, 644. On *kosmios*, Bushnell cited 1 Tim. 2:9; *hagnos* can be found in Phil. 4:8; 1 Tim. 5:22; James 3:17; 1 John 3:3; 2 Cor. 7:11, 11:2; Tit. 2:5; and 1 Peter 3:2. Bushnell had introduced her critique of *hagnos* and other mistranslations years earlier in the pages of the *Union Signal* (June 14, 1894, 2–3).

90. Bushnell, *GWTW*, 682.

91. Bushnell, *GWTW*, 687.

92. Bushnell, *GWTW*, 674.

93. Bushnell, *GWTW*, 692.

94. Uncial manuscripts are ancient parchment texts, which tended to be more reliable than their papyri counterparts. For a brief overview of uncial manuscripts, see J. Harold Greenlee, *Introduction to New Testament Textual Criticism* (Peabody, MA: Hendrickson, 2005), 27–33. I am grateful to Nevada DeLapp for assistance in navigating this area of historical theology.
95. Bushnell, *GWTW*, 675.
96. Bushnell, *GWTW*, 677.
97. Bushnell, *GWTW*, 678.
98. Bushnell, *GWTW*, 680.
99. Bushnell, *GWTW*, 677.
100. Bushnell, *GWTW*, 683.
101. Bushnell, *GWTW*, 691. Bushnell reminded her readers "of the days when monks fled to the wilderness, that they might never be defiled by looking upon the face of a woman; and when celibacy was so exalted that marriage was looked upon as a mild sort of adultery" (685).
102. Bushnell, *GWTW*, 685. See Augustine, *De Conj. Adult.* 2.6.
103. Bushnell, *GWTW*, 685.
104. Bushnell, *GWTW*, 682.
105. Bushnell, *GWTW*, 682, 684.
106. Bushnell, *GWTW*, 684.
107. Bushnell, *GWTW*, 687.
108. Bushnell, *GWTW*, 688.
109. Bushnell, *GWTW*, 690.
110. Bushnell, *GWTW*, 633. Had theologians correctly translated and interpreted biblical passages, Bushnell argued, women "would have been far better equipped to guard their virtue,—since the ruin of girls is usually due to weak character and general unfitness to cope with the world."
111. Bushnell, *GWTW*, 378, 379. Bushnell conceded that there had been male teachers who had shown the importance of "humility" and "meekness" for men as well as for women, but she did not deem it necessary to pause at each step to call attention to the exceptions to the rule.
112. Bushnell, *GWTW*, 391.
113. Bushnell, *GWTW*, 382.
114. Bushnell, *GWTW*, 66.
115. Bushnell, *GWTW*, 411, 466. If women were truly men's subordinates, Bushnell explained, they would be nonentities, reckoned neither good nor bad, since morality and immorality alike originated in free choice.
116. Bushnell, *GWTW*, 385–386.

CHAPTER 6

1. Bushnell, *GWTW*, 44. Bushnell noted that though some scholars attributed the words in Gen. 2:24 to Adam, in Matt. 19:4–5 Jesus "speaks of them as God's

own language." Earlier editions of Bushnell's "Women's Correspondence Bible Class" contain very little on the idea of the matriarchate, but the thesis plays a prominent role in her 1923 edition that is the source of modern reprints of *God's Word to Women*.

2. Bushnell, *GWTW*, 53.

3. Bushnell, *GWTW*, 421.

4. Bushnell, *GWTW*, 458.

5. Bushnell, *GWTW*, 489.

6. Bushnell, *GWTW*, 46. Bushnell found further evidence for female kinship in passages where the Scriptures referred to "whole cities and nations of people" with feminine pronouns. Bushnell insisted that this was "not a mere meaningless human 'custom' observed by the Holy Spirit who inspired the Word," but rather a reflection of God's will for humanity (Bushnell, *GWTW*, 468). Also see paragraphs 64, 470.

7. Bushnell, *GWTW*, 439. Bushnell pointed as well to Deborah's waging war against Sisera "for his crimes against women" recounted in Judg. 4 (55).

8. Bushnell, *GWTW*, 474.

9. Bushnell, *GWTW*, 56; see also 277.

10. Bushnell, *GWTW*, 59.

11. Bushnell, *GWTW*, 59, 530. Citing William Robertson Smith, Bushnell also suggested that the word "Israel" shared the same stem as "Sarah," in accordance with matriarchal custom (278).

12. Bushnell, *GWTW*, 529.

13. Bushnell, *GWTW*, 542.

14. Bushnell, *GWTW*, 541.

15. Bushnell, *GWTW*, 548; see also 277, 301, 110.

16. Bushnell, *GWTW*, 549–550.

17. Bushnell, *GWTW*, 521–522.

18. Bushnell, *GWTW*, 550. And both needed to grow in faith, Bushnell added. She explained how God took one hundred years to prepare Adam and ninety years for Sarah, waiting until all sensuality was dead, and "fleshly desire" displaced "by holier aspiration" (525).

19. Bushnell, *GWTW*, 279.

20. Bushnell, *GWTW*, 281.

21. Bushnell, *GWTW*, 495, 510, 512. Bushnell recommended James Orr's *Virgin Birth of Christ* (New York: Charles Scribner's Sons, 1907), "lest feminine prejudices might be alleged."

22. Bushnell, *GWTW*, 494, 443.

23. Bushnell, *GWTW*, 223.

24. Bushnell, *GWTW*, 497.

25. Bushnell, *GWTW*, 497.

26. Bushnell, *GWTW*, 501.

27. Bushnell, *GWTW*, 498.

28. Bushnell, *GWTW*, 499. Bushnell added that male kinship "rests always for proof, on hearsay evidence; female kinship, on *prima facie* evidence. Uncertainty must always haunt the former; and that is the great reason why it should never have been made the basis of human records" (500).

29. Bushnell, *GWTW*, 418.

30. Bushnell, *GWTW*, 450.

31. Bushnell, *GWTW*, 452.

32. Bushnell, *GWTW*, 450.

33. See Elazar Barkan and Ronald Bush, "Introduction," in *Prehistories of the Future: The Primitivist Project and the Culture of Modernism*, ed. Barkan and Bush (Stanford, CA: Stanford University Press, 1995), 15.

34. Bushnell, *GWTW*, 489. Bushnell also rejected the anthropological theory that linked promiscuous social relations to the prehistoric matriarchy as incompatible with God's will as revealed in Genesis.

35. Bushnell, *GWTW*, 441.

36. Bushnell, *GWTW*, 438.

37. Bushnell, *GWTW*, 443.

38. Bushnell, *GWTW*, 511

39. Bushnell, *GWTW*, 496.

40. Bushnell, *GWTW*, 511. Bushnell was likely playing on the subtitle of her distant relative Horace Bushnell's *Women's Suffrage: The Reform Against Nature* (1869).

41. Bushnell, *GWTW*, 443.

42. Bushnell, *GWTW*, 447.

43. Bushnell, *GWTW*, 289.

44. *Union Signal*, January 3, 1895, 3. Bushnell quipped, "Perhaps woman should be 'ashamed of her face,' because if unveiled, it shines forth to the detriment of the theological theory of its having only a glory reflected from man's face, and it is a shame that nature should thus be allowed to contradict dogma."

45. Bushnell, *GWTW*, 234.

46. Bushnell, *GWTW*, 641.

47. Bushnell, *GWTW*, 236. Bushnell pointed to instances of the same word in Rev. 2:26, 14:18, and 20:6, and argued that "if it be allowable to treat this verse so, then we may read elsewhere, 'The Son of Man hath a *token of being under* authority,' instead of reading that He '*hath power*' to forgive sin."

48. Bushnell, *GWTW*, 260.

49. Bushnell, *GWTW*, 218.

50. Bushnell, *GWTW*, 224.

51. Bushnell, *GWTW*, 240. Here Bushnell cited Rom. 8:1.

52. Bushnell, *GWTW*, 241; see also 245–246, where Bushnell cited 1 Thess. 2:19 and 2 Cor. 3:18.

53. Bushnell, *GWTW*, 245.

54. Bushnell, *GWTW*, 240.

55. Bushnell, *GWTW*, 243.

56. Bushnell, *GWTW*, 240.

57. Bushnell, *GWTW*, 249.

58. Bushnell, *GWTW*, 239. Here Bushnell was referring in particular to Tertullian's suggestion that women needed to veil before angels lest women seduce them (264–270).

59. Bushnell cited Matt. 5:5, 18:4, 20:25, 23:12, 28:12; Mark 9:35, 10:42–43; Luke 14:11, 18:14, 22:26; 1 Pet. 5:2–3, 5–6; Rom. 12:10; Gal. 3:27–28, 5:23; Eph. 5:21; Phil. 2:3, 2:6; among others (*Union Signal*, June 7, 1894, 3–4).

60. *Union Signal*, June 14, 1894, 2.

61. *Union Signal*, June 21, 1894, 3.

62. *Union Signal*, June 7, 1894, 3.

63. Bushnell, *GWTW*, 4. Bushnell cited Eph. 6:5; 1 Cor. 7:21–23; 1 Tim. 6:1.

64. Bushnell, *GWTW*, 4. Bushnell explained this clause in the context of 1 Cor. 7:21–23 and Col. 3:23, 24. The Ephesian woman ought to submit "not because of her husband's commands," but in the spirit of the Gospel teaching found in Matt. 5:39–41; 1 Cor. 4:12; 1 Cor. 6:7; 2 Cor. 4:8, 9; 2 Cor. 6:4; 2 Cor. 12:10; 2 Tim. 2:24–25, 4:5; Heb. 10:30, 34.

65. Bushnell, *GWTW*, 4.

66. Bushnell, *GWTW*, 291. Bushnell compared New Testament women to Chinese women with bound feet, who, when they unbound their feet, first needed to re-bind each toe to individual splints until they gained strength enough to walk. While the original foot-binding deprived women of freedom, the latter restored lost freedom, and this was precisely the nature of Paul's advice; he first declared that the bandages of women's oppression be removed, and then that husbands be "used as individual splints to each broken and crushed woman" (358).

67. Bushnell, *GWTW*, 355.

68. Bushnell, *GWTW*, 358.

69. Bushnell, *GWTW*, 292–299. Bushnell further explained that in the Old Testament "subjection" often meant "waiting on God," and she offered this as a possible interpretation for both 1 Cor. 14:34 and 1 Tim. 2:11. "Where 'subjection' is spoken of as a woman's duty, without further immediate specification, it has been too readily assumed that this means subjection *to a husband*," she claimed, while "the thought of a spirit of humility *towards God*, may be all that is intended."

70. Bushnell, *GWTW*, 293.

71. Bushnell, *GWTW*, 296. Willard also made this point in *Woman in the Pulpit*, 35.

72. Bushnell, *GWTW*, 298. Bushnell cited Titus 2:5, 5:22, and Col. 3:18. She also noted that when Peter exhorted wives to win over their heathen husbands by being "in subjection" to them, this could not have entailed absolute obedience lest women be commanded to worship other gods (1 Peter 3:1–2).

73. Bushnell, *GWTW*, 304.

74. Bushnell, *GWTW*, 305. Bushnell referenced Matt. 6:24, 23:11, and Luke 16:13.

75. *Union Signal*, June 7, 1894, 4; see also *GWTW*, 367–369.

76. *Union Signal*, June 14, 1894, 2.

77. Bushnell, *GWTW*, 127.

78. Bushnell, *GWTW*, 221.

79. Bushnell, *GWTW*, 344. Similarly, Bushnell referenced Lev. 20:18 as evidence that "God holds woman as a free agent in the marriage relation" (111; see also 302).

80. Bushnell, *GWTW*, 290.

81. Bushnell, *GWTW*, 392. Bushnell cited John 2:24–25, where it was recorded that though many believed in Christ's name, Jesus "did not commit Himself unto them, because He knew all men," and she advised: "Let women do the same; they have a very safe example to follow."

82. Bushnell, *GWTW*, 392.

83. Bushnell, *GWTW*, 397.

84. Bushnell, *GWTW*, 250, 307. In her index, Bushnell added that "every woman should be well acquainted" with Mill's *Subjection of Women*.

85. As Barbara Epstein makes clear, WCTU women held a variety of views on divorce, and disagreed with each other on how best to protect women and pursue morality when it came to the accessibility of divorce (*Politics of Domesticity*, 133–135).

86. Bushnell, *GWTW*, 63. The passage can also be found in Mark 10:7–9.

87. Bushnell, *GWTW*, 370. See also 616–644.

88. Bushnell, *GWTW*, 395.

89. Bushnell, *GWTW*, 468.

90. Bushnell, *GWTW*, 398.

91. *Union Signal*, September 12, 1889, 7; see also *GWTW*, 189–214.

92. Bushnell, *GWTW*, 191, 199.

93. Bushnell, *GWTW*, 200.

94. Bushnell, *GWTW*, 201.

95. *Union Signal*, September 12, 1889, 7.

96. Bushnell, *GWTW*, 201; see also 204–208.

97. *Union Signal*, September 12, 1889, 7; *GWTW*, 203. What Paul meant by this, Bushnell argued, was "just what the Bible teaches, viz.: that the word came unto *women* also" at Pentecost, as recorded in Acts 2.

98. Bushnell, *GWTW*, 207. Here Bushnell quoted Acts 2:16–18.

99. Bushnell also pointed to Psalm 68:11: "The Lord giveth the word; the women that publish the tidings are a great host" (Bushnell, *GWTW*, 190).

100. *Union Signal*, September 12, 1889, 7. She directed readers to 1 Cor. 15:29–34, where male commentators attributed the phrase "let us eat and drink, for tomorrow we die" to an interlocutor, and she was confident that male commentators would have treated 1 Cor. 14 in the same way had the passage placed limitations upon the male sex.

101. Bushnell, *GWTW*, 306–307.

102. Bushnell, *GWTW*, 308.
103. Bushnell, *GWTW*, 309.
104. Bushnell, *GWTW*, 307.
105. Bushnell, *GWTW*, 314.
106. Bushnell, *GWTW*, 325.
107. Bushnell, *GWTW*, 325. Bushnell cited Ramsay's *Church in the Roman Empire* (1893).
108. Bushnell, *GWTW*, 317.
109. Bushnell, *GWTW*, 319.
110. Bushnell, *GWTW*, 319, 321. "We must not forget," Bushnell reminded her readers, that "*an accusation* against a woman's virtue throughout all time, has generally been treated more severely than *a proved deed* of the same sort in a man" (322).
111. Bushnell, *GWTW*, 322. Here Bushnell quoted F. W. Farrar's *Early Days of Christianity.*
112. Bushnell, *GWTW*, 323.
113. Bushnell, *GWTW*, 317.
114. Bushnell, *GWTW*, 320.
115. Bushnell, *GWTW*, 324.
116. Bushnell, *GWTW*, 326.
117. Bushnell, *GWTW*, 338.
118. Bushnell, *GWTW*, 341.
119. Bushnell, *GWTW*, 326. Bushnell also cautioned against "thoughtlessly" assuming that the Bible ought to be "corrected" in "the light of profane history," but nevertheless insisted that "the Bible, when carefully tested by well-known ancient customs or conditions set forth in reliable profane history, will be found to ring true to contemporary facts."
120. Bushnell, *GWTW*, 337. Bushnell reminded her readers, too, of Priscilla's role as Paul's helper, and of his appreciation for the role Timothy's mother and grandmother played in instructing him in the faith. In addition to contextualizing the passage, Bushnell identified instances of erroneous punctuation or additions to the text in the English translation that further obscured the meaning of key verses, errors she interpreted as "an index of the spirit which has prompted the interpretation of this entire passage,—an assumption, against proof to the contrary, that it is man's exclusive right to teach woman and his right to rule her."
121. Bushnell, *GWTW*, 338.
122. Bushnell, *GWTW*, 343.
123. Bushnell, *GWTW*, 343.
124. Bushnell, *GWTW*, 423. Bushnell also cited Matt. 23:9.
125. Bushnell, *GWTW*, 342–343.
126. Bushnell, *GWTW*, 161.
127. Bushnell, *GWTW*, 344.

128. Bushnell, *GWTW*, 413. In the KJV the passage was translated: "How long wilt thou go about, O thou backsliding daughter? For the Lord hath created a new thing in the earth, A woman shall compass a man."

CHAPTER 7

1. "Comments on the First Edition," n.d., Anne Henrietta Martin Papers, ca. 1892–1951; Bancroft Library, University of California, Berkeley.

2. Jessie Penn-Lewis, *The Magna Charta of Woman According to the Scriptures: Being Light upon the Subject Gathered from Dr. Katherine Bushnell's Text Book, "God's Word to Women"* (Bournemouth, UK: The Overcomer Book Room, 1919), 4–6. Penn-Lewis praised Bushnell for taking up this task with "scholarly dignity and soberness of language," even as she acknowledged Bushnell's penchant for "a little sarcasm"; as the evangelist explained, "knowing what she knows, and having seen what she has seen, of the results in the world of the Gen. iii. 16 misinterpretation, nothing but the grace of God has enabled her to write so temperately."

3. Review of *GWTW*, *Moody Bible Institute Monthly* (May 1921): 416.

4. Bushnell to Ethel Dummer, May 20, 1921, Ethel Sturges Dummer Papers, ca. 1866–1954, Schlesinger Library, Radcliffe Institute, Cambridge, MA.

5. Excerpt from review of *GWTW* in *The Baptist*, June 5, 1924, from " 'God's Word to Women' Review Notes," n.d., Anne Henrietta Martin Papers, ca. 1892–1951, Bancroft Library, University of California, Berkeley. Montgomery herself incorporated several of Bushnell's insights into her 1924 *Centenary Translation of the New Testament* (see Sharyn Dowd, "Helen Barrett Montgomery's *Centenary Translation* of the New Testament: Characteristics and Influences," *Perspectives in Religious Studies* 19 [Summer 1992]: 133–150, and Roger A. Bullard, "Feminine and Feminist Touches in the Centenary New Testament," *Bible Translator* 38 [January 1987]: 118–122).

6. Review of *GWTW*, *Watchman-Examiner* (September 10, 1925): 1180.

7. Review of *GWTW*, *Biblical Recorder*, April 1, 1924, Vol. XVI, no. 4, 98–99, 103–104. The editor of the *Biblical Recorder* later requested Bushnell's biography, which resulted in her publication of *A Brief Sketch*.

8. Excerpt from review of *GWTW* in *The Christian of London, England*, May 15, 1924, from " 'God's Word to Women' Review Notes." A reviewer in the *Record of Christian Work* characterized Bushnell's argument as "one-sided," yet "challenging, to say the least," a "serious original work" worthy of careful study (Review of *GWTW*, *Record of Christian Work*, Vol. 43, 1924, 278).

9. The reviewer particularly resisted Bushnell's suggestion that Paul was quoting from and critiquing other sources (Review of *GWTW*, *The Glory of Israel* [May–June, 1924], Vol. XXII, no. 3, 82–83). Similarly, a reviewer in *The Evangelical Christian and Missionary Witness* (Toronto, Canada), though "disposed often to refuse" some of Bushnell's New Testament translations, conceded that her

arguments, though unique, were "rarely to be set aside as not plausible." The reviewer took issue with her interpretation of 1 Cor. 14:35, but assessed her version of 1 Tim. 2:8–15 to be "beyond serious objection" (see Review of *GWTW, The Evangelical Christian* [September 1924], 370).

10. Review of *GWTW* in *The Sunday School Times* (Philadelphia) March 22, 1924, 200–201. The reviewer found some of her explanations "suggestive, convincing, and truly helpful," but others he dismissed as "unconvincing and not a few positively wrong," and he feared that her erroneous conclusions might "prejudice many readers against the points that are both true and illuminating," spoiling "the undoubted value of the rest of the work."

11. Grant Wacker, "The Holy Spirit and the Spirit of the Age in American Protestantism, 1880–1910," *Journal of American History* 72 (June 1985): 54.

12. Janet Forsythe Fishburn, *The Fatherhood of God and the Victorian Family: The Social Gospel in America* (Philadelphia: Fortress Press, 1981), 135; Christine Rosen, *Preaching Eugenics: Religious Leaders and the American Eugenics Movement* (New York: Oxford University Press, 2004), 16.

13. Claude Welch, *Protestant Thought in the Nineteenth Century*, 165.

14. William A. McLoughlin, *Billy Sunday Was His Real Name* (Chicago: University of Chicago Press, 1955), 140; *Watchman-Examiner* (August 13, 1915): 1066; and George Marsden, *Fundamentalism and American Culture* (New York: Oxford University Press, 1980), 81–83, 91–92. Marsden notes, however, that evangelicals continued to hold a variety of views on the relation between personal salvation and social action. For more on this realignment, see David O. Moberg, *The Great Reversal: Evangelism versus Social Concern* (Philadelphia: Lippincott, 1972), Dayton, *Discovering an Evangelical Heritage* (New York: Harper & Row, 1976), and Jean Miller Schmidt, *Souls or the Social Order: The Two-Party System in American Protestantism* (Brooklyn, NY: Carlson Publishing, 1991).

15. Rosen, *Preaching Eugenics*, 12, 14; Fishburn, *Fatherhood of God*, 6, 15, 29; William R. Hutchison, *The Modernist Impulse in American Protestantism* (Durham, NC: Duke University Press, 1992), 164–165.

16. For this reason, scholars have generally placed Bushnell within the context of conservative Protestantism. See, for example, Donald Dayton, *Discovering an Evangelical Heritage*; Janette Hassey, *No Time for Silence*; and Letha Dawson Scanzoni and Susan Setta, "Women in Evangelical, Holiness, and Pentecostal Traditions," in *Women and Religion in America, Volume 3: 1900–1968*, ed. Rosemary Radford Ruether and Rosemary Skinner Keller (San Francisco: Harper & Row, 1986).

17. *Biblical Recorder* Review, 100–101. Bushnell insisted that "God has never given to any body of men whatsoever, a chartered right to lock up heaven, and let the people perish for lack of knowledge," and declared that in such "days of apostasy," it was "wicked for any human being to shut the mouth of anyone, male or female, who will sound forth a testimony to the truth."

18. Madeline Southard, Journal, December 23, 1923, M. Madeline (Mabel Madeline) Southard Papers, ca. 1878–1998; Schlesinger Library, Radcliffe Institute, Cambridge, MA.

19. Madeline Southard, "The Theology of Women Preachers," *Woman's Pulpit* 3, no. 7 (December 1927): 3.

20. Madeline Southard, "Woman and the Ministry," 1919 (pamphlet in Southard Papers, ca. 1878–1998; Schlesinger Library, Radcliffe Institute, Cambridge, MA). Other observers agreed that women might help bridge the liberal/conservative divide. In 1925, for example, the year of the famous Scopes Trial, a writer in the *Woman Citizen* expressed hope that a growing number of women ministers might help to bring "a speedy end to the fundamentalist-modernist controversy" (Frances Drewry McMullen, "Women in the Pulpit," *Woman Citizen*, February 21, 1925: 12–13, 27–28). Historians have also pointed to the reluctance of holiness Methodists to side with either fundamentalists or modernists; see, for example, Susie C. Stanley, "Wesleyan/Holiness Churches: Innocent Bystanders in the Fundamentalist/Modernist Controversy," in *Re-Forming the Center: American Protestantism, 1900 to the Present*, ed. Douglas Jacobsen and William Vance Trollinger, Jr. (Grand Rapids, MI: Eerdmans, 1998), 172–193, and Schmidt, *Souls or the Social Order*, 173.

21. Gail Bederman, " 'The Women Have Had Charge of the Church Work Long Enough': The Men and Religion Forward Movement of 1911–1912 and the Masculinization of Middle-Class Protestantism," *American Quarterly* 41, no. 3 (September 1989), 432–465. As Bederman explains, churchmen ignored the fact that "the churches had been two-thirds female for over two hundred years," and instead "discovered—or, more accurately, constructed—a 'crisis,' pointing to the 'excess of women over men in church life' as a new and dangerous threat, requiring immediate attention" (438). By the mid-1920s, many churches had not only adopted masculine business models, but male church leaders had also successfully seized control of once-flourishing women's organizations.

22. Bendroth, *Fundamentalism and Gender*, 31. See also Betty De Berg, *Ungodly Women: Gender and the First Wave of American Fundamentalism* (Minneapolis: Fortress Press, 1990). Bendroth explains how dispensational teachings "depended heavily on notions of order and obedience," and fundamentalists themselves noted that the loose translation for the Greek word for "dispensation" was in fact the "ordering of a household" (8).

23. Bendroth, *Fundamentalism and Gender*, 65–67, 100–103.

24. Bendroth, *Fundamentalism and Gender*, 54–72.

25. Fishburn, *Fatherhood of God*, 53.

26. By promoting this static view of the Victorian family, Social Gospel leaders departed from their otherwise progressive social and political views. As Fishburn

notes, the "only plank in the Republican platform of 1912 that Rauschenbusch refused to endorse was that of woman suffrage" (*Fatherhood of God*, 124).

27. David J. Pivar, *Purity and Hygiene: Women, Prostitution, and the "American Plan," 1900–1930* (Westport, CT: Greenwood Press, 2002), 224; Rosen, *Preaching Eugenics*, 120–121, 127.

28. Bendroth, *Fundamentalism and Gender*, 81.

29. See Virginia Lieson Brereton, "United and Slighted: Women as Subordinated Insiders," in William R. Hutchison, ed., *Between the Times: The Travail of the Protestant Establishment in America, 1900–1960* (Cambridge: Cambridge University Press, 1989), 143–167; and Michael S. Hamilton, "Women, Public Ministry, and American Fundamentalism, 1920–1950," *Religion and American Culture* 3, no. 2 (Summer 1993): 182–183. Hamilton notes that the relative number of women ordained by mainline churches likely fell in the interwar years, mainline divinity schools were reluctant to enroll women, and most mainline Protestants were unenthusiastic about the possibility of women pastoring their churches.

30. See Maureen Fitzgerald, "Losing Their Religion: Women, the State, and the Ascension of Secular Discourse, 1890–1930," in *Women and Twentieth-Century Protestantism*, ed. Margaret Lamberts Bendroth and Virginia Lieson Brereton (Urbana: University of Illinois Press, 2002), 285–286.

31. The history of Protestant women's foreign missions organizations from the 1870s to the 1920s reveals this pattern distinctly; as the associations increasingly embraced "scientific" and "professional" identities, they distanced themselves from many of their once-devoted supporters, rendering the organizations vulnerable to takeovers by male denominational leaders in the 1920s. See, for example, Hill, *The World Their Household*; Elizabeth Howell Gripe, "Women, Restructuring and Unrest in the 1920s," *Journal of Presbyterian History* 52 (Summer 1974): 188–199; Lois A. Boyd and R. Douglas Brackenridge, *Presbyterian Women in America: Two Centuries of a Quest for Status* (Westport, CT: Greenwood Press, 1983); and Brereton, "United and Slighted." On these developments within Methodism, see Section IV, "The Status of Women in Institutional Church Life," in Rosemary Skinner Keller and Hildah F. Thomas, *Women in New Worlds: Historical Perspectives on the Wesleyan Tradition* (Nashville, TN: Abingdon Press, 1981), vol. 1, 217–289.

32. See, for example, *Woman's Pulpit* 2, no. 5 (December 1925): 1–2, and Euphemia Drysdale, "Woman and the Ministry," *Homiletic Review* 33, no. 5 (May 1922): 347–353.

33. Inez M. Cavert, *Women in American Church Life: A Study Prepared under the Guidance of a Counseling Committee of Women Representing National Interdenominational Agencies* (New York: Friendship Press, published for the Federal Council of the Churches of Christ in America, 1949), 10, 18–19.

CHAPTER 8

1. Pivar, *Purity and Hygiene*, 212–217.

2. Pivar, *Purity and Hygiene*, 212; see also Bushnell, "Compulsion for Women—License for Men," *The Light* (Jan.–Feb. 1921): 17–20.

3. Bushnell to Ethel Dummer, April 12, 1920, Ethel Sturges Dummer Papers, ca. 1866–1954, Schlesinger Library, Radcliffe Institute, Cambridge, MA. Bushnell was not alone among Methodist women. Jane Hunter writes that "[i]n 1920, despite the acquiescence of the major women's suffrage organization in the war effort, the Methodist Woman's Foreign Missionary Society (WFMS) allied its enthusiasm for the passage of the Nineteenth Amendment enfranchising women to a global antimilitarist stand" ("Women's Mission in Historical Perspective," 33).

4. Bushnell to Alison Neilans, January 13, 1936, Records of the Association for Moral & Social Hygiene, The Women's Library collections at LSE, 3AMS/B/09/06.

5. Bushnell's pamphlets included *Compulsory Notification; Well-Intentioned Blundering; A Nostrum Worse Than the Disease; What Saith the Doctor?; Wicked and Unjust Measures; Beware of Slanderous Exaggerations; Physician, Heal Thyself; A Call to Arms; A Correction of False Alarms.* She printed and distributed at least 18,000 of these. See "List: The Printer's Bills," Records of the Association for Moral & Social Hygiene, The Women's Library collections at LSE, 3AMS D/51/01.

6. "The Union to Combat the Sanitation of Vice," Records of the Association for Moral & Social Hygiene, The Women's Library collections at LSE, AMS/D/51/01/02; Pivar, *Purity and Hygiene*, 212.

7. Alison Neilens, "Neo Regulation in the United States," containing excerpts from Bushnell's address to the Biennial Conference of the World's Purity Federation, Chicago, 1921, Records of the Association for Moral & Social Hygiene, The Women's Library collections at LSE, 3AMS/D/51/01.

8. Bushnell, "Compulsion for Women," 18.

9. "Union to Combat the Sanitation of Vice." Bushnell suggested that Christ's words to the woman taken in adultery did not merely express "an ideal justice as between man and woman," but in fact offered "the only practicable means of a legislative attack upon the social evil."

10. Bushnell to Dummer, March 15, 1920, Ethel Sturges Dummer Papers, ca. 1866–1954, Schlesinger Library, Radcliffe Institute, Cambridge, MA.

11. Bushnell, *Brief Sketch*, 26–27; see also Pivar, *Purity and Hygiene*, 214.

12. Ethel M. Walters, M.D., to the Surgeon General, December 15, 1919; T. A. Storey to C. C. Pierce, Assistant Surgeon General, September 22, 1919, National Archives, RG 90, quoted in Pivar, *Purity and Hygiene*, 214.

13. Pivar, *Purity and Hygiene*, 212.

14. Bushnell to Neilans, January 31, 1920, Records of the Association for Moral & Social Hygiene, The Women's Library collections at LSE, 3AMS/D/51/02.

Bushnell's writings were also sent to Jane Addams and Katharine Anthony (Dummer to Bushnell, March 13, 1920, Ethel Sturges Dummer Papers, ca. 1866–1954, Schlesinger Library, Radcliffe Institute, Cambridge, MA).

15. Bushnell to Neilans, February 11, 1918; Bushnell to Neilans, August 2, 1918, Records of the Association for Moral & Social Hygiene, The Women's Library collections at LSE, 3AMS/D/51 01.

16. Pivar, *Purity and Hygiene*, 212; see Maurice Gregory, "State-Regulation of Vice; Its Various Forms," Records of the Association for Moral & Social Hygiene, The Women's Library collections at LSE, 3AMS/D/51; "Address before the International Purity Conference Dec. 27, 1921, Chicago, IL," printed in *The Light* (March–April, 1922): 21–27; and "What's Going On? A Report of Investigations by Katharine C. Bushnell Regarding Certain Social and Legal Abuses in California That Have Been in Part Aggravated and in Part Created by the Federal Social Hygiene Programme" (Oakland, CA: n.d.).

17. Bushnell to Dummer, April 12, 1920, Ethel Sturges Dummer Papers, ca. 1866–1954, Schlesinger Library, Radcliffe Institute, Cambridge, MA.

18. Bushnell to Neilans, August 16, 1917, Records of the Association for Moral & Social Hygiene, The Women's Library collections at LSE, 3AMS/D/51/01. They also decided against sending Bushnell as their delegate to President Wilson, deeming her "hardly the right kind of person, being too sentimental" (George W. Johnson to Dr. Helen Wilson, September 16, 1917, Records of the Association for Moral & Social Hygiene, The Women's Library collections at LSE, 3 AMS/D/51/01).

19. "List: The Printer's Bills," Records of the Association for Moral & Social Hygiene, The Women's Library collections at LSE, 3AMS/D/51/01.

20. Bushnell to Neilans, February 11, 1918, Records of the Association for Moral & Social Hygiene, The Women's Library collections at LSE, 3AMS/D/51/01. Bushnell admitted that she feared allowing others to join lest they begin to divert the organization from her unflinching antiregulationist goals.

21. Bushnell, *Brief Sketch*, 27. Bushnell was able to incite a small public outcry in San Diego against the compulsory examination of prostitutes under the American Plan, but she and her fellow reformers were dismissed as uninformed (Pivar, *Purity and Hygiene*, 215).

22. See Bushnell to Neilans, February 21, 1920, Records of the Association for Moral & Social Hygiene, The Women's Library collections at LSE, 3AMS/D/51/01.

23. Pivar, *Purity Crusade*, 259.

24. According to Ginzberg, female reformers started to abandon moral suasion in favor of more "scientific" or "efficient" methods as far back as the 1850s, a trend expedited by the Civil War (*Women and the Work of Benevolence*, 173).

25. Bushnell to Dummer, June 30, 1920, Ethel Sturges Dummer Papers, ca. 1866–1954, Schlesinger Library, Radcliffe Institute, Cambridge, MA; Pivar, *Purity and Hygiene*, 43. The Alliance had formed in response to Josephine Butler's activism, and Bushnell herself had served as a vice president in the 1880s.

26. *California State Board of Health Monthly Bulletin* 5, no. 10 (April 1910), Records of the Association, 3AMS/D/51/01; Pivar, *Purity and Hygiene*, 139–142.

27. Bushnell to Dummer, June 30, 1920, Ethel Sturges Dummer Papers, ca. 1866–1954, Schlesinger Library, Radcliffe Institute, Cambridge, MA.

28. Pivar, *Purity and Hygiene*, 201.

29. Pivar, *Purity and Hygiene*, xiv.

30. Pivar, *Purity and Hygiene*, xvii, 148.

31. George W. Stocking, *Victorian Anthropology* (New York: Free Press, 1987), 199.

32. Bushnell to Dummer, July 5, 1922, Ethel Sturges Dummer Papers, ca. 1866–1954, Schlesinger Library, Radcliffe Institute, Cambridge, MA.

33. Regina G. Kunzel, *Fallen Women, Problem Girls: Unmarried Mothers and the Professionalization of Social Work, 1890–1945* (New Haven, CT: Yale University Press, 1993), 52–53. As Kunzel points out, the category to replace feeblemindedness—sex delinquency—was similarly gendered (55).

34. Pivar, *Purity and Hygiene*, 157.

35. Bushnell to Dummer, March 15, 1920, Ethel Sturges Dummer Papers, ca. 1866–1954, Schlesinger Library, Radcliffe Institute, Cambridge, MA.

36. July 1917–August 1918 Expenditures, Records of the Association for Moral & Social Hygiene, The Women's Library collections at LSE, 3AMS/D/51/01/02. The following year Bushnell received a $477.00 donation from Belle Huntington Mix, by far her most substantial support (Bushnell to Neilens, January 2, 1919, Records of the Association for Moral & Social Hygiene, The Women's Library collections at LSE, 3AMS/D/51/01.)

37. Bushnell to Neilans, August 2, 1918, Records of the Association for Moral & Social Hygiene, The Women's Library collections at LSE, 3AMS/D/51/01.

38. Pivar, *Purity and Hygiene*, 224; see also Rosen, *Preaching Eugenics*, 120–121.

39. Bushnell to Neilens, June 13, 1919, Records of the Association for Moral & Social Hygiene, The Women's Library collections at LSE, 3AMS/D/51/01.

40. Kunzel describes the "embattled and protracted transfer of power" from female reformers to professional social workers in her study of maternity homes for unwed mothers (*Fallen Women*, 3–4).

41. Gordon, *Moral Property*, 83.

42. Bushnell, "Birth-Control: Where's the Harm?" *The Light* (March–April 1923): 11.

43. Pivar, *Purity and Hygiene*, xiv–xv.

44. Pivar, *Purity and Hygiene*, 158.

45. Christine Stansell, *American Moderns: Bohemian New York and the Creation of a New Century* (New York: Metropolitan Books, 2000), 2.

46. Cott, *Grounding of Modern Feminism*, 38, 15. Women of this generation coined the term "Feminism" (which they initially capitalized). In this chapter I have followed this usage, capitalizing the term when referring to the specific early twentieth-century movement that emerged in the 1910s.

47. Cott, *Grounding of Modern Feminism*, 36.

48. Stansell, *American Moderns*, 241.

49. See Joanne Meyerowitz, "Sexual Geography and Gender Economy: The Furnished Room Districts of Chicago, 1890–1930," *Gender & History* 2, no. 3 (Autumn 1990); and Cott, *Grounding of Modern Feminism*, 42.

50. Gordon, *Moral Property*, 121–126.

51. Meyerowitz, "Sexual Geography," 288.

52. Carroll Smith-Rosenberg, "The New Woman as Androgyne: Social Order and Gender Crisis, 1870–1936," in *Disorderly Conduct: Visions of Gender in Victorian America* (New York: A. A. Knopf, 1985), 284; Gordon, *Moral Property*, 210.

53. Christina Simmons, "Modern Sexuality and the Myth of Victorian Repression," in *Passion and Power: Sexuality in History*, ed. Kathy Peiss and Christina Simmons (Philadelphia: Temple University Press, 1989), 165.

54. As Gordon notes, the "sexual revolution" often associated with the 1920s was in fact well under way before World War I, and changes in women's sexual behavior "constituted the very essence of this revolution" (*Moral Property*, 128–130).

55. Gordon, *Moral Property*, 3, 66–67.

56. Bushnell, *Brief Sketch*, 27. Bushnell feared that birth control would "encourage illicit relations among old and young enormously," and she regretted that "just as many of the churches had led" in the "mischievous" social hygiene movement, so, too, had they "followed on into the second infamy" ("Birth-Control: Where's the Harm?" 13–14).

57. "God Shall Send Them Strong Delusion," Records of the Association for Moral & Social Hygiene, The Women's Library collections at LSE, 3AMS/B/09/06. According to Gordon, other women, too, shared Bushnell's fears of state control (*Moral Property*, 204–208).

58. Bushnell, *GWTW*, 527.

59. Bushnell, "Birth-Control: Where's the Harm?" 11–14.

60. Bushnell to Neilans, January 13, 1936; Bushnell to Neilans, December 28, 1934, Records of the Association for Moral & Social Hygiene, The Women's Library collections at LSE, 3AMS/B/09/06. Bushnell quoted from Sanger's speech "The Civilizing Force of Birth Control" (1929), published in *Sex in Civilization*, ed. V. F. Calverton and Samuel Daniel Schmalhausen (New York: The Macaulay Co., 1939).

61. Bushnell to Neilans, January 13, 1936, Records of the Association for Moral & Social Hygiene, The Women's Library collections at LSE, 3AMS/B/09/06.

62. Bushnell to the Executive Committee of the Association for Moral and Social Hygiene, June 7, 1935, Records of the Association for Moral & Social Hygiene, The Women's Library collections at LSE, 3AMS/B/09/06.

63. Bushnell to the Executive Committee of the Association for Moral and Social Hygiene, June 7, 1935, Records of the Association for Moral & Social Hygiene, The Women's Library collections at LSE, 3AMS/B/09/06.

64. Bushnell to Neilans, December 28, 1934, Records of the Association for Moral & Social Hygiene, The Women's Library collections at LSE, 3AMS/B/09/06.

65. Bushnell to Neilans, July 12, 1934, Records of the Association for Moral & Social Hygiene, The Women's Library collections at LSE, 3AMS/B/09/06.

66. Neilans to Mr. Gillett, November 19, 1936, Records of the Association for Moral & Social Hygiene, The Women's Library collections at LSE, 3AMS/B/09/06.

67. "Exploitation of Vice" *Edinburgh Evening Dispatch*, February 20, 1937, Records of the Association for Moral & Social Hygiene, The Women's Library collections at LSE, 3AMS/B/09/06.

68. Simmons, "Modern Sexuality," 158, 170–171.

69. Jonathan Ned Katz, *The Invention of Heterosexuality* (New York: Dutton, 1995).

70. Smith-Rosenberg, "New Woman," 246, 265; Stansell, *American Moderns*, 249; Gordon, *Moral Property*, 122–123. According to Gordon, "the sexual revolution was not a general loosening of sexual taboos but only of those on nonmarital heterosexual activity" (131). Bushnell participated in the intimate female friendships common among members of her generation, most notably with her long-time coworker Elizabeth Andrew, yet as Carroll Smith-Rosenberg details in her classic essay, "The Female World of Love and Ritual: Relations Between Women in Nineteenth-Century America" (*Signs* 1, no. 1 [Autumn 1975]: 1–29), such relationships resist classification according to present-day conceptions of heterosexuality or homosexuality. As Smith-Rosenberg makes clear, "defining and analyzing same-sex relationships involves the historian in deeply problematical questions of method and interpretation" (2); situated in their proper context, intimate friendships in the Victorian era were "both sensual and platonic" (4). In Bushnell's case, while there is no evidence to suggest the presence of physical intimacies between her and her close companions, the emotional intimacy she shared with her most devoted friends and coworkers is undeniable.

71. Gordon, *Moral Property*, 123; 161–163. Like Bushnell, Gilman turned to religion to offer a more comprehensive vision for social reform, in *His Religion and Hers: A Study of the Faith of our Fathers and the Work of our Mothers* (1923).

72. Stansell, *American Moderns*, 267.

73. Stansell, *American Moderns*, 227.

74. Gordon, *Moral Property*, 163.

75. Stansell, *American Moderns*, 248; 262–267, 307. At the same time, both Stansell and Smith-Rosenberg ("New Woman," 296) advise against an overly critical or anachronistic view of the radicals' apparent short-sightedness.

76. Lida M. Herrick, a member of the Association of Women Preachers, felt that "all the talk about the evils of flapperism is doing more harm than good," and insisted that "modern girls" were in many ways "better than their mothers were" (". . . Says Modern Girls Better Than Mothers Were," unmarked clipping, MC 647, folder #1.2, M. Madeline [Mabel Madeline] Southard Papers, ca. 1878–1998; Schlesinger Library, Radcliffe Institute, Cambridge, MA).

77. *Woman's Pulpit* 2, no. 5 (December 1925): 2.

78. *Woman's Pulpit* 1, no. 11 (September 1924): 3.

CONCLUSION

1. Bushnell to Neilens, April 28, 1928, Records of the Association for Moral & Social Hygiene, The Women's Library collections at LSE, 3AMS/D/51/01.

2. Bushnell to Dummer, October 7, 1929, Ethel Sturges Dummer Papers, ca. 1866–1954, Schlesinger Library, Radcliffe Institute, Cambridge, MA. It was at one of Yu's revivals in 1920 that Watchman Nee was converted.

3. Hardwick, *Oh Thou Woman*, 79.

4. In addition to a series of "Bible Interleaves," pages meant to be placed in readers' Bibles to correct common mistranslations of key biblical passages (*Bible Interleaves: A Series of Notes*, 1920, available at the British Library, BL 03107.ee.3), Bushnell published a number of additional writings, including *The Supreme Virtue* (Oakland, CA: by the author, 1924); *The Reverend Doctor and His Doctor Daughter* (Oakland, CA: by the author, 1927); *Mother's Catechism on Adam and Eve* (Oakland, CA: by the author, 1938); *Mother's Catechism on The Seventh of First Corinthians* (Oakland, CA: by the author, 1938); and *The Vashti-Esther Bible Story* (Piedmont, CA: by the author, 1945).

5. Tyrrell, *Woman's World*, 117. In 1918 and 1919, Bushnell notes sharing her home with her older sister, but after her sister was injured in an accident, Bushnell found herself caring for her sibling and struggling to keep up with her own demanding schedule. Bushnell to Neilans, February 11, 1918, and January 16, 1919, Records of the Association for Moral & Social Hygiene, The Women's Library collections at LSE, 3AMS/D/51/01.

6. Bushnell to Anne Martin, September 2, 1943; September 7, 1943, Anne Henrietta Martin Papers, ca. 1892–1951; Bancroft Library, University of California, Berkeley.

7. Bushnell to Martin, September 7, 1943, Anne Henrietta Martin Papers, ca. 1892–1951; Bancroft Library, University of California, Berkeley.

8. "Last Will and Testament of K. B. Bushnell," Personal Files of Ruth Hoppin, Daly City, CA.

9. "Dr. Kate Bushnell Completes Her Work," *Union Signal*, April 6, 1946, 152, 159.

10. Ruth Hoppin, "The Legacy of Katherine Bushnell," *Priscilla Papers* 9, no. 1 (Winter 1995): 8–10.

11. Bushnell was "lost to generations of unsympathetic historians," asserts Ian Tyrrell (*Woman's World*, 284–285).

12. "Literature List," Anne Henrietta Martin Papers, ca. 1892–1951; Bancroft Library, University of California, Berkeley. In Germany the text was available in German translation, *Was Sagt Gott der Frau?*

13. Penn-Lewis's *Magna Charta* was reprinted again in 1975 by the evangelical publishing house Bethany Fellowship (Minneapolis, MN), and Starr's *Bible Status* in 1987 (New York: Garland Publishing).

14. Southard to Weigle, October 18, 1940, M. Madeline (Mabel Madeline) Southard Papers, ca. 1878–1998; Schlesinger Library, Radcliffe Institute, Cambridge, MA. Southard expressed her hope that "scholars in the middle of the twentieth

century may be open-minded enough to give the same translation when a word is used for a woman that they do when it is used for a man—but we doubt if they will notice this unless it is called to their attention."

15. Weigle to Southard, July 25, 1941, M. Madeline (Mabel Madeline) Southard Papers, ca. 1878–1998; Schlesinger Library, Radcliffe Institute, Cambridge, MA. Responding to Southard's suggestion, Weigle wrote that he "had not thought of asking a woman scholar to read the manuscript before publication, but that probably is an excellent idea," and that he would propose it to the committee at their next meeting. But no record of such a proposal can be found in the minutes of the Standard Bible Committee, and Starr's book does not appear on the "List of Books Used by the Bible Revision Committee, 1939–51, 1968" (Papers of the Standard Bible Committee, Yale Divinity School, New Haven, CT). See also letter to Moffatt, March 27, 1941, Luther Allan Weigle Papers, Sterling Memorial Library, Yale University, New Haven, CT.

16. Kroeger, "Legacy of Katherine Bushnell," 1–4.

17. Virginia Hearn, "New Publishers of Katherine Bushnell," *Update: Newsletter of the Evangelical Women's Caucus* 11, no. 4 (Winter 1987–1988): 7–8.

18. See Ann Braude, "A Religious Feminist—Who Can Find Her? Historiographical Challenges from the National Organization for Women," *Journal of Religion* 84, no. 4 (October 2004): 555–572.

19. Bethany Moreton, "Why Is There So Much Sex in Christian Conservatism and Why Do So Few Historians Care Anything about It?" *Journal of Southern History* 75, no. 3 (August 2009): 717–738. Moreton links evangelicals' pronatalism to larger economic shifts, claiming that "reproduction became central as the American economy shifted from production to reproduction, or service" (724).

20. Those who have helped recover Bushnell's life and teachings for the Christian community include Dee Alei, Gilbert Bilezikian, Donald Dayton, Patricia Gundry, Stanley Gundry, Nancy Hardesty, Dana Hardwick, Janette Hasscy, Susan Hyatt, Laurence R. Iannaccone, Catherine Clark Kroeger, L. E. Maxwell, Russell Prohl, Rosemary Radford Ruether, Aida Besançon Spencer, and Rosemary Skinner. Catherine Clark Kroeger, in particular, was inspired by Bushnell to address the issue of the abuse of women. See, for example, Catherine Clark Kroeger and James R. Beck, ed., *Women, Abuse, and the Bible: How Scripture Can Be Used to Hurt or to Heal* (Grand Rapids, MI: Baker Books, 1996; Catherine Clark Kroeger, *No Place for Abuse: Biblical and Practical Resources to Counteract Domestic Violence* (Downers Grove, IL: InterVarsity Press, 2001); and Nancy Nason-Clark and Catherine Clark Kroeger, *Refuge from Abuse: Hope and Healing for Abused Christian Women* (Downers Grove, IL: InterVarsity Press, 2004).

21. The Evangelical Women's Caucus later became the Evangelical and Ecumenical Women's Caucus (EEWC). Godswordtowomen.org was founded by Barbara Collins, Gay Anderson, and Pat Joyce; the site has recently been brought under the leadership of Susan Hyatt, and includes an expanded social media presence,

a published newsletter, and, in collaboration with the International Christian Women's History Project & Hall of Fame (www.icwhp.org), a series of "GWTW College Courses."

22. Andrew F. Walls, "Christian Scholarship in Africa in the Twenty-first Century," *Journal of African Christian Thought* 4, no. 2 (December 2001): 46; Philip Jenkins, *The New Faces of Christianity* (New York: Oxford University Press, 2006), 9. See also Kristin Kobes Du Mez, "Reorienting American Religious History: The Case of Katharine Bushnell," in *American Evangelicalism: George Marsden and the Shape of American Religious History*, ed. Darren Dochuk, Thomas S. Kidd, and Kurt W. Peterson (Notre Dame, IN: University of Notre Dame Press, 2014).

23. Carrie A. Miles, president of Empower International Ministries, a ministry working to mobilize "local clergy and communities to promote gender equality" in various African countries, refers to Bushnell, along with Lee Anna Starr, as "the grandmothers of us all," and has promoted Bushnell's teachings through study guides and missionary work (Carrie A. Miles, e-mail message to author, July 13, 2009). Since 2004, Christians for Biblical Equality has held international conferences in Durham, England; Bangalore, India; Toronto, Canada; Melbourne, Australia; and Limuru, Kenya.

24. Godswordtowomen.org includes blogs in Spanish and Hungarian, as well as profiles on women and men across the globe who have benefited from reading Bushnell's *God's Word to Women*.

25. Jenkins, *New Faces*, 15–16; see also Mark A. Noll, *The New Shape of World Christianity* (Downers Grove, IL: IVP Academic, 2009), 11–15. On the significance of women in the growth of global Christianity, see Dana L. Robert, "World Christianity as a Women's Movement," *International Bulletin of Missionary Research* 30, no. 4 (2006): 180–188.

26. For a sampling of the rich reflections that African women have already offered on Christianity and women's liberation, see Mercy Amba Oduyoye, *Beads and Strands: Reflections of an African Woman on Christianity in Africa* (Maryknoll, NY: Orbis Books, 2004) and *Daughters of Anowa: African Women and Patriarchy* (Maryknoll, NY: Orbis Books, 1995); Isabel Apawo Phiri, *Women, Presbyterianism and Patriarchy: Religious Experience of Chewa Women in Central Malawi* (Blantyre, Malawi: Christian Literature Association, 1997); Musimbi R. A. Kanyoro and Nyambura Njoroge, ed., *Groaning in Faith: African Women in the Household of God* (Nairobi, Kenya: Acton Publishers, 1996); Nyambura Njoroge and Musa Dube, ed., *Talitha Cum: Theologies of African Women* (Pietermaritzburg, South Africa: Cluster Publications, 2001); and Angela Dwamena-Aboagye, "An Analysis of the Hierarchicalist and Egalitarian Debate on Gender Relations in the Western Evangelical Church from the Perspective of an African Christian Woman" (master's thesis, Akrofi-Christaller Institute of Theology, Mission and Culture, 2013).

27. Gary A. Haugen, *Good News about Injustice: A Witness of Courage in a Hurting World*, rev. ed. (Downers Grove, IL: InterVarsity Press, 2009), 68–70; and Lisa Thompson, "Fighting the Other Slave Trade: Women Against Sexual Trafficking," *Christian History & Biography* 90 (Spring 2006): 43–45.

28. Mary A. Renda, "Conclusion: Doing Everything: Religion, Race, and Empire in the U.S. Protestant Women's Missionary Enterprise, 1812–1960," in *Competing Kingdoms*, 377–378.

29. See Elizabeth Bernstein, "Militarized Humanitarianism Meets Carceral Feminism: The Politics of Sex, Rights, and Freedom in Contemporary Antitrafficking Campaigns," *Signs* 36 (Autumn 2010): 62–65; and Melani McAlister, "The Politics of Persecution," *Middle East Report*, no. 249 (Winter 2008): 18–27. In contrast to contemporary antitrafficking campaigns, Bushnell remained highly skeptical of state regulation and carceral feminism.

30. Robert D. Putnam and David E. Campbell, *American Grace: How Religion Divides and Unites Us* (New York: Simon & Shuster, 2010), 113–119, 131, 237, 244.

31. Donna Freitas, *Sex and the Soul: Juggling Sexuality, Spirituality, Romance, and Religion on America's College Campuses* (New York: Oxford University Press, 2008), 75–92.

32. Adelle M. Banks, "Evangelicals Say It's Time for Frank Talk about Sex," Religion News Service, http://archives.religionnews.com/culture/gender-and-sexuality/Evangelicals-say-its-time-for-frank-talk-about-sex (accessed January 9, 2013).

33. Freitas, *Sex and the Soul*, 148. See also Heather R. Hlavka, "Normalizing Sexual Violence: Young Women Account for Harassment and Abuse," *Gender & Society* 28: 337–358 (published online February 28, 2014).

34. Bushnell, *GWTW*, 413.

Scripture Index

Subject Index